APOCALYPSE

The Bible & Liberation

An Orbis Series in Biblical Studies

Norman K. Gottwald and Richard A. Horsley,
General Editors

The Bible & Liberation Series focuses on the emerging range of political, social, and contextual hermeneutics that are changing the face of biblical interpretation today. It brings to light the social struggles behind the biblical texts. At the same time it explores the ways that a "liberated Bible" may offer resources in the contemporary struggle for a more human world.

Already published:

The Bible and Liberation: Political and Social Hermeneutics
    (Revised edition), Norman K. Gottwald and Richard A. Horsley, Editors

Josiah's Passover: Sociology and the Liberating Bible, Shigeyuki Nakanose

The Psalms: Songs of Tragedy, Hope, and Justice, J. David Pleins

Women and Jesus in Mark: A Japanese Feminist Perspective,
    Hisako Kinukawa

Liberating Paul: The Justice of God and the Politics of the Apostle,
    Neil Elliott

Becoming Children of God: John's Gospel and Radical Discipleship,
    Wes Howard-Brook

Discovering the Bible in the Non-Biblical World, Kwok Pui-lan

Biblical Hermeneutics of Liberation, Gerald West

The Bible & Liberation Series

APOCALYPSE

A People's Commentary on The Book of Revelation

Pablo Richard

Translated by Phillip Berryman

ORBIS BOOKS
Maryknoll, New York 10545

Second Printing, April 1998

Library of Congress Cataloging-in-Publication Data

Richard, Pablo.
    [Apocalipsis. English]
    Apocalypse : a people's commentary on the book of Revelation /
Pablo Richard.
       p.   cm. — (Bible & liberation series)
    Includes bibliographical references and index.
    ISBN 1-57075-043-2 (alk. paper)
    1. Bible. N.T. Revelation—Commentaries.   I. Title.
II. Series.
BS2825.3.R497   1995
228'.07–dc20   95-42970
                                         CIP

Contents

Acknowledgments

To mention here all the people and institutions that have aided in the preparation of this book on Revelation would be impossible. I would first like to thank DEI (Ecumenical Research Department), which has supported me in my work during the last fifteen years, and likewise the Ecumenical School of the Sciences of Religion at the National University of Costa Rica. I would also like to thank the Christian Theological Seminary in Indianapolis, where I spent a sabbatical semester as guest professor in 1988 and devoted myself to studying the bibliography on Revelation and apocalyptic literature. Among the people at the seminary I should especially thank Richard Dickinson, Dean Michael Kinnamon, and David Vargas. I must also thank Union Theological Seminary in Virginia, where I was a guest professor in 1994 and was able to examine the most recent literature on Revelation and to proofread the final manuscript of this book. At that seminary I must give special thanks to Dean Charles M. Swezey and to Mary Jane Winter. I would like to thank DEI team members Elsa Tamez, Franz Hinkelammert, Jung Mo Sung, and Francisco Cruz, who read the final manuscript and offered very valuable criticism and suggestions. Finally, this book would not have been possible without the patience and affection of my family.

I must also thank thousands of other people: the members of Christian base communities, and especially the peasant delegates of the Word of God and the indigenous theologians and pastoral agents who have communicated to me the Spirit with which the Bible was written. I would also like to thank the Catholic bishops for the biblical work done in their dioceses, which has been an encouragement to me: Pedro Casaldáliga and Paulo Evaristo Arns (Brazil); Víctor Corral, Gonzalo López, and Luis Alberto Luna (Ecuador); Carlos María Ariz (Panama); Julio Cabrera (Guatemala); and Fernando Ariztía (Chile); and also our bishops Sergio Méndez Arceo, Oscar Arnulfo Romero, and Leonidas Proaño, who are now in the risen Christ, even as their personal friendship, their spirit, and their blessing are still at work within me.

Introduction

BIRTHPLACE OF THIS BOOK

This book arose out of two different but converging contexts. One context has been study and scholarly research into the text of Revelation, apocalyptic literature, and the related bibliography. I have been engaged in this research for five years at DEI, where I have been able to work on a team along with other theologians, social scientists, and economists. The most intensive research was done during two sabbatical semesters in the United States. In addition, I have delved further into the matter during my courses at the Ecumenical School of the Sciences of Religion at the National University and the Latin American Biblical Seminary in Costa Rica. The Latin American Network of Biblical Scholars, which produces *RIBLA (Revista de Interpretación Bíblica Latinoamericana)*, has provided an important space for my biblical work.

The other and perhaps more important context in which this work gradually arose has been that of ongoing biblical workshops with pastoral agents from Latin America and the Caribbean, especially in Central America. These have been intensive week-long workshops with an average of eighty persons each. I have been able to carry out a number of biblical workshops on Revelation (and Daniel) in Costa Rica, Panama, Nicaragua, El Salvador, Guatemala, Mexico, Haiti, Ecuador, Brazil, Bolivia, and Chile. The main participants in these workshops have been peasants and indigenous people, leaders of Christian base communities, and similar groups.

Scholarly research and work with pastoral agents of Christian base communities have been converging labors. This book is the outgrowth of a close connection between scholarship and the Spirit.

HOW THIS BOOK IS ORGANIZED
AND HOW TO READ IT

The first chapter is a general introduction in which we examine three kinds of keys for understanding Revelation: (1) historical and theological keys, (2) sociological and theological keys, and (3) literary and structural keys.

In chapters 2 to 8 we present our commentary on the whole book of Revelation. We divide these chapters along the lines of what we take to be the structure of Revelation. Thus, the commentary divides into seven parts:

- Revelation 1:1–8 and 22:6–21: The beginning and end of the book of Revelation.

- Revelation 1:9–3:22: Apocalyptic vision of the church.

- Revelation 4:1–8:1: Prophetic vision of history.

- Revelation 8:2–11:19; 15:5–16:21: The seven trumpets and the seven bowls.

- Revelation 12:1–15:4: Center of Revelation — center of history: the Christian community confronting the beasts.

- Revelation 17:1–19:10: Prophetic vision of history.

- Revelation 19:11–22:5: Apocalyptic vision of the future.

Each of the seven chapters is divided into two parts: an introduction to the reading and the structure of the text, followed by keys for interpreting it. It is absolutely necessary to study the text well first — to read it and delve into its structure. Our aim in proposing an overall structure and the structures for each section is to help the reader enter deeply into the text. When dealing with Revelation — more than with any other book of the Bible — it is absolutely necessary to read the text carefully and discover its literal meaning. After the introduction to the reading and the structure of the text, we provide the keys for interpreting it. Rather than a verse-by-verse commentary we are providing the interpretative keys necessary for better understanding the text in its literal, historical, and spiritual meaning.

At the end we have added a bibliography of the works that we have found especially helpful for interpreting Revelation. The bibliography is divided into two sections: the first part includes specific works on Revelation and apocalyptic literature, while the second includes general works on the theoretical and historical background that constitute the hermeneutical horizon for my interpretation of Revelation.

INTENDED AUDIENCE FOR THIS COMMENTARY ON REVELATION

I first want this book to be read by pastoral agents working with the churches and the basic Christian communities. I have written this book jointly with them, and now I am giving it back to them. At all times they have been my primary interlocutors. Pastoral agents are women and men devoted to serving the people of God, and that includes bishops, priests, male and female pastors, men and women theologians, and men and women religious, who work with the people of God, catechists, trainers, coordinators of communities, and delegates of the Word of God, and especially this new generation of biblical specialists arising among the people: men and women at the service of the Word of God in the midst of the people. I also include Christian leaders working in economic, social, cultural, or political arenas, for whom the book of Revelation provides great inspiration.

Second, I want this book to be read by biblical scholars and professional exegetes, North and South, from "every race, language, people, and nation." They have also been interlocutors while I have been working. I have sought to produce a work that is scholarly and exegetically well grounded, but from the standpoint of the oppressed: the poor, indigenous people, blacks, women, young people, the cosmos and nature, and all those who endure the discrimination of the oppressive and idolatrous system.

BASIC GUIDELINES OF MY INTERPRETATION OF REVELATION

I would like to present in summary form some of the main ideas and principles guiding me in my work on Revelation.

1. Revelation arises in a time of persecution — and particularly amid situations of chaos, exclusion, and ongoing oppression. In such situations, Revelation enables the Christian community to rebuild its hope and its awareness. Revelation transmits a spirituality of resistance and offers guidance for organizing an alternative world. Revelation is a liberating book, one full of hope; its utopia is political and unfolds in history.

2. Revelation represents an important movement at the very beginning of Christianity, one rooted in the history of the people of Israel and in the prophetic-apocalyptic movement within which the Jesus movement, the apostolic mission, and the first Christian communities take their rise. Revelation draws together and transforms the Jewish and Judeo-Christian apocalyptic traditions; within the church its function is one of critique of, and resistance to, the Hellenization of Christianity and its authoritarian and patriarchal institutionalization. Over the long run, it was disregard of Revelation that opened the way for the incorporation of the church into the dominant imperial system and the construction of an authoritarian Christendom. To retrieve Revelation is to retrieve a fundamental dimension of the Jesus movement and of the origins of Christianity. Revelation is not an isolated book, one belonging to a sectarian or desperate tiny group, but rather a universal book that presses for radical reform of the church and a new way of being Christian in the world.

3. The eschatology of Revelation takes place basically in the present. The central fact transforming history is the death and resurrection of Jesus. Revelation is not oriented toward the "second coming of Jesus" or the "end of the world," but is focused on the powerful presence of the risen Jesus now, in the community and in the world. His resurrection transforms the present into a *kairos:* a moment of grace and conversion, a time of resistance, witness, and building of the reign of God. The central message of Revelation is this: if Christ arose, the time of resurrection and of the reign of God has begun.

4. Revelation is a book about the process of history. In this book history has two dimensions: one that is visible and empirical (which the author calls "earth")

and another that is deep and transcendent (which the author calls "heaven"). There is only one history and it unfolds simultaneously in heaven and on earth. God and the risen Messiah are active in our history, liberating us from oppression and death and building an alternative world. The utopia of Revelation is not achieved beyond history, but beyond oppression and death in a new world, where God's glory becomes visible over all the earth. This transcendent and liberating utopia of Revelation can be anticipated and furthered in our current history and even now is guiding all our thought and activity.

5. Revelation discloses (*apocalypse* = un-covering) the transcendent and liberating presence of the risen Christ in history. Revelation is wrath and punishment for the oppressors, but good news (gospel) for those excluded and oppressed by the empire of the beast. Revelation is the opposite of what we would today call ideology (which conceals oppression and legitimizes domination). The Spirit of Revelation is summed up in Jesus' cry: "I give praise to you, Father, Lord of heaven and earth, for although you have hidden these things from the wise and the learned you have revealed them to the childlike" (Matt. 11:25). The book of Revelation is God's revelation in the world of the poor, the oppressed, and the outcast.

6. Revelation is expressed through myths and symbols. Myth is within history and seeks to provide the community with an identity and to mobilize it in situations of chaos, oppression, and exclusion. Myth rebuilds the collective consciousness and the social praxis of the people of God. Myth is polysemic (has many senses) and is ever open to new interpretations. Revelation creates liberating myths and subverts dominant myths. Revelation teaches us to discover the power of myths.

7. The visions in Revelation transmit a fundamental conviction and a historical certainty. These visions must be not only interpreted, but also contemplated and transformed into action. Vision transmits power and expresses a spirituality that is within history. Vision is also memory and *parenesis* (exhortation). Finally, vision develops the creative imagination of the people and the search for alternatives.

8. The hatred and violence found in certain texts of Revelation express the limit-situation of extreme oppression and anguish that the community is undergoing. Revelation reproduces these feelings in order to produce a catharsis (release and purification) in those listening and thereby transform their hatred into awareness. The violence in Revelation is more literary than real: the risen Jesus appears as a lamb beheaded; his victory is on the cross; the martyrs defeat Satan with their witness; Jesus defeats the kings of the earth with his word. Apocalyptic praxis is the force of the Spirit, the force of consciousness, the power of myths, of witness, and of the Word (what we would call today the spiritual power of the oppressed and their strategy of nonviolence).

9. The Revelation of John unites apocalypse and prophecy. The myths and symbols it utilizes are not static fixed representations of reality but tools and criteria for a prophetic discernment of history. The book of Revelation calls to conversion and offers a universal salvation. Revelation is not a book of absolute archetypes and Manichaean dichotomies, but a reconstruction of the Exodus at

the heart of the Roman empire. With its prophetic Spirit, the book of Revelation moderates and transforms radical apocalyptic ideals.

10. Revelation brings together eschatology and politics, myth and praxis, consciousness and transformation of history. Revelation is not merely vision, catharsis, or protest. History does not lie in God's hands alone. Revelation is not about passivity or inactivity. The martyrs, the prophets, those who refuse to adore the beast or its image or to accept its mark really make history: they defeat Satan, destroy the powers of evil, cause an earthquake in Babylon, and reign over the earth. In Revelation the future is being built; this future, however, can be advanced and built in the present. In Revelation we find an analysis of the situation, and we are provided with materials and inspiration for building an alternative society. Revelation furnishes us with a decisive key for transforming history. The basic historical context of Revelation is the economic, political, cultural, social, and religious clash of the people of God and the Christian community with the Roman empire and the supernatural powers of evil.

11. Revelation should be understood in the historical context in which it arose (Asia Minor at the close of the first century) and must be interpreted in the Spirit in which it was written (see Vatican II, *Dei verbum*, no. 12). The book of Revelation is not abstract, universal, and eternal, equally valid for all ages and everywhere. Nor does it contain in enigmatic code form all of history from John to the end of the world. It is not a news report of the future nor is it science fiction. We reject every kind of fundamentalist, dispensationalist, or neoconservative interpretation of Revelation. We seek to interpret it in a positive manner in its literal and historical meaning, but we are likewise striving to interpret our present era in the light of Revelation. That is what we call the spiritual sense of Scripture.

1

General Introduction to Revelation

HISTORICAL AND THEOLOGICAL KEYS
FOR UNDERSTANDING REVELATION

From Prophecy to Apocalyptic (after the Destruction of Jerusalem in 586 B.C.E.)

In the history of the people of Israel we find an evolution from the prophetic literature toward the apocalyptic. It is a slow evolution in which the prophetic for some time is still mixed with the apocalyptic. It is not so important to attempt to find the dates when this change took place, but rather to discern the qualitative change from the prophetic to the apocalyptic in both the literary genre and the kind of theology produced. As a rule prophecy takes place in an orderly world, one in which the prophet announces God's word. Apocalyptic, by contrast, arises when this organized world has been destroyed and when the believer is excluded from the orderly world and thrown out into the chaos of marginality. Apocalyptic strives to rebuild consciousness, so as to make it possible to rebuild a different world. In the history of Israel the classical prophetic movement takes place primarily before the destruction of Jerusalem in 586. Before that date the people own the land, and they have a monarchy and a ruling class (priests, scribes, officials, and so forth); the capital, Jerusalem, and other cities exist, as do temple and worship. In 586 all of this world comes crashing down, and the "people of the land"[1] are left without any economic, political, cultural, or religious reference point. Apocalyptic is born at that point, and it strives to rebuild consciousness by creating new symbols and myths to make possible the rebuilding of the people.[2]

The prophet acts within the existing world; apocalyptic condemns the existing order and announces the building of another world. The prophet is the man of

---

1. See Jorge Pixley, *Historia sagrada, historia popular: Historia de Israel desde los pobres (1220 a.c.–135 d.c.)* (San José, Costa Rica: DEI, 1991), 91.

2. See Paul D. Hanson, *The Dawn of Apocalyptic: The Historical and Sociological Roots of Jewish Apocalyptic Eschatology,* rev. ed. (Philadelphia: Fortress Press, 1983), especially the appendix, 427–44.

God in the political and religious world of his own age; he seeks to bring about God's plan in this world. Apocalyptic arises when this world has been destroyed or is so deeply corrupted that God is going to destroy it. Apocalyptic rebuilds God's plan in consciousness (with visions, symbols, and myths) in order to build a new world. The world is just as historical in apocalyptic as it is for the prophet; it is only the perspective that changes. The prophet seeks to rebuild the world that is on the earth; apocalyptic seeks to rebuild awareness and hope so as to build a different world — within history nonetheless.

We could take an example from our own history of Latin America and the Caribbean in order to better understand these observations. What the year 586 meant in the history of Israel took place in the history of our continent in 1492. That year was also one of complete destruction, in this instance of the indigenous people — a destruction that was economic, political, cultural, and religious.

In this context and through the positive influence of a certain liberating evangelization there arises a new awareness in the indigenous people of Mexico that will find expression in the legend of Tepeyac. This story is apocalyptic and is intended precisely to rebuild indigenous consciousness. It is a syncretistic myth, built up from indigenous and Christian traditions (the goddess Tonantzin and the Virgin of Guadalupe), thus making it possible for the indigenous people first, followed by the Mexican (and Latin American) people, to build their own identity as part of a process of a complete rebuilding of the Amerindian people.[3] Alongside this apocalyptic indigenous story we find the prophetic response of Fray Bartolomé de las Casas. Because he is Spanish and a bishop, this prophet is able to act within the system. We thus observe an apocalyptic response that arises out of the chaos into which the indigenous people have been plunged and a prophetic response within the system.

Origins of Apocalyptic (after the Exile)

In the year 538 the Israelite elite returns to Palestine from exile in Babylon. An initial apocalyptic movement or, better, a reform movement is born, with its accompanying eschatology and an apocalyptic symbolic world, which then moves in two opposite directions.[4] The dominant tendency is hierocratic (priestly), draws inspiration from the apocalyptic eschatology of Ezekiel, and is led by the Zadokite priestly group. Its program is to rebuild the people by first rebuilding the temple and reinstating worship. It draws inspiration from Ezekiel 40–48. With the prophets Haggai and First Zechariah (Zech. 1–8), the movement creates its own symbolic universe in opposition to the Persian imperial world. This movement soon loses its eschatological and apocalyptic dimension and becomes a movement for controlling the community (Ezra, Nehemiah, and Chronicles).

---

3. See Clodomiro L. Siller Acuña, *Flor y canto del Tepeyac: Anotaciones y comentarios al Nican Mopohua* (Mexico, D.F.: Servir-Estudios Indígenas-Cenami, 1981).

4. See Hanson, *The Dawn of Apocalyptic,* especially the appendix mentioned in note 2.

The other tendency has a prophetic and popular character and draws inspiration from the apocalyptic eschatology of Second Isaiah. It seeks to rebuild Israel, not primarily on the basis of structures, but rather by rebuilding the people. Its program is Isaiah 60–62. This popular movement with an apocalyptic eschatology will produce writings like Isaiah 34–35, 24–27, all of Third Isaiah (Isa. 56–66), and later on Second Zechariah (Zech. 9–14), Second Joel (Joel 3–4), and perhaps Malachi. This movement will last about a century.

It is interesting to compare these two reform movements, the priestly-institutional and the popular-prophetic. Both seek to rebuild the people of God, the first by restoring structures and the second by restoring the people.[5] The subsequent apocalyptic movement will conserve the language and symbolism of the former, but in historical terms it will be the extension of the latter. The first movement was strongly influenced by the elite returning from exile. "Returnees" always try to rebuild the institutions of the past. The second movement grows primarily among the people of the land, who did not go into exile; they tend to see the institutions of the past as the cause of all the disasters that have befallen the people. This popular movement then strives for a utopian rebuilding of the people by creating a new awareness (new symbols and myths) and by criticizing dominant institutions. Perhaps both movements were historically necessary but the second one — prophetic and popular — was more creative and had a greater influence on the Jesus movement and on the origins of Christianity. It is quite obvious that liberation theology today follows the prophetic and popular model (drawing inspiration primarily from Isaiah 56–66). Today it also finds itself facing the restorationist priestly movement, which seeks to rebuild the people of God by restoring institutions and the law. Just as in biblical times, both movements are legitimate, provided that the institutional does not kill the prophetic and apocalyptic.

From Daniel to Revelation (Three Centuries of Apocalyptic)

Daniel and Revelation are the only apocalyptic books that became part of the canon of Scripture. Daniel (composed between 167 and 164 B.C.E.) and Revelation (between 90 and 96 C.E.) are the two visible extremes of a horizon spanning three centuries during which an almost uninterrupted popular apocalyptic movement expressed itself in a flourishing apocryphal literature that was both apocalyptic and connected to history.[6] Often the Revelation of John looks strange and seemingly isolated within the canon, but when we reconstruct the whole history and the apocalyptic literature between Daniel and Revelation, we have a meaningful context of three centuries in which Revelation again finds its

---

5. It is impressive to compare Ezekiel 40–48 (priestly project) with Isaiah 60–62 (popular project).

6. See Pablo Richard, "El Pueblo de Dios contra el Imperio: Daniel 7 en su contexto literario e histórico," *Revista de Interpretación Bíblica Latinoamericana* (San José, Costa Rica-Santiago de Chile) 7 (1991): 43–46. In general on this period see George W. E. Nickelsburg, *Jewish Literature between the Bible and the Mishnah: A Historical and Literary Introduction* (Philadelphia: Fortress Press, 1981), and John J. Collins, *The Apocalyptic Imagination: An Introduction to the Jewish Matrix of Christianity* (New York: Crossroad, 1987).

true historical place and meaning. This context becomes even more significant if we situate the Jesus movement and the apostolic church within it.

We have the following pattern:

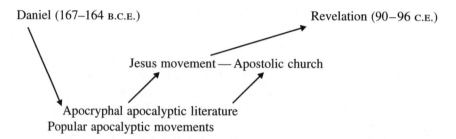

Daniel (167–164 B.C.E.)   Revelation (90–96 C.E.)

Jesus movement — Apostolic church

Apocryphal apocalyptic literature
Popular apocalyptic movements

To understand the Revelation of John historically we must begin with the peasant insurrection led by the Maccabees in 167 B.C.E. and the history of all the popular Jewish movements from that moment up to 135 C.E.[7] We must likewise study the apocalyptic literature that testifies to these movements, especially 1 Enoch, 2 Baruch, and 4 Ezra. It is within this broad context that we must situate the Judeo-Christian apocalyptic movement.

It is a qualitative advance for exegesis that the Jesus movement is now situated in the historical context of the popular movement of his time and primarily in the context of the apocalyptic movement.[8] Discussion has finally gotten beyond the question of whether Jesus was or was not a Zealot or a friend of Zealots, since it has been established that as an organized group the Zealots began to come on the scene only in the war against Rome in 66 C.E. Prior to that date we find only people who are fiercely devoted to the law, but such a stance is more religious than political.

Jesus stands against the historical backdrop of apocalyptic as a world of ideas, symbols, and myths that energized the peasant movements of his own time, especially in Galilee. It is apocalyptic rather than Zealot ideals that explain the Jewish resistance by the poor against the Roman empire in the time of Jesus.

The clear implication is that our idea of an apocalyptic movement and of apocalyptic must change (we will deal with this later). Liberal exegesis misinterpreted apocalyptic, and that is why it understood the preaching of the reign of God in terms of a completely otherworldly eschatology, one that was cosmic, outside of history, and divorced from social and political change. Properly understood, the apocalyptic context offers us a completely different vision of the Jesus movement: of Jesus' vision of the reign, his struggle with the devils, his identification with the son of man, the meaning of his parables, and especially all the historical meaning that it gives to his resurrection and his victorious presence in the midst of history and of the church. The apocalyptic perspective enables us to rescue the historical, economic, political, and social dimension of the Jesus

---

7. Here we refer to the exceptional work of Richard A. Horsley and John S. Hanson, *Bandits, Prophets, and Messiahs: Popular Movements in the Time of Jesus* (Minneapolis: Winston Press, 1985), and likewise Pixley, *Historia sagrada, historia popular.*

8. Horsley and Hanson, *Bandits, Prophets, and Messiahs.*

movement and to appreciate its peasant and popular character and at the same time its transcendent dimension within history. We thus come to see how the Jesus movement, the synoptic tradition, and the Revelation of John are drawn much closer together.

One key to interpreting Revelation is its relationship to early Christian prophecy and to the apostolic (and especially Pauline) movement. Another key is the rootedness of this prophecy and theology in Jewish and Judeo-Christian apocalyptic. It has been a mistake to contrast prophecy and apocalyptic in the New Testament too radically. In dealing with the Old Testament, we make a historical distinction between prophecy and apocalyptic because there was a deep change in literary genre and in theology, but the prophetic movement and apocalyptic converge in early Christianity. Today we are discovering, for example, how close Paul of Tarsus and the book of Revelation are.[9] While there are deep theological and literary differences, there is also continuity. A blend of prophecy and apocalyptic is being discovered in Jesus and the first communities, Judeo-Christian as well as Hellenistic. The Pauline writings manifest a strong apocalyptic dimension,[10] while the Revelation of John makes a very serious claim to be Christian prophecy.

Revelation in the Post-apostolic Period (70–120 C.E.)

We distinguish the apostolic period (30–70 C.E.) from the post-apostolic period (70–120 C.E.). The apostolic period is the lifetime of the first Christian generation (men and women), the apostles, those witnesses to Jesus who are charged with a mission in both the Jewish and Hellenistic world. Our basic direct witness to this period is Paul.

Our concern here is to focus on the post-apostolic period, that of the second Christian generation, the disciples of the apostles and of the witnesses to Jesus. Jerusalem has been laid waste in the Jewish war against Rome (66–74 C.E.), the mother church in Jerusalem has disappeared, the apostles are all dead, and the clash between the Christian movement and the synagogue is becoming more severe. It now becomes necessary to put the apostolic tradition and the other Christian traditions into writing (and thus the New Testament is born); during this period the church is being institutionalized. This is the period when Revelation is written. As a key to interpreting it, we must situate it in relation to all the other currents during this period.

James Dunn[11] distinguishes four currents in first-century Christianity: Jewish Christianity, Hellenistic Christianity, early Catholicism — which we prefer

---

9. Elisabeth Schüssler Fiorenza, *The Book of Revelation: Justice and Judgment* (Philadelphia: Fortress Press, 1985), chapter 5.

10. See J. Christiaan Beker, *Paul's Apocalyptic Gospel: The Coming Triumph of God* (Philadelphia: Fortress Press, 1982).

11. James D. G. Dunn, *Unity and Diversity in the New Testament: An Inquiry into the Character of Earliest Christianity,* 2d ed. (London: SCM Press; Philadelphia: Trinity Press International, 1990).

to call early Christendom[12] — and finally apocalyptic Christianity. He insists that these currents are not mutually exclusive and that they are to some extent overlapping (most Christians came from Judaism and almost all Jews were quite Hellenized). Nevertheless, these four currents unquestionably represent four different types of Christianity, especially by the end of the century.

Dunn also finds that the various heresies that appear toward the end of the second century correspond to these tendencies: the Ebionite sects come from Judeo-Christianity, the gnostic sects from Hellenic Christianity, and the Montanists from apocalyptic Christianity. Early Christendom is destined to prevail as the dominant orthodox tendency, especially beginning with Constantine in the fourth century. (Could we not also speak of an authoritarian and patriarchal heresy during the early centuries of Christianity?)

The interesting thing in this examination of history is that from the outset Christianity was deeply pluralistic within the unity of the church. Our usual idea is just the opposite: Christianity is believed to have been born monolithically, as a single trunk, and then subsequently to have become diversified into heretical sects. The historical truth is that Christianity is plural in character, especially in the post-apostolic period. This plurality and diversity is deep: it gives rise to different theological currents and models of church, which are to last for several centuries. Equally true is the unity of the church in the first century, which was never broken except for a few instances in the Johannine communities.

In order to have a key for understanding Revelation, it is important to compare apocalyptic Christianity to the other three tendencies. First we must note the distinction between *Jewish Christianity* and apocalyptic Christianity. While they are both rooted in the tradition of the people of Israel and both constitute "messianic sects" within the Jewish people, the differences are nonetheless equally significant. Judeo-Christianity will remain completely attached to the law, and some of its adherents will be radically opposed to Paul's mission and theology (Gal. 2; 2 Cor. 10–13; Acts 21). After the destruction of the Jerusalem temple, the academy of Jamnia under the sway of the pharisaic tendency will create a rabbinic Judaism quite opposed to messianic and apocalyptic ideas. More radical Jewish Christians who early in the second century will splinter off from the broader church and form Ebionite sects will also be anti-apocalyptic. Apocalyptic Christianity, which is very close to the prophetic-apocalyptic tradition of Jesus, Paul, and the early communities, will draw further and further away from orthodox Jewish Christianity. It is thanks to works like the Gospel of Matthew and the letter of James, which derive from moderate Judeo-Christianity, that the later broad church will be able to avoid being utterly cut off from the wealth of the Jewish tradition.

Hellenic Christianity and apocalyptic Christianity have much in common, particularly their radical opposition to the tendency that is to unfold as gnosticism in the second century. These future gnostics are the adversaries in

---

12. See Pablo Richard, *Morte das cristandades e nascimento da igreja,* 2d ed. (São Paulo: Paulinas, 1984). English translation: *Death of Christendoms, Birth of the Church* (Maryknoll, N.Y.: Orbis Books, 1987).

1 Corinthians, Philippians, Colossians, the pastoral letters, Jude, and Revelation. Paul, Mark, and the tradition of the Beloved Disciple raise up against them the theology of the cross, and Revelation likewise opposes them with its theology of martyrdom. Revelation stands apart from Hellenic Christianity in its ability to confront the negative aspects of the Hellenization of Christianity.

During the post-apostolic period the church becomes institutionalized. This process does not follow any single model. Quite the contrary, we have different models of institutionalization. The pastoral letters (1, 2 Timothy and Titus) represent one model; the post-Pauline tradition of Colossians/Ephesians and the other post-Pauline tradition of Luke-Acts represents another; a third model of institutionalization is that of Matthew, which in combining the traditions of Paul and James will be the founding model for the broad church; we also have the model of the Petrine tradition in the first letter of Peter; and finally, the model of institutional critique that unfolds in the tradition of the Beloved Disciple (Gospel of John and Epistles of John), which will ultimately acknowledge the apostolic model of the broader church (this is what we find in chapter 21 of John).[13]

Throughout this process of the institutionalization of the church during the post-apostolic period one clear tendency stands out and will later come to prevail with Constantine and Eusebius of Caesarea, that which we call *early Christendom*. This tendency simultaneously evidences a Hellenization and a de-eschatologization of Christianity (faith becomes doctrine — indeed, eschatology is already merely doctrine in the second letter of Peter — or it has to do only with the salvation of the individual soul, as in the Shepherd of Hermas). This tendency will likewise prompt the church to become more at home in the dominant political system (the Roman empire) and also lead to a gradual exclusion of women from church ministry (such exclusion was not the case in the early apostolic tradition). This tendency, called early Christendom, is clearly present in the pastoral letters and in 1 Clement in particular.

Finally we have *apocalyptic Christianity,* within which the Revelation of John is located. We have already said that this Christianity is very deeply rooted in the tradition of the Jewish people, and especially in Jewish apocalyptic. Apocalyptic Christianity likewise has roots in the Jesus movement, in the prophetic movement of the early communities, and even in Pauline theology. Hence, apocalyptic Christianity is not something isolated and bizarre at the end of the first century. Rather this tradition is part of the foundation and is decisively important in the birth of Christianity and of the church throughout the first century. Dunn states: "Christianity began as an apocalyptic sect within Judaism, a sect which in its apocalypticism was in substantial unity with the messages of both John the Baptist and of Jesus."[14]

The Gospel of Mark and the so-called Q generally retain their apocalyptic

---

13. For this description of models of the church in the post-apostolic period see the interesting work of Raymond E. Brown, *The Churches the Apostles Left Behind* (New York: Paulist, 1984). For the tradition of the Beloved Disciple see his *The Community of the Beloved Disciple* (New York: Paulist Press, 1979).

14. Dunn, *Unity and Diversity in the New Testament,* 325.

roots and inspiration.[15] Mark 13 is the primary expression of this apocalyptic tradition, which Mark has sought to preserve with special fidelity. Nevertheless, as we have already said, Jesus' whole conception of the reign of God, the struggle against the devils, the tradition of the son of man, and especially his resurrection, is inspired by apocalyptic, at least in its eschatological dimension. This tradition likewise survives in the Gospels of Matthew and Luke, especially in Matthew 24–25 and Luke 21.[16] We have already mentioned the apocalyptic background to Paul, particularly in the first letter to the Thessalonians (the entire letter, but especially 1 Thess. 4:13–5:11; also 1 Cor. 15; Gal. 1; Rom. 1–8). The second letter to the Thessalonians, which is almost certainly not Paul's, nevertheless clearly derives from the Pauline tradition and may be contemporary with the Revelation of John.[17] 2 Thessalonians 2:1–12 is enormously important for interpreting Revelation. Ephesians 6:1–20 also reflects a very lively apocalyptic Christianity. Outside the Pauline and post-Pauline tradition we may also mention the letter of Jude, an apocalyptic text that is contending with gnosticism.[18]

Function of Revelation in the Birth of Christianity

Thus far we have presented the roots of Christian apocalyptic, stressing that it is part of the foundation of the apostolic movement, and have indicated its identity, specificity, legitimacy, and importance in the post-apostolic period. All of this has often been denied, downplayed, or set aside in the Christian tradition with tragic consequences for both Christianity and the church. Hence in order to interpret the Revelation of John it is very important to examine briefly the function of Christian apocalyptic and of Revelation in the history of Christianity.

Christian Apocalyptic and Revelation in Relation to Judaism and Judeo-Christianity

First, Christian apocalyptic served as a bridge between the Jewish apocalyptic tradition and Christianity. That such was the case is indicated by the impact of the book of Daniel on the Jesus movement, in early Christian tradition, and throughout the subsequent history of Christianity, especially in popular Christian circles. Christian apocalyptic served as a bridge between the popular Jewish apocalyptic movements, with all their symbolic and theological riches, and Christian liberating movements throughout the history of Christianity. The Jewish apocalyptic books (such as 1 Enoch, 4 Ezra, 2 Baruch, etc.) survived thanks to the Christian churches.

---

15. N. Perrin and D. C. Duling, *The New Testament: An Introduction,* 2d. ed. (New York: Harcourt, 1982), 11ff. and 233ff., where Mark's Gospel is called "the apocalyptic drama."

16. Jacques Dupont, *Les trois apocalpyses synoptiques* (Paris: du Cerf, 1985).

17. Helmut Köster, *Introducción al Nuevo Testamento: Historia, cultura y religión en la época helenística e historia y literatura del cristianismo primitivo* (Salamanca: Sígueme, 1988), 765ff., on the renewal of the apocalyptic genre. English translation: *Introduction to the New Testament* (Philadelphia: Fortress Press, 1988).

18. Köster, *Introducción al Nuevo Testamento,* 770ff., on the apocalyptic genre and gnosticism; the epistle of Jude.

Second, Christian apocalyptic was very helpful for blending the prophetic and the apocalyptic traditions. That took place in Jesus' own life and in the post-Easter community from the outset, and it lasted throughout the whole first century. From the very beginning Christianity was a prophetic and apocalyptic movement. This fusion made the Old Testament prophetic tradition relevant for the apostolic communities and endowed that tradition with all its popular and liberating drive. That blend was subsequently lost in the church, especially when the church marginalized or completely forgot the apocalyptic tradition, turned it into an abstract doctrine, or reduced it to salvation of the individual soul (a process already underway in the second letter of Peter and in the Shepherd of Hermas).

Christian apocalyptic also corrected or moderated some negative aspects of Jewish apocalyptic. It was helpful for overcoming its sometimes excessively nationalistic and violent character, and it likewise corrected its fundamentalist enthusiasms and its disproportionate expectation that the Messiah would come soon. Jewish apocalyptic literature often got lost in otherworldly and cosmic speculations, drawing it away from the historical responsibility of the believer within the world. Many of these apocalyptic deviations reappear in the Christian churches precisely when the churches marginalize and forget the genuine tradition of Christian apocalyptic.

Revelation likewise played an important role in the second century in dealing with Montanism. This heresy is certainly rooted in apocalyptic Christianity and shows us the power of this Christianity, as well as its distortions. Montanism arose in Pepusa near Philadelphia around the year 156.[19] It was an apocalyptic movement that battled fiercely with the Roman empire, as well as with the members of the hierarchy who collaborated with the empire. The Montanists suffered many persecutions and furnished many martyrs. This movement represented a kind of popular Christianity, in which women figured prominently. It was likewise an explosion of prophecy, in which the presence of the oppressed classes can be felt. The great theologian of the church Tertullian was involved in this movement in the early years of the third century. Ultimately Montanism split away from the broader church.

A connecting thread runs from Montanism, through Novatianism and Donatism, to the medieval movements of the Cathari, Bogomils, and Albigensians, the "spirituals" of Joachim of Fiori, and the "fraticelli" of St. Francis — and indeed to subsequent movements such as the Hussites and Anabaptists, in which the inspiration of the original Christian apocalyptic survives, often combined with the apocalyptical deviations mentioned above. If the church admitted Revelation into the canon it was largely in order to legitimize this prophetic-apocalyptic dimension that is essential to Christianity, although it was also in order to discern between what was positive and negative in popular apocalyptic movements, and at the same time to moderate apocalyptic Chris-

---

19. For what follows, see Eduardo Hoornaert, *La memoria del pueblo cristiano: Una historia de la Iglesia en los tres primeros siglos* (Madrid: Paulinas, 1986), 113ff. English translation: *The Memory of the Christian People* (Maryknoll, N.Y.: Orbis Books, 1989).

tianity and avoid the exuberant manifestations of fundamentalist apocalyptic. The Revelation of John fits this double intention of the church perfectly: it rescues the prophetic-apocalyptic dimension of the church and restrains alienating apocalyptical enthusiasm.

Christian Apocalyptic and Revelation vis-à-vis Hellenism and Gnosticism

Ernst Käsemann's position that Apocalyptic themes form "the real beginning of primitive Christian theology" is well known.[20] Elsewhere he calls apocalyptic the "mother of Christian theology." Even more important is his warning against the risks of abandoning apocalyptic:

> My own contention tends to be that Apocalyptic of the time after Easter designates the earliest variant and interpretation of the kerygma. Admittedly, we can then no longer ask the question whether it was more help or more hindrance in getting a grip on the necessary theological task. Certainly it was the first to acknowledge and attack the task. It cannot be disputed that the theology of the Church has to a large extent seen its task as consisting in the vanquishing of apocalyptic. Are the early Fathers therefore the first theologians? Is classical Greece the godparent of Christian theology? The New Testament scholar may be permitted to ask what price we should have to pay and what gamble we should embark upon if, as theologians, we were to become heirs of Greek thinking in our systematics. One does not conquer apocalyptic and escape scot-free.[21]

This assessment of apocalyptic as the mother of theology, the acknowledgement that the church subsequently eliminated apocalyptic, and pointing out the price we pay for the excessive Hellenization of theology are very important for rediscovering the function of apocalyptic in the church. All of this is quite acceptable. What is questionable is the way Käsemann reduces apocalyptic to the imminent parousia (coming) of Jesus.[22] Apocalyptic is centered not on the parousia but on Jesus' resurrection. Resurrection is common in apocalyptic thought in general; what is new in Christian apocalyptic is that resurrection has already taken place in Jesus. If Jesus arose from the dead, then the resurrection of the dead is possible and the time of resurrection has already begun. Further on we will see how the parousia as "second coming" is not so important in Revelation (and generally in the New Testament). What is important is the parousia as the "victorious presence of the risen Christ in history." The experience that Jesus is alive in the community and the experience of his Spirit are what is basic in the eschatology of the early church as a whole, and especially in Christian

---

20. Ernst Käsemann, *Ensayos exegéticos* (Salamanca: Sígueme, 1978), 211, on the origins of Christian theology.

21. Ibid., 223ff., n. 7, on the issue of early Christian apocalyptic.

22. See I. Howard Marshall, "Is Apocalyptic the Mother of Christian Theology?" G. F. Hawthorne, and O. Bets, eds., *Tradition and Interpretation in the New Testament* (Grand Rapids: William B. Eerdmans, 1987), 33–42.

apocalyptic. That is how apocalyptic is the mother of Christian theology, and that is how it will oppose gnosis and the over-Hellenization of Christianity.

Apocalyptic is the mother of theology because it is rooted historically in Jewish and Judeo-Christian apocalyptic, it is a part of popular apocalyptic movements, and it is the background to the Jesus movement and the early church. Precisely because of these origins, however, apocalyptic is not the mother of any theology whatsoever, but of a very specific type of theology: a theology that is historical, political, popular, eschatological, and opposed to an excessively Hellenized Greco-Latin theology. Let us briefly examine the negative effects of Hellenism in Christianity, how Christianity dealt with Hellenism, and how apocalyptic played an important role in resistance to Hellenism.

Further on we will discuss Christendom, and the relationship of the church with the ruling classes, especially starting in the fourth century. For now let us examine something earlier and more fundamental, namely, the *penetration of Hellenism into the church:* into its theology, official teaching, liturgy, and its ways of acting and relating to the world and to God.[23] This process has been taking place from the second century up to our own times, and indeed there are Hellenizing tendencies in the first century: Paul's opponents in 1 Corinthians and Philippians and in the period after Paul in Colossians and the pastoral letters. We also find such tendencies within the dissidents in the communities of the Gospel of the Beloved Disciple (fourth Gospel); 1 John combats those tendencies. The Revelation of John will subsequently struggle against similar opponents (those who are called "Nicolaitans," as we will later explain). Likewise the letter of Jude is contending with a similar tendency.

In continuity with these Hellenizing enthusiasts (future gnostics), subsequent Greco-Latin theology will engage in a mistaken rereading and interpretation of the origins of Christianity. Paul and John will be read in a Hellenizing way, the synoptics will be set aside as edifying reading, and apocalyptic and the Revelation of John will be left out. Hellenism will establish an intellectual class poles apart from the people, standing in continuity with the philosopher class in Hellenistic society. A Hellenistic theology thereby comes into being, one that is intellectualist, individualist, elitist in nature, and foreign to the Christian life of the people. Such Christian elites never undertook a discernment of Hellenism, or evangelized it, but took it on as it was. Plato and Aristotle replaced the historical memory of Jesus and the apostolic tradition. It was Hellenism that changed Christianity; Christianity did not evangelize Hellenism. The church was unable to evangelize the dominant culture, because that culture had already changed the ruling group in the church. The intellectual elites in Christianity were tied to the political elites of the empire. Hellenism and Christianity were blended in a way that served domination.

One of the negative aspects of Hellenism in theology is that the image of God that comes to prevail is that of the Greek philosophers: a cosmic God, not a

---

23. For the question of Hellenism in the church I am following José Comblin, *Tiempo de acción: Ensayo sobre el Espíritu y la historia* (Lima: CEP, 1986), chapter 3, "El Espíritu ante el helenismo." Likewise José Comblin, *A força da palavra* (Petrópolis, Brazil: Vozes, 1986), chapter 2, "A palavra de Deus e o desafío do helenismo."

God of history; an ordering God rather than a liberating God.[24] The order of the universe is taken as the image of God. Hellenism thoroughly imbues theology with idealism. It was such Christianity that popularized Hellenic idealism, with two effects: contempt for matter (the body, sex, and so forth) and the isolation of the Spirit (foreign to bodiliness and history). The result was a Hellenized Christianity that projected into the people a spirituality that was anti-material, un-social, intellectualist, individualistic, and patriarchal. The Hellenization of Christianity also led to neglect of the Holy Spirit. Hellenistic culture had no room for the Spirit and hence no room for the spiritual transformation of history, matter, the body — forgetting the resurrection! The movement of the Spirit that survives within the people of God will thus inevitably find itself contending with the Hellenizing intellectual focus of the ecclesiastical institution.

Resistance to Hellenism and to Hellenization is already beginning in Jewish apocalyptic, even in the first half of the second century B.C.E. in the war of the Maccabees (see the books of Maccabees and Daniel). Although Palestine is quite Hellenized at the beginning of the first century B.C.E., Jesus' preaching, deeply inspired by apocalyptic, stands in radical opposition to the wise and learned who rule over the people:

> I give praise to you, Father, Lord of heaven and earth, for although you have hidden these things from the wise and learned you have revealed[25] them to the childlike. (Matt. 11:25–27; Luke 10:21–22: texts from the Q source, which is strongly apocalyptic)

Neither Jesus nor the synoptic tradition (Q, Mark, Matthew, Luke) reflects any Hellenistic influence. The preaching of the reign of God, which is transcendent but is carried out on earth; the struggle against the demons; teaching in parables; the cross and bodily resurrection of Jesus — all draw their inspiration from apocalyptic and are contrary to the culture of Hellenism already present in Palestine in the time of Jesus. Paul will also have a wretched experience with the philosophical schools of Hellenism (Acts 17:16–34), which then shapes his negative attitude toward the wise of this world (1 Cor. 1–4). Paul will struggle against Hellenizing enthusiasts in 1 Corinthians and Philippians, and his followers will do so in the letters to the Colossians and the pastoral letters. Against them Paul raises up his "theology of the cross." The Revelation of John struggles with opponents of the same kind (Nicolaitans), against whom it raises a very similar theology, its "theology of martyrdom." The letter of Jude likewise struggles against Hellenizing theology from an apocalyptic perspective.

In short, we can say that from the second century B.C.E. until the middle of the second century C.E., apocalyptic played a decisive role in the struggle against the radical Hellenizing philosophy and the Hellenization of both Judaism and Christianity. The triumph of the Hellenization of Christian theology meant the failure of Christian apocalyptic. As Käsemann says in the passage quoted above,

---

24. José Comblin, *Cristo en el Apocalipsis* (Barcelona: Herder, 1969), 195ff.
25. The verb used is *apocalypsas,* the verbal form of the noun *apokalypsis* = revelation.

the church eliminated apocalyptic but paid a high price: theology became the heir of Greek thought. We could add that theology became elitist, intellectualist, and idealist and came to serve the oppressors. One does not conquer apocalyptic and escape scot-free!

Even if Hellenization had a major impact on Christianity starting in the second century, it did not sweep the field entirely. A popular kind of Christianity that resisted Hellenized culture developed, particularly in the East. The struggle against gnostic heresies was also of the people. Gnosticism represents a perverse inculturation of Christianity into the Roman empire's philosophy of domination.[26] Christian gnosticism is a failed attempt to blend Hellenism and Christianity (Comblin). Throughout history somehow the people of God have preserved the memory of the tradition of Jesus and of the early Christian communities, which is a tradition of poor people and for poor people, one that is apocalyptic and non-Hellenistic.[27] Hellenism held sway over the oppressor classes, but it never managed to hold sway over the memory and the popular Christian consciousness of Christianity. If Hellenism prevailed within the ruling elites, the apocalyptic tradition survived in the consciousness of the faith of the people of God.

In closing this section we should also acknowledge certain positive features of Greco-Latin culture in Christianity.[28] This culture provided the Christian religion with a certain sense of what is human and a rational conception of religion that freed us from certain irrational religious excesses connected to devils, magic, sorcery, superstition, fear, and other kinds of collective madness. Hellenism furnished Christianity with a sense of universality and an optimistic vision of religion. Hellenism likewise was an aid in the theoretical formulation of the faith, leaving aside the negative factors already noted. Greek humanism also freed Christianity from sensationalism and religious enthusiasm and opened it to the profane, to culture, and to the meaning of freedom (rejection of totalitarianism).

The excessive Hellenization of Christianity nullified these positive elements of Greco-Latin culture. The excluding and dominating Hellenization that prevailed in Christianity threw the Christian tradition and the life of the church out of balance, with the negative effects that we have already noted. Hence it is extremely important to retrieve apocalyptic in general and the Revelation of John in particular in order to offset this negative Hellenization. The point is not to fall into the opposite error of building up an exclusively apocalyptic church and theology. It is rather to rediscover the balance that we lost due to excessive Hellenization and the neglect of apocalyptic and to rebuild a synthesis in which the positive elements of Hellenic culture and tradition can make a modest and positive contribution to the original Christian tradition so that apocalyptic and Revelation may occupy the proper historical place that they originally merited.

---

26. Some writers distinguish between the dominant philosophical gnosticism, linked to the ruling classes, and certain "popular gnosticism," i.e., the incorporation of some gnostic ideas into movements of popular, and especially feminist, protest.

27. See Hoornaert, *La memoria del pueblo cristiano*.

28. Comblin, *Tiempo de acción*, 180ff.

Christian Apocalyptic and Revelation vis-à-vis Early Christendom

What has been called the system of Christendom begins in the fourth century with the conversion of the emperor Constantine. The period of major persecutions of the church draws to a close, and the time of the alliance of the hierarchical church with the political power of the Roman empire begins.[29] The church also undergoes deep internal changes: the Hellenization of the church already underway in the second century is made official, and the power of the intellectual elites gradually prevails over the apostolic tradition, which is still alive in the consciousness and memory of the Christian people and the communities. Power is sacralized: the Roman empire is now compared to Moses and David. The church's enemies are no longer the structures of the empire, the rich and the oppressors, but heretics, Jews, and pagans. The moving force of history is no longer the people of God, its communities and its poor, but those who organize the church (bishops, priests, and deacons).

Worse than the Constantinization of the church's structures, however, is its theological Constantinization. The person chiefly responsible for this development is Eusebius of Caesarea (263–339), the bishop of Caesarea in Palestine, a great theologian and church historian and major advisor to the emperor Constantine. Eusebius wrote a ten-volume History of the Church, which is truly a very useful work for church history. The theology underlying that history, however, would be the source of a deep disruption in the history of Christianity. Eusebius reconstructs the history of the church from the perspective of the Roman empire and from the standpoint of Christendom and the Hellenization of Christianity. The "official history" of Christianity thus comes into being in order to justify and legitimize Christendom, the alliance between church and empire. This official church history is not the actual history but history imagined as it would have to be so that imperial Christendom might be accepted as legitimate. No doubt his work has many positive features and many items of information that are very useful for the history of Christianity. Nevertheless, the underlying theological and "ideological" direction of the work profoundly disfigures and falsifies the history of the first three centuries of Christianity. Even though Christianity arose out of the poor and outcast as a prophetic and apocalyptic movement and its message was one of profound liberation from the law, sin, and death, it was now transformed into its opposite, an institution of law and power.

Hence we are not surprised to find that Eusebius is the main founding figure of anti-Semitism. Christianity thus loses contact with its Jewish origins (its origins in the Exodus, the prophets, and apocalyptic). Nor is it surprising that he should cast doubt on whether the Revelation of John is part of the canon of Scripture. Hence in order to reconstruct the real history of Christianity from its origins we must turn Eusebius of Caesarea's vision upside down. We must reconstruct the history of those origins from their roots, that is, interpret the history of the books of the New Testament in the spirit in which they were written and not in the Hellenistic, Constantinian, imperial spirit of Eusebius. As we will see later, retrieving the Revelation of John and apocalyptic in general

---

29. In this section, we are following Hoornaert, *La memoria del pueblo cristiano*.

will be fundamental for this reconstruction of the real history of the origins of Christianity.

We have already noted that so-called early Christendom was one of the major currents during the post-apostolic period and that it was marked by the Hellenization and de-eschatologization of early Christianity. This tendency was embodied in the process of the institutionalizing of the church and of faith that is especially observable in the pastoral letters. That the church had to become institutionalized to some degree during this post-apostolic period is beyond question. Had this process not taken place, perhaps today we would know nothing of the first Christian generation and of the origins of Christianity. The problem is not the institutionalization of the early church, but a certain kind of institutionalization that runs counter to the apostolic-charismatic tradition and the prophetic-apocalyptic tradition of the first Christian generation and its communities. The tradition of Mark and of the Beloved Disciple (Gospel and letters of John) represents a strong protest even in the post-apostolic period against an authoritarian and patriarchal institutionalization of the early church. Such protest is even more radical in Christian apocalyptic and in the Revelation of John.

During the first century the Spirit achieves a certain balance between apocalyptic and prophetic Christianity and institutionalizing Christianity (which we have called early Christendom), and during the second century this balance is reflected in the formation of the canon. Both the pastoral letters and Revelation remain in the canon. The Spirit and the church recognize this pluralism of the post-apostolic period of which we have spoken. This balance and pluralism disappear, however, in the rereading of the origins of Christianity carried out by Eusebius and Christendom. As we have noted, Eusebius puts Revelation outside the canon with impunity, and with his anti-Semitism he breaks the connection between Christianity and the Jewish tradition. That is why it is important to retrieve the apocalyptic tradition and Revelation and to reconstruct the function that this literature fulfilled throughout the first century, not only in order to reconstruct the genuine history of the origins of Christianity, but also in order to reconstruct its meaning in our own contemporary history.

In this confrontation between the prophetic and apocalyptic tradition and the institutionalization of the church — a legitimate confrontation that is accepted by the church — we must still refine several points.[30] Some admit that Revelation is part of the apocalyptic-prophetic movement of the early church, but they think that it represents a marginal group in the church of Asia Minor, perhaps a group that comes from Jerusalem or from Syria-Palestine, which founded its own communities. The aim is thereby to isolate or marginalize the reality of church lying behind Revelation. The book is said to have its origins in groups that are marginal, desperate, fanatical, and that do not have much to do with the life of the broader church and of all its more recognized communities. It is true that if we compare Revelation with the Acts of the Apostles, Colossians, Ephesians, 1 Peter, the pastoral letters, Ignatius of Antioch, and the letter of Polycarp, we see a very different church structure. In Revelation we find a

---

30. Schüssler Fiorenza, *The Book of Revelation,* chapter 5.

church led by prophets, whereas in other writings the church is seen to be led by bishops, presbyters, and deacons. Although that is true, we must nonetheless not forget that Ignatius of Antioch is a *prophet* bishop. It is the prophetic that gives ministries their power. The Didache represents the shift from a church that depends on prophets to a church that depends on bishops who play the role of prophets. The problem posed is not the opposition between prophets and bishops or between a prophetic church and another church that is hierarchical. That is not the problem. The issue raised by Revelation is the opposition between true and false prophets. The problem is not the shift from a prophetic church to another church that is hierarchical, but the loss of the prophetic spirit. There is a movement from prophet bishops to authoritarian bishops who are no longer prophets. Revelation seeks to renew this prophetic spirit throughout the church and in all the churches. In this sense the churches of Revelation are the very same churches that make up the broader church in Asia Minor and elsewhere. The alleged marginal churches do not exist; what exists is an apocalyptic current lived and accepted in the broader church, which is still a community in which all the traditions of the apostolic and post-apostolic period exist together.

SOCIOLOGICAL AND THEOLOGICAL KEYS
FOR UNDERSTANDING REVELATION

We now move from historico-theological analysis to socio-theological analysis. In what follows, we will distinguish "apocalypse" as literary genre from "apocalyptic" as symbolic universe in which an apocalyptic movement codifies its identity and interpretation of reality.[31] We will investigate the historical context or social origins of both apocalyptic and apocalypse, as well as the function that apocalyptic and apocalypse fulfill in society. A social movement that sustains apocalyptic and apocalyptic literature is called an "apocalyptic movement."

Economic, Political, Cultural, and Religious Context of Apocalyptic

Exegesis today is devoting special attention to examining apocalyptic movements and apocalyptic from a sociological standpoint. Such socio-historical analysis provides us with an explanation of the origins and character of apocalyptic movements. There is a consensus that apocalyptic literature is "a literature of oppressed people"[32] that expresses the worldview of the poorest and most oppressed, humiliated, and outcast sectors of society; those who do not feel that their own authorities understand them or speak for them; those who have an alternative view of history or theological vision, one that is different from that of the ruling groups. These are not marginal sects, as has been maintained so

---

31. Hanson, *The Dawn of Apocalyptic,* appendix.
32. André Lacocque, "Naissance de l'apocalyptique," *Lumière et Vie* 160 (1982): 7.

often in order to relativize or downplay apocalyptic. The oppressed are the social agents in apocalyptic, but their thinking can also be universal, foundational, creative, constitutive, and all-encompassing and can have its own identity and legitimacy.

With the consensus mentioned above as a starting point, we must examine the specific and differentiated situation of each apocalyptic movement. Some apocalyptic movements arise in situations of *breakdown* after major catastrophes, when all the social and religious structures that used to reproduce the life and myths of the people are falling apart. In such situations apocalyptic strives to create new myths and to build a new awareness, so that life will not fall into chaos, as, for example, in the apocalyptic that emerges after the destruction of all Israel's structures in 586 B.C.E. or 70 C.E. Another specific situation is *persecution* by local authorities or by a foreign power with the complicity of local ruling groups, such as occurred under Antiochus IV Epiphanes. That persecution jeopardized not only the faith of the people of God but all the economic, political, and cultural structures of the people as well. The book of Daniel (167–164 B.C.E.) arose out of such a context. A third possibility occurs when the people are living under *ongoing oppression.* An example is the situation of the Jewish people in Palestine, oppressed simultaneously by the temple and the ruling Jewish groups (Sadducees, Herodians, scribes) and by the Roman empire.

In short, these are three different situations: breakdown, persecution, and oppression. Each situation can give rise to different kinds of apocalyptic. The main problem underlying the Revelation of John is not so much persecution, which certainly exists, but oppression and exclusion: because of their consciousness and their faith, Christian communities can neither "buy nor sell" — they cannot participate in society and culturally they are outcasts. They are enduring ongoing oppression and complete exclusion: economic, political, cultural, and religious, in everyday life and in their families as well. The "tribulation" mentioned in Revelation 1:9 and 7:14 is not basically a persecution but a situation of ongoing oppression and exclusion.

Exclusion is something worse than exploitation and oppression, for the excluded are completely outside and do not count; their death has no effect on the system. As Paul says in 1 Corinthians 1:28: "God chose the lowly and despised of the world, those who count for nothing, to reduce to nothing those who are something." To a certain extent the exploited are privileged, insofar as they are still part of the system. Degradation increases when the poor are not only poor but also oppressed, and when they go from being oppressed to being excluded. The excluded suffer not only the dominant violence, but also the violence among the excluded themselves; exclusion destroys social relations between one poor person and another, between man and woman and between adult and child. In such a situation of exclusion, rebuilding community and person becomes both urgent and liberating. This is the basic social context out of which Revelation arises, which is not to deny situations of ongoing oppression and particular moments of persecution, which are also a fact. In the Third World today, exclusion is becoming more universal and more defining of the situation than the reality of poverty, oppression, and persecution.

A possible working hypothesis for explaining the rise of apocalyptic in the history of Israel is that it arose out of the transition of a tributary mode of production to an *imperial slave-based mode of production.* In the tributary mode, protest can be made within the system, especially against the religion of the system; in the slave mode, protest places one outside the system and outside the religion of the system. Prophecy is then proper to the tributary mode of production, while apocalyptic arises in the transition to an imperial slave-based mode of production. The Revelation of John would thus be an attempt to affirm Christian identity in opposition to the slave system and in building an alternative community. Something similar is happening today in the Third World vis-à-vis a total market system that imposes on us a single system of values and a market religion that is utterly opposed to Christian faith. Prophetic protest against the system becomes more difficult with each day; apocalyptic protest outside the system is the most significant and effective mass protest.

Far from being all alike, apocalyptic responses are varied. What they all have in common is the creation of a symbolic universe on which the life of the community depends, an alternative to the previous system that has fallen apart or an alternative to the dominant system that is persecuting, oppressing, or excluding the community. This alternative symbolic universe may be radically otherworldly if the community withdraws to set up a society on its own; or it may be a clandestine underground subworld if the community goes below the surface and disappears in order to engage in resistance that is silent and invisible to the visible political world; finally, it may be an alternative universe that responds actively against the dominant world: one that protests, denounces, resists, struggles, and seeks to create an alternative visible community and society, standing in opposition to the dominant and oppressive world. This oppressor world may be foreign or internal to the society or community in question.[33] All these responses are found in the Revelation of John, although the prevailing response is that of an active resistance and the positive building of a community that is a visible alternative to the dominant oppressive system. Such is the meaning of testimony, about which we will speak further.

Although purely sociological analysis is absolutely necessary, it is insufficient. A socio-theological analysis is required as well. The contradiction between rich and poor, oppressor and oppressed, persecutor and persecuted, can be interpreted theologically in terms of "wicked-just" or "theocratic-visionary," in theologico-cosmic terms like "earth and heaven" and "dwellers on earth and dwellers in heaven," or in theologico-temporal terms like "this world and the coming world." Apocalyptic abounds in such socio-theological polarities: the opposition between empire and people is interpreted by means of the symbols of Beast-Human Figure (Daniel 7), Beast-Lamb, and Mark of the Beast-Mark of the Lamb (Rev. 13–14). The Revelation of John creates its own imaginary world and socio-literary code, thus enabling it to achieve distance from and oppose the imagination or literary code prevailing in society as well as in certain established or authoritarian models of church.

---

33. Hanson, *The Dawn of Apocalyptic.*

The sociological context likewise helps us to discern within apocalyptic theological dimensions that are especially important when groups are being persecuted within a religious community. An example is the apocalyptic notion of the kingdom of God in Jesus' preaching, which stands in opposition to the nationalistic conception of the kingdom of Israel held by the dominant religious groups in Palestine. The kerygma of the resurrection in the early Christian communities likewise stands in opposition to the enthusiastic Hellenistic theology of some groups of rich Christians (future gnostics). Another example is the very concept of revelation that the seer or prophet receives directly from God and that surpasses or contradicts the theological erudition that is under the control of the religious or political authorities, for example, Daniel 2, Matthew 11:25, Galatians 1, and 4 Esdras 14:1–48 — where the seer, like a new Moses, wrote seventy books beyond the twenty-four of the Hebrew canon — in other words, a divine revelation that triples what is in the Torah, one that does not pass through it and cannot be controlled by the power groups.[34] All these alternative theological visions enable persecuted or oppressed groups to have their own identity and to struggle against the dominant political or religious structures.

World Vision of Apocalyptic Movements

We have defined apocalyptic as the symbolic universe in which an apocalyptic movement codifies its identity and interpretation of reality. Now that we have examined the social origins of apocalyptic, let us also examine its constitutive symbolic elements.

Heaven and Earth

Although in the Bible the expression "heaven and earth" normally refers to creation, the cosmos, and the universe, in apocalyptic literature the meaning it acquires is primarily symbolic or mythical. The earth refers to the world as it appears to be, the empirical world, the world in which human powers, the unjust, and the wicked prevail. Heaven, on the other hand, is the deep dimension of the world, and it is beyond the political control of the wicked; heaven is the transcendent world in which supernatural powers, both God and the devil, are at work; it is the world of the saints and the believers. The Revelation of John systematically employs the expression "inhabitants of the earth" (*hoi katoikountes epi tes ges*) to designate the wicked and the expression "inhabitants of heaven" for the saints and the just. Hence the earth appears to be the place of the powerful and the oppressors; heaven, by contrast, is the place of the poor, the persecuted, and the excluded.

The expression "heaven and earth" is mythical and symbolic; hence it cannot be interpreted literally (as the fundamentalists do), but requires a theological interpretation. Every myth is spatial and temporal, and hence there is a spontaneous tendency to situate its elements directly in space and time (we say that

---

34. J. Severino Croatto, "Apocalíptica y esperanza de los oprimidos: Contexto socio-político y cultural del género apocalíptico," *Revista de Interpretación Bíblica Latinoamericana* (San José, Costa Rica-Santiago de Chile) 7 (1990): 11ff.

the earth is "below" and heaven "above"). The proper procedure is to discern the theological content of myth and of course to interpret it within history. (We will return to myth further on.) Heaven and earth are two dimensions of the same history; there is but one history, and heaven and earth point to the two dimensions of that single history. Heaven is history's deep and transcendent dimension, while earth is its apparent and superficial dimension.

Apocalypse as Unveiling

The basic meaning of "apocalypse" in apocalyptic literature is "unveiling." The meaning of apocalypse — whose literal sense is "to reveal" — is to make visible, tangible, audible, and understandable something that was hidden, invisible, and unintelligible. Moreover, what is unveiled is something that is primarily of interest to the saints, the just, and the poor. As unveiling, apocalypse seeks to make visible the reality of the saints and to legitimize their cause, their resistance, and their struggle. In modern parlance, we could say that apocalypse is the opposite of ideology. In its pejorative sense, ideology is what *conceals* reality and *legitimizes* domination. The function of ideology is to hide oppression and legitimize domination. Apocalypse unveils the reality of the poor and legitimizes their liberation. That is why apocalypse is liberating and is good news for the poor. Taking up the mythical and theological notion of "heaven and earth," we can say that apocalypse reveals heaven; it makes visible the hidden transcendent depths of history.

Apocalyptic revelation is different from the traditional kind. In apocalyptic there is a "plus" beyond the revelation that has already been transmitted (Torah, prophets, writings) and that is now regarded as insufficient for understanding new crisis situations.[35] A breakdown of the previous world, persecution, or oppression poses new questions to apocalyptic and to the people. It is no longer enough to recall or interpret the received Scripture. It is useful and necessary to do so, but to uncover the current situation and to find where God lies in the new historical situation and what God's will or plan of salvation is, something new is required. That is why apocalyptic does not present its arguments in a theological reflection based on earlier texts, but presents its message as a new and direct revelation from God. In Galatians 1:11–12 Paul says,

> Now I want you to know brothers, that the gospel preached by me is not of human origin. For I did not receive it from a human being, nor was I taught it, but it came through a revelation of Jesus Christ [*di' apokalypseos Iesou Christou*].

Paul is not speaking as an excited or haughty visionary, but simply as one who is apocalyptic. No doubt this conception of revelation can lead to abuses (as later happened among the Montanists, who misused their "new" revelations of God). Hence apocalypse can occur only if it is built upon a powerful spiritual

---

35. J. Severino Croatto, "Desmesura y fin del opresor en la perspectiva apocalíptica: Estudio de Daniel 7–12," *Revista Bíblica* (Argentina) 39 (1990): 130f.

experience of the community and in continuity with the whole previous revelation, which is accepted as a criterion for discerning current revelation in history. The meaning of apocalypse can be compared with what in hermeneutics we call the allegorical or spiritual meaning.[36] This spiritual (apocalyptic) meaning is also legitimate when it is "controlled" by the literal and historical meaning, as well as by the community (magisterium) and by biblical scholarship. As St. Augustine says: "The Bible, God's second book, was written to help us decode the world, to give back to us the gaze of faith and of contemplation, and to *transform all of reality into one great revelation of God.*"[37]

Apocalypse is precisely this "great revelation of God." The Bible reveals to us not only God's Word, but where and how God is revealed today. The Bible trains us to be apocalyptic in every new set of circumstances, new crisis, or new world in which we are called to live.

Vision of History and of Eschatology

Scholars distinguish between historical apocalypses and otherworldly apocalypses (built on journeys to other worlds).[38] In historical apocalypses (the only kind we are considering here) the revelation is always connected to resistance and subversion, and its location in society is with the oppressed.[39] What is proper to such apocalyptic is that it has a history-oriented theology and a political eschatology. Hence it stands opposed to dominant theology, both Greek and gnostic, and to modern liberal theology, which basically tends toward spiritualism, idealism, and individualism (and is therefore ahistoric, atemporal, anti-body, un-social, anti-communitarian, and anti-feminist). Apocalyptic theology is theology that connects the economic, the political, the social, and the cultural, and is accordingly a theology of poor and oppressed people seeking liberation. "One of the features of twentieth-century theology is the split between eschatology and politics."[40] Within apocalyptic, eschatology is not simply a teaching or an individual eschatology (salvation of the soul) but is experienced as historical and political eschatology. With its mythical and cosmic language, its exuberant visions, its talk of heaven, angels, and devils, and its (seeming) lack of a notion of praxis, apocalyptic gives the impression that it is not oriented toward ongoing history. Such a judgment, however, remains on the level of ap-

---

36. Pablo Richard, "Lectura popular de la Biblia en América Latina: Hermenéutica de la liberación," *Revista de Interpretación Bíblica Latinoamericana* (San José, Costa Rica-Santiago de Chile) 1 (1988): 32–40.

37. Quoted by Carlos Mesters, *Flor sin defensa: Una explicación de la biblia a partir del pueblo* (Bogota: CLAR, 1984), 28 (emphasis added). English version: *Defenseless Flower.* Maryknoll, N.Y.: Orbis Books, 1989.

38. Collins, *The Apocalyptic Imagination,* chapter 1.

39. E. P. Sanders ("The Genre of Palestinian Jewish Apocalpyses") locates Daniel, 1 Enoch, Jubilees, 4 Ezra, 2 Baruch, the Apocalypse of Abraham, and perhaps the testament of Levi in this kind of apocalypse. What they all have in common, he says, is "the combination of revelation with a promise of restoration and subversion." For a broader list see Pablo Richard, "Editorial," in *Revista de Interpretación Bíblica Latinoamericana* (San José, Costa Rica-Santiago de Chile) 7 (1991).

40. Christopher Rowland, "Mantener viva la peligrosa visión de un mundo en paz y justicia," *Concilium* 220 (November 1988): 429.

pearance and fails to understand apocalyptic's specific way of expressing itself (we will return to this point later).[41]

In apocalyptic, history has a present, a past, and a future (in that order). The fundamental thing is the present in which the writer and the book's hearers find themselves. The present is a time of crisis (a period following a catastrophe or a time of extreme persecution or oppression) but it is likewise *kairos* (a unique and limited time for conversion and grace). The author writes in order to give encouragement to his hearers in their resistance, their hope, their struggle, and in building the reign. He offers encouragement by proclaiming an *end,* which is going to bring to a close the sufferings of the present period and will begin a new world. In order to convince his hearers that this end has credibility, the author returns to the past. In order to present this past the writer identifies himself fictitiously with some figure from the past (Adam, Enoch, Moses, Elijah, Daniel, Baruch, Ezra, John) who lived in a situation similar to that in which his hearers are now living and who is a significant figure for those hearers. This past is presented as a revelation made to that imaginary figure in which what is to happen in the future is announced. This future has already occurred just as it has been revealed, for the real, nonfictitious author is in the present. The fact that what is revealed has already happened is what provides the author with credibility in announcing the certainty of the end: if the past has been fulfilled, the approaching end is also certain to arrive. This phenomenon, which is typical of apocalyptic, is called "prophecy after the fact" and also "pseudonymous" or "predated" prophecy; it has a rhetorical and kerygmatic function of exhorting and convincing.[42] Nevertheless, its function is more than rhetorical: it shows the author's interest in history. Inspired by the Spirit, the author studies and discerns the past in order to draw consequences and teachings for the present.

We have spoken about how the author understands present and past. What about the future? Eschatology is not an abstract discourse on the end or the future, but a concrete discourse on what is bringing to an end the present period. Just as apocalyptic speaks of the past for the sake of the present, it likewise speaks of the future for the sake of the present. Revelation 1 and 4:8 present God as "He who is, who was and who will be." The future "is" not, but "is coming" — that is, it breaks into the present. The end is not something static, but the action of *bringing to an end* the sufferings of the present moment. The eschatological is what puts an end to suffering and crisis. What brings the present period to an end is God's judgment. In Daniel 7, for example, God's judgment means the destruction of the empires and the raising up of the people of the saints. God's judgment is always good news for the saints and something fearful for the beasts and the wicked.

What comes after the judgment that brings the present period to an end? At this point the author is talking about the unknown, and the images of such a future after the end vary considerably within apocalyptic. The most important

---

41. Richard A. Horsley, *Jesus and the Spiral of Violence: Popular Jewish Resistance in Roman Palestine* (San Francisco: Harper & Row, 1987), chapter 5, 121–45.

42. Croatto, "Desmesura y fin del opresor en la perspectiva apocalíptica," 130–33.

point is that there is not just one future, but many futures, or one future that has many stages. The future is divided into periods; hope and utopia are set into periods. In the Revelation of John, for example, the future has the following stages: destruction of the beasts, chaining up of Satan, one-thousand-year reign, freeing and destruction of Satan, last judgment, and the creation of a new heaven and a new earth. Our prevailing eschatology reduces the entire future to the last judgment, which is usually understood as an individual judgment (spiritualized and emptied of history). Apocalyptic eschatology, on the other hand, is eminently historical and political. The building of the future is what gives meaning to the present moment and to all of history. Moreover, this future can be advanced in the community, which is the first fruit of that future (Rev. 14:4). The most important point is that this eschatological future is part of history and takes place in history. It is a transcendent future insofar as it is achieved by God and is beyond the end, beyond death, beyond this world, but it takes place within history and represents the complete and final achievement of this history.

Myths, Symbols, and Visions in Apocalyptic

Studies of apocalyptic have been flawed by a lack of interest in the social and historical context and by a literalist and doctrinal approach. Liberalism and modernity, moreover, have rendered us incapable of understanding symbols and myths in historical terms. Popular cultures in Latin America and the Caribbean, particularly the indigenous cultures, have reeducated us to understand myths and symbols, not literally but in a historical and liberating key.

Myth usually employs elements of the cosmos: the sun, moon, stars, sky, earth, chaos, earthquakes, signs in the sky, beasts coming out of the abyss, eagles flying in the sky, locusts stripping the land, horseback riders from hell, rivers with the water of life, trees of life, and so forth. It also constructs symbols out of human realities: twenty-four elders, all kinds of angels, a human figure, a woman clothed with the sun, Babylon, the prostitute riding the beast, the new Jerusalem, the heavenly books, the marks and signs on the body, reaping and harvesting, and so forth. With their cosmic and human sets of symbols myths are not ahistorical symbols, archetypes, or universal essences, but rather they express realities and processes within history, and that is how they must be read. The Bible itself teaches us how to read myths: in Isaiah 65:17 we find the myth of "new heavens and new earth," and in vv. 21–23 the historical meaning of this myth is interpreted: "they shall live in the houses they build, and eat the fruit of the vineyards they plant." The book of Daniel is full of myths, but almost all are explained directly or we are given a key for interpreting them. Something similar happens in Revelation. Liberalism put myth and history at odds with each other. Something could be either mythical or historical; if it was mythical it was not historical, and was therefore false, fictitious, deceitful, and did not exist. Today we are affirming the historical nature of myths; indeed even overly cosmic myths express realities in history. If cosmic reality is invoked, the aim is to provide drama and urgency to processes within history.

It is of most interest here to analyze the *use* or *function* of myths and symbols. First, myth and symbol are polysemic (that is, they have multiple meanings) and thus are able to communicate different messages at the same time. When Rome is symbolized as Babylon (Rev. 17), the intention is to assert that it is both oppressive and idolatrous. The woman clothed with the sun (Rev. 12) is a myth used to signify simultaneously humankind (new Eve) opting for life, the people of God that begets the Messiah, the Christian community, and Mary the mother of the Messiah. Myth always remains open and ready for new meanings, provided that its internal consistency and the historical context in which it arose and made history are respected.

Second, myth strives to provide an identity to and mobilize a community or specific group, especially in a situation in which the community's previous identifying structures have been completely destroyed, or in circumstances of extreme oppression or persecution, in which the community is on the brink of disappearing. In such circumstances, by creating myths apocalyptic seeks to re-build the consciousness of the people so that it may have an identity and may rebuild itself as a people. In situations of oppression or persecution, myth also allows the people to work out their identity and mobilize against the oppressive or persecuting system. Myth breaks the logic and discourse of the oppressive system and allows the oppressed to create a discourse, a logic, and an alter-native community. Myth is an organic representation of the consciousness of the oppressed community. It likewise fulfills the critical function of unmasking reality: it calls the empire "beast" and treats Rome like a prostitute.

Myth is by no means passive or alienating, but on the contrary, it serves to mobilize. The function of myth is the productive structuring of social practice, and it can be understood and deciphered only if the hearer takes part in that social praxis.[43] Myth and praxis are essentially connected. Today in becoming mobilized our people identify with liberating myths. Of course there are also oppressive myths, and apocalyptic strives to subvert them. Popular culture gen-erally functions on the basis of myths, contrary to ruling elite culture, which is more conceptual and abstract. A new understanding of apocalyptic entails a new appreciation of myths, and will indeed be an essential key for our rereading of the Revelation of John.

Apocalyptic vision (dreams, ecstasies, tableaux) combines many symbols and myths in a single view. The vision cannot be read as a theological text dealing with ideas (as a text from St. Thomas would be read, for example). The vision is above all to be contemplated and thereby to be translated into action. The vision seeks to transmit a fundamental conviction or to develop a spirituality. That is why the liturgy plays so central a role in the Revelation of John; it is there that almost all Revelation's visions take place. This liturgy leads us to the heart of the community, where the hymns sung by the community provide us with keys for interpreting the texts of Revelation. The vision fulfills the same function as the *parenesis*.[44] Revelation provides visions of an alternative world to give heart to Christians and increase their ability to resist under persecution.

---

43. Pedro Trigo and Gustavo Gutiérrez, *Arguedas: Mito, historia y religión: Entre las calandrias* (Lima: CEP, 1982), 27.

44. Schüssler Fiorenza, *The Book of Revelation,* chapter 7.

Like poetry, a vision seeks to organize the people's imaginative experience; its function is that of creative imagination. Apocalyptic creates visions to help the people to imagine and create a world that is an alternative to the world that is no more or to the oppressive dominating world. It is especially through its myths and visions that apocalyptic serves to keep memory alive. The people recall the past and the message of Revelation because they have the apocalyptic visions stamped in their memory. By means of vision, apocalyptic leads us into God's world, into the transcendent world, not in order to remove us from history, but to make us live history in a different manner.

Ethics: Violence and Discernment

An ethical issue that gives rise to a great deal of discussion about apocalyptic is that of the violence and hatred that many texts would seem to transmit. The function of these texts is not to generate violence or hatred, but rather to express the situation of extreme oppression and suffering that the people of God are experiencing. The language of people living in dire want or under cruel persecution today is not very different. We cannot expect the poor to speak the refined diplomatic language of the powerful. The language of Revelation is a language of people in situations of extreme oppression and suffering. If Revelation uses such language it is partly in order to bring about a catharsis in its hearers,[45] but it is also so that they may feel that they have attained their identity and through the message of Revelation may transform their hatred into awareness.

Another ethical issue in apocalyptic is *discernment.*[46] Some believe that Revelation does not make a distinction between the kind of law-authority that kills and a law-authority that may be illegitimate but is in effect and is needed for safeguarding life. Revelation would thus regard all authority on earth as beast and Babylon. Such a view would fall into the Manichaean polarity of "beast or people of the saints." The kind of discernment found in Romans 13 and 1 Peter is more realistic. A Christian must make a discernment: if there is a law that kills it should be eliminated; if there is a law that protects life, it should be respected. Such a lack of discernment would explain the fact that Revelation is sometimes turned upside down and used against the people. The people's hatred for the beast is changed into the beast's hatred for the people.

That objection is not entirely valid. Something of this sort can be found in some noncanonical apocalyptic literature, but apocalyptic — especially when it is Christian — is profoundly blended with prophetic discernment. The prophetic aspect must be taken seriously in the Revelation of John. Furthermore, we should not take the visions (for example, those referring to the two beasts in chapter 13) as direct reflections of the situation or as photographs of the Roman empire. These visions are mythical, and hence they should not be interpreted literally, but as symbols whose very purpose is to enable us to discern when an

---

45. Adela Yarbro Collins, *Crisis and Catharsis: The Power of the Apocalypse* (Philadelphia: Westminster Press, 1984).

46. Franz J. Hinkelammert, *Las armas ideológicas de la muerte,* 2d ed. (San José, Costa Rica: DEI, 1981); English translation: *The Ideological Weapons of Death: A Theological Critique of Capitalism* (Maryknoll, N.Y.: Orbis Books, 1986).

authority is beast and when it is not. With these symbols the hearers of Revelation identified the Roman empire as beast, but we could likewise identify other things as beast: a father can be beast to his children; a man can be beast to his wife; a leader can be beast with his or her group.

Visions are myths that are open to being employed as instruments for making a discernment of the situation, although not mechanically or in a concordistic way. As an apocalyptic-prophetic book, Revelation also engages in other acts of discernment: it distinguishes between the kings of the earth who prostitute themselves with Rome, the great harlot (17:2–18:3), and the kings of the earth who bring the treasures of the nations to the new Jerusalem (21:24–26). Revelation furthermore has a universal vision of salvation: all are called to conversion. In the plagues of the first four trumpets (8:2–12), the punishment falls on only a third of history; two-thirds is a time of grace and is open to salvation. Between the sixth and seventh trumpets (present age) stands the action of the prophets who seek the conversion of all and are partly successful (see 11:13). The organization of the people of God into twelve tribes of twelve thousand each (7:5 and 14:1) is a symbol of organizing the community in an alternative way, thus giving us a distinction between an organization or law of the people of the saints and an organization or law that is beast.

Practice within History and Witness

Revelation is accused of passivity. Revelation is said to reflect a Christian community that merely listens to the reading of Revelation and mentally conjures up all the visions and stories it hears. Some compare Revelation to Greek tragedies: Revelation would accordingly be a pageant intended to produce a catharsis (purification and internal transformation) in a passive spectator public. Many say that apocalyptic is dream, vision, myths, and utopias that lead Christians to an imaginary world outside of history. Others say that in Revelation God alone effects history; human beings only pray, wail, shout, desire, and hope, but are not offered any way of carrying out any action to change history. Finally, many note the failure of Revelation: everything proclaimed there (fall of Rome and of the beasts) never took place; instead the Roman empire defeated the church when one of the beast's leaders became "Catholic" (Constantine).

All such accusations tend to be the result of an ignorance of apocalyptic or to derive from a liberal, Hellenistic, rationalistic vision of history that looks down on, or is ignorant of, the power of the mythical and symbolic, the power of hope and of utopia for transforming history, the efficacy of a transformation of the collective awareness of a people, and finally the force, power, and efficacy of the Spirit in history and the power of the spirituality of the poor and the oppressed. In the previous sections we have stressed that apocalyptic is historical and seeks to lead the community to action within history. Revelation combines eschatology and politics, myth and praxis, within history. It may not be politics and praxis in the modern sense, but it is an organized and conscious action by the people of God against the oppressive empire or system: "Revelation has been the basis for what is called radical social and political change throughout the history of the church."[47]

In Revelation there is indeed a practice within history, and in each chapter we will be drawing attention to it. It is not a practice as a positivist or modern rationalist would understand it. It is different and specific to the historical, social, and spiritual context in which apocalyptic is born. A basic element of this practice in Revelation is Testimony (*martyría* in Greek). The content of Revelation is "the Word of God and the Testimony of Jesus Christ" (1:2); and that is why the martyrs are beheaded (6:9 and 20:4) and John is exiled (1:9). "Testimony" is not just any word but a public word (spoken or acted out) that commits the one pronouncing it vis-à-vis society and the authorities. It is like the word spoken in the courtroom that continues to stand and is active either for or against us. Finally, it is a word that remains until death. In Greek "witness" means martyr: the martyrs are those who give testimony, even with their blood. In Revelation, testimony always has a power to change history, both in heaven and on earth. We will return to all of this in detail when commenting on the texts.

LITERARY AND STRUCTURAL KEYS
FOR UNDERSTANDING REVELATION

Here we will present only the overall structure of Revelation and will leave the structure of each of its parts for the following chapters. We will first present the overall structure, followed by its literary and structural justification, and finally we will show how it is to be understood theologically.

Overall Structure

Prologue and greeting (present period): 1:1–8

    A. 1:9–3:22: apocalyptic vision of the church

      B. 4:1–8:1: prophetic vision of history

        C. 8:2–11:19: the seven trumpets (rereading of Exodus)

          Center: 12:1–15:4: the Christian community among the beasts

        C. 15:5–16:21: the seven bowls (rereading of Exodus)

      B. 17:1–19:10: prophetic vision of history

    A. 19:11–22:5: apocalyptic vision of the future

Epilogue (present period): 22:6–21

Explanation of the Overall Structure

First we detect a neat match between the prologue and initial greeting (1:1–8) and the epilogue (22:6–21); likewise there is a match between the seven

---

47. Rowland, "Mantener viva la peligrosa visión de un mundo en paz y justicia," 432.

trumpets (8:2–11:19) and the seven bowls (15:5–16:21). Both sections are an apocalyptic rereading of the Exodus and both have the same theology of Exodus: God's liberating intervention in history. The only thing that the section about the seven seals (4:1–8:1) has in common with that of the seven trumpets and seven bowls is that it is built around seven elements, since the literary genre and theology of this section are very different from those of the trumpets and bowls and it resembles instead 17:1–19:10. For this and for other internal structural and theological reasons that we will examine later we propose a concentric structure: A-B-C-center-C-B-A.[48]

Revelation does not contain a chronological or step-by-step vision of history, nor does it in any systematic way claim to be a history of salvation. Its content is instead eschatological, which means three basic things: (1) a prophetic interpretation of the present situation of the Christian community; (2) the present time as *kairos,* as the short time before the end; and (3) God's intervention that puts an end to the powers of death and begins the definitive establishment of the reign of God.[49] The structure of the book is in line with this fundamental theological conception. The present time, the *kairos,* the short time before the end, is between 4:1 and 19:10. This section begins with a grand liturgy: chapters 4 and 5, and ends with another major liturgy: 19:1–10. At the center we find the prophetic interpretation of the Christian community in the midst of the world (the community as sign of the defeat of the oppressor powers in the world). This center is literally bounded by apocalyptic rereadings of Exodus:

> Rereading of Exodus (the seven trumpets: 8:2–11:19)
>
> The community in the midst of the beasts (12:1–15:4)
>
> Rereading of Exodus (the seven bowls: 15:5–16:21)

The author stands between the sixth and seventh trumpet (10:1–11:13): this is the present moment, when the prophets and witnesses are active; he likewise stands between the sixth and seventh bowl (16:13–16), which is also the present moment, when the demonic spirits are at work. To live history as exodus is to live the present moment as the moment of God's liberating action in history. Within this present history there also occurs the "great day of the wrath of the Lamb" (6:1–8:1) and the "judgment on the famous harlot" (17:1–18:24). All this constitutes the *present of Revelation* (4:1–19:10).

Before this present the author gives us an apocalyptic vision of the churches (1:9–3:22), that is, the communities as they are vis-à-vis the presence and prophetic message of the Risen Christ in their midst. It is not exactly the past, but it is certainly the eschatological reality in which Revelation is situated and which

---

48. Schüssler-Fiorenza, *The Book of Revelation,* especially chapters 1 and 6. The author likewise proposes (176) a concentric structure in which the center of the book is the prophetic interpretation of the political and religious situation of the community. She believes that that center is 10:1–15:4. In my outline, by contrast, the center is 12:1–15:4 but, as we will see later, 10:1–11:13 and 16:13–16 also have to do with the present of the community.

49. Schüssler-Fiorenza, *The Book of Revelation,* chapter 1.

serves as its starting point. After the present comes the final eschatological reality, what comes after the end, the apocalyptic vision of the future (19:11–22:5). This apocalyptic vision of the churches and of the end also has the nature of judgment: Jesus and God become present in history in order to discern between the good and the wicked. Jesus first renders judgment in the church, and then Jesus and God render judgment over humankind and the cosmos. It is in this judgment context in the church (1:9–3:22) and in the whole of humankind and the cosmos (19:11–22:5) that the present time is being played out, the *kairos* in which the community lives its prophetic witness standing up to the beasts and the wicked: 4:1–19:10. The structure revolves around the present and not around the "end of time" (as happens in fundamentalist readings of Revelation).

Present moment

1:9–3:22	**4:1** ——————————————————— **19:10**	19:11–22:5
(judgment on the churches)	**The community in the midst of the world**	(judgment on the world)

2

Beginning and End of
the Book of Revelation

Revelation 1:1–8 and 22:6–21

BEGINNING OF THE BOOK:
PROLOGUE AND GREETING (1:1–8)

Structure of the Text

> Title of the Book: v. 1a
> Subtitle or Explanation of the Title: vv. 1b–3
> Greetings: vv. 4–8

Text (Complete Text Arranged in Terms of Its Structure)

v. 1.   Revelation of Jesus Christ

        God gave it to him (Jesus)
          to show his servants
          what must happen soon
        (Jesus) made it known — by sending his angel — to his servant John

v. 2. (John) gives witness
          to the Word of God and to the testimony of Jesus Christ
          by reporting what he saw.

v. 3.   Blessed is the one who reads aloud and blessed are those
          who listen
        to this prophetic message
        and (those who) heed what is written in it,
        for the appointed time is near.

v. 4. (John:) John to the seven churches in Asia.
    Grace and peace to you
    from: Him who is and who was and who is to come
    from: the seven spirits before his throne,

v. 5.   and from: Jesus Christ,
    the faithful witness,
    the firstborn of the dead, and
    the ruler of the kings of the earth.

(Community:) To him who loves us
    and has freed us from our sins by his blood

v. 6.   who has made us into a kingdom,
    priests for his God and Father
    to him be glory and power forever [and ever]. Amen.

v. 7. (John:) Behold, he is coming amid the clouds,
    and every eye will see him,
    even those who pierced him.
    All the peoples of the earth will lament him.

  (Community:) Yes. Amen.

v. 8. (John:) "I am the Alpha and the Omega," says the Lord God,
    "the one who is and who was and who is to come,
    the almighty."

Keys for Interpretation

Revelation [Apocalypse] of Jesus Christ (1:1a)

This is the book's title. John is the first to use the word "apocalypse" as the title of a book. Apocalypse means revelation. As we saw in the introduction, it has the sense of unveiling, that is: the revelation of something that was concealed, hidden, and inaccessible. It is not neutral: what the wicked and the oppressors cannot understand is revealed to the upright, to the childlike, to the oppressed:

> I give praise to you, Father... for although you have *hidden* these things from the wise and the learned, you have *revealed* them to the childlike. (Matt. 11:25)

The content of revelation is the reality of heaven, that is, the transcendent world of the presence of God in history. The opposite of revelation is covering up, what today we would call ideology. Ideology serves to conceal injustices and legitimize domination. Apocalypse un-conceals the world of the poor and legitimizes their struggle for the reign of God, which is life and liberation. This liberation is therefore good news for the poor. Apocalypse seeks to un-conceal the reality of God and the reality of the poor in history. Apocalypse does something that none of the media generally do.

In chapter 2 of the book of Daniel we find an example of the value of apocalypse as revelation. God reveals to Daniel the liberating meaning of history, something that the theologians of the empire fail to understand. Paul uses the term in this same sense in the New Testament:

> ... the gospel preached by me is not of human origin. For I did not receive it from a human being, nor was I taught it, but it came through a *revelation of Jesus Christ.* (Gal. 1:12)

It is not out of pride that Paul is speaking, nor as a visionary who is carried away, but as an apocalyptic prophet. In other words, Paul builds his gospel and legitimizes it directly on the grace of God that has enabled him to discern, experience, and know Jesus risen within history. It is this Jesus, not the law, that has revealed to him the meaning of history and of mission (see also Gal. 1:16 and 2:2; Eph. 3:3). Another text from the Pauline school, which may be from the same period as Revelation, gives us a similar sense of what the term "apocalypse" means:

> For it is surely just on God's part to repay with afflictions those who are afflicting you, and to grant rest along with us to you who are undergoing afflictions, at the *revelation of the Lord Jesus* from heaven with his mighty angels.... (2 Thess. 1:6–7)

Similarly,

> Therefore, gird up the loins of your mind, live soberly, and set your hopes completely on the grace to be brought to you at the *revelation of Jesus Christ.* (1 Pet. 1:13)

Subtitle (1:1b–3)

There are three main verbs here: gave, made known, and gave witness. (*édoken, esémanen, emartyresen*). In simplified form, the sentence structure is as follows:

> God gave (*édoken*) the revelation to Jesus
> Jesus made it known (*esémanen*) to John
> John witnessed (*emartyresen*) it to the community.

The community appears in three participles:

> the one who is reading
> those who are listening
> those who are waiting.

It is quite clear that apocalypse is a living text, one that lives in a gathered community where there is one who is reading it and a community that listens and commits itself to keeping it. They receive this text from John, John receives it from Jesus, and Jesus receives it from God. God grants it as a gift. Jesus signifies it through symbols and visions. John gives testimony. It is this structure that gives legitimacy and power to apocalypse.

The content of this apocalypse becomes apparent in the following phrases:

what must happen soon
the word of God and the testimony of Jesus Christ
what he saw
this prophetic message.

In apocalypse God reveals "what must happen soon." This phrase appears here and in the epilogue, 22:6. In 22:6, however, where the speaker is Jesus himself, he immediately adds, "Behold, I am coming soon" (*érchomai tachú*). The same expression is repeated in 22:12, 20. In the prophetic messages to the churches this phrase also occurs (2:16 and 3:11). The same idea is expressed in different terms in 2:5, 3:3, and 3:20. In these texts what must happen soon is the coming of Jesus. The texts are not about Jesus' second coming at the end of time, however, but his glorious manifestation now in the present. Jesus is coming soon, in this present time that is the subject matter of the section between 4:1–19:10. This is the *kairos* that we are likewise told is near at hand: "the appointed time is near" (*ho kairós eggús*): 1:3 and 22:10. In this *kairos* Jesus is coming to live and to struggle within the Christian community that is confronting the beasts. Revelation is not focused on the second coming of Jesus but on his glorious manifestation (*parousía*) now in the historical present of the community. Moreover, one cannot speak properly of a "coming" of Jesus, as though he had gone somewhere else. Jesus never left: since his resurrection he is ever in the midst of the communities ("And behold, I am with you always, until the end of the age"). The community does not want him to "come" but to show himself, to act, to free, to reign.

Revelation also contains "the word of God and the testimony of Jesus Christ." The same expression appears in 1:9, 6:9, and 20:4 as the reason why Christians are persecuted. This is what John receives in the apocalyptic visions: what he saw. The content of the revelation is also designated as "the prophetic message." We find the same thing in 22:7, 10, 18, and 19. The author clearly regards Revelation as a prophetic book. John regards himself as a prophet (10:8–11). In 1:1 God manifests to him what must happen soon to his servants, which according to the parallel texts 22:6 and 22:9 means his servants the prophets (see also Amos 3:7: "Indeed, the Lord God does nothing without revealing his plan to his servants, the prophets").

In 1:3 we find a beatitude for the community:

Blessed is the one who reads aloud and blessed are those who listen to this prophetic message and heed what is written in it, for the appointed time is near.

This is the first of seven beatitudes that appear in Revelation: 1:3, 14:13, 16:15, 19:9, 20:6, 22:7, 22:14. Revelation is important not as abstract doctrine, but as joyous experience in the community in the present time, in the *kairos* that is now beginning.

Salutation: 1:4 – 9

We find a salutation as though in a letter. The conclusion of Revelation in 22:21 also resembles a letter. The apocalyptic literary genre is thus combined with the epistolary genre. The author shows his free approach to the apocalyptic genre and reflects elements that are proper to the Christian apocalyptic movement. Second Thessalonians is similarly an apocalyptic text in the form of a letter. Nevertheless, this salutation in Revelation is more than a salutation: it is a liturgical text that amounts to a theological and political manifesto. In the structured text we presented at the beginning of the chapter, we indicated that there is a liturgical dialogue between John and the community. All of Revelation reflects the community's liturgy, primarily in chapters 4 and 5 and in 19:1–10, but the community's liturgical life also appears in 11:15–18; 12:10–12; 14:1–5; 15:1–4; 16:5–7; and 22:17, 20. This liturgical tone throughout Revelation situates the text at the heart of the prayerful and militant Christian community. The liturgy furthermore reflects and communicates the power and spirituality of the community.

Besides having a liturgical form, the salutation is a theological manifesto with a forceful political thrust. There are two clear allusions to Exodus: the name of the liberating God: "I am who am" (Exod. 3:14) is echoed in the God "who is and who was and who is to come" of Revelation 1:4, 8. The people are also seen to be constituted as a "kingdom, priests for . . . God" in Revelation 1:6 (Exod. 19:6). It is not "a kingdom of priests" as most translations render it, but a people constituted as reign, that is, as power. This people constituted as reign is furthermore said to be entirely made up of priests. Jesus' title as "ruler of the kings of the earth" is likewise political, as is the "Behold, he is coming amid the clouds." This is a reference to Daniel 7, and it means the political triumph of the risen Jesus in present history (as son of man, representative of the people of the holy ones, who receives all power and the reign).[1] Designating God as the "Almighty" (*ho pantocrator*) is a characteristic feature of Revelation within the New Testament.[2] The term appears six times in a liturgical context (1:8, 4:8, 11:17, 15:3, 16:7, 19:6), always with a political coloration. In 16:14 and 19:15 it appears in a context of judgment, also with a political meaning. This God is not abstract and universal, but the God of the holy ones, of the upright, of those oppressed by the empire: the God of the poor is an all-powerful God.

The initial salutation is trinitarian, in its triple use of "from." God is first named the "one who is and who was and who is to come." We find two depar-

---

1. Pablo Richard, "El Pueblo de Dios contra el Imperio: Daniel 7 en su contexto literario e histórico," *Revista de Interpretación Bíblica Latinoamericana* (San José, Costa Rica-Santiago de Chile) 7 (1991): 25–46.

2. In the New Testament the term appears only in 2 Corinthians 6:18, in an Old Testament citation, and nine times in Revelation.

tures from custom here: the present is mentioned first, then the past, and then the future; and the verb "to come" is used for the future, not the verb "to be." This is in keeping with the notion of history in apocalyptic, in which the present is what is central; the past is reconstructed to give the community encouragement in the present; and finally, God is not one who will be, but the God who is coming, who breaks in to end the sufferings of the present age. The beautiful thing about this expression is that God does not appear as a universal abstract being (like the God of the Greek philosophers) but as the God of history. The Spirit is presented in an ambiguous form: "the seven spirits before his throne." A similar expression is found in 3:1, 4:5, and 5:6. In this trinitarian context, it represents the Spirit of God in the fullness of its activity and power (fullness signified by the number seven). The community receives grace and peace from this experience of the Spirit. The greatest number of references is to Jesus; their Christology is very compact but not abstract. This Christology is built on John's experience and that of the Christian community in the world. Three references are put on John's lips, and the community responds three times. John says

the faithful witness, the firstborn of the dead, the ruler of the kings of the earth.

In Greek "witness" means "martyr." The martyr is the one who publicly gives testimony, giving his or her life if necessary. In 3:14 Jesus is also called the faithful and true martyr. The community in Pergamum likewise had its faithful martyr, Antipas (2:13); the church is represented by two martyr-prophets in chapter 11. Rome, the prostitute, appears in 17:6, getting drunk on the blood of the saints and martyrs of Jesus. In a church of martyrs, to call Jesus the faithful witness (= martyr) was very much a sign of hope and an example for the community. Jesus is likewise the Firstborn, that is, the first one born from among the dead (which assumes that there are to be others born-resurrected from among the dead): it is also a sign of hope in a community in which many have been killed for the word of God and the testimony of Jesus (6:9; 2:4). Jesus, announced as sovereign Ruler (*ho árchon*) or governor over the kings of the earth, is also a sign of hope for Christians oppressed by the political powers of the empire. This expression also appears in 17:14 and 19:16 with a clear political meaning. The community responds to this liturgical salutation on John's part by referring to Jesus not so much with Christological titles, but expressing its own experience of the risen Jesus within the community:

To him who loves us and has freed us from our sins by his blood, who has made us into a kingdom, priests for his God.

The community feels loved and liberated by Jesus, by his martyrdom to death for the for the sake of the reign of God. The community also feels constituted with power. Jesus has made it a reign; they are a people powerful with priests:

...you are "a chosen race, a royal priesthood, a holy nation, a people of his own, so that you may announce the praises" of him who called you out of darkness into his wonderful light. Once you were "no people" but now you are God's people. (1 Pet. 2:9–10)

We will return to this point in our commentary on 5:5, where we find the same expression.

Verse 7 speaks of the present coming of the risen Jesus (verb in present tense: *érchetai*): "behold, he is coming"; Jesus comes in the historical "today" that the community is living in the world (with the political categories of Daniel 7 that we have already observed) and likewise speaks of his future coming (verbs in the future tense: *ópsetai...kópsontai*): "every eye will see him...[they] will lament." Jesus will also one day manifest himself to bring the present age to an end and inaugurate the reign of God in history (19:11–22:5). Verse 8 ends by connecting to v. 4 (beginning resembling the end). The expression, "I am the Alpha and the Omega" is added, thus expressing the beginning and end of history.

THE CONCLUSION OF THE BOOK: EPILOGUE (22:6–21)

Structure of the Text

Entry of Jesus (vv. 6–16)

    A. Jesus: vv. 6–7 (reassumes the message of the angel-guide)

        B. John: v. 8
        B. Angel: v. 9

    A. Jesus: vv. 10–16

Liturgy (vv. 17–20)

    A. Acclamation-invitation: v. 17

        B. warning: vv. 18–19 (apparently issued by Jesus himself)

    A. Acclamation: 20

Final epistolatory salutation (v. 21)

Text (Complete Text Presented in Structured Form)

v. 6.   And he said to me:

    (Jesus:) These words are trustworthy and true,
            and the Lord, the God of prophetic spirits,
            sent his angel to show his servants
            what must happen soon.
v. 7.   — Behold, I am coming soon. —
    Blessed is the one who keeps the prophetic message of this book.

v. 8.   (John:) It is I, John, who heard and saw these things,
and when I heard and saw them I fell down to worship
at the feet of the angel who showed them to me.

v. 9.   But he said to me:

(Angel:) Don't!
I am a fellow servant of yours and of your brothers
the prophets
and of those who keep the message of this book.
Worship God.

v. 10. (John:) Then he said to me:
(the angel is indicated, but it is Jesus who speaks)

(Jesus:) Do not seal up the prophetic words of this book,
for the appointed time is near.

v. 11.   Let the wicked still act wickedly,
and the filthy still be filthy.
The righteous must still do right,
and the holy still be holy.

v. 12.   — Behold, I am coming soon. —
I bring with me the recompense
I will give to each according to his deeds.

v. 13.   I am the Alpha and the Omega
the first and the last,
the beginning and the end.

v. 14.   Blessed are they who wash their robes
so as to have the right to the tree of life
and enter the city through its gates.

v. 15.   Outside are the dogs,
the sorcerers, the unchaste,
the murderers, the idol-worshipers,
and all who love and practice deceit.

v. 16.   I, Jesus, sent my angel
to give you this testimony for the churches.
I am the root and offspring of David,
the bright morning star.

(Liturgical celebration of the community)

v. 17.   The Spirit and the bride say, "Come."
Let the hearer say, "Come."
Let the one who thirsts come forward,
and the one who wants it receive the gift of life-giving
water.

v. 18. (Jesus:) I warn everyone who hears
the prophetic words in this book:
if anyone adds to them, God will add to him
the plagues described in this book,

v. 19.   and if anyone takes away from the words in
this prophetic book,
God will take away his share in the tree of life and
in the holy city described in this book.

v. 20. (John:)   The one who gives this testimony says:

      (Jesus:)   Yes, I am coming soon.

(Community:)   Amen! Come Lord Jesus (Marana tha)

v. 20. (John:)   The grace of the Lord Jesus be with all. Amen.

Keys for Interpretation

This is a dialogue between Jesus (his angel) and John. The community is also present celebrating its liturgy. In vv. 6 and 7 the speaker would still seem to be the angel who has been John's guide in the vision of the New Jerusalem (21:9) but actually the one who speaks is Jesus, who says, "I am coming soon." There is no difference between Jesus and his angel. In v. 8 John uses emphatic expressions. In v. 9 the angel appears by himself. Jesus is speaking from v. 10 to v. 16. Between vv. 17 and 20 we have the final liturgy in which the Spirit enters, along with the New Jerusalem and the Christian community: Jesus speaks up in the middle of the liturgy with a typically apocalyptic imprecation: vv. 18–19. The book ends with a final salutation as though it were a letter, thus connecting with the initial epistolary salutation in 1:4–8.

This epilogue emphatically highlights the prophetic character of Revelation. The author refers to the entirety of Revelation four times with the expression "the prophetic words of this book" (vv. 7, 10, 18, 19), thus returning to the similar expression in 1:3, "this prophetic message." God is called "the God of prophetic spirits" (v. 6). This is often understood to mean the God who inspires the prophets, although it is better to translate it more literally as the God who lives in the hearts of the prophets. The angel is called a "fellow servant of John and of his brothers the prophets," thus indicating that John is associated with a group of prophets. This prophetic community would explain the plural "you" in v. 16 as the intended audience of Revelation. The angel likewise acts as a prophet: he is a prophet like John and his brothers the prophets; they both play the same role. It may be that the seven angels of the seven churches in chapters 2 and 3 are these prophets who together with John lead the Christian communities in Asia Minor.[3] It is to these prophets that God reveals "what must happen soon" (22:6, reflecting 1:1). These prophets are called servants of God, in keeping with

---

3. Elisabeth Schüssler Fiorenza, *The Book of Revelation: Justice and Judgment* (Philadelphia: Fortress Press, 1985), chapter 5.

a text that is very significant for Revelation: "Indeed, the Lord God does nothing without revealing his plan to his servants the prophets" (Amos 3:7). All of this receives a broader treatment in chapters 10 and 11 of the book.

The fundamental content of this epilogue is summed up in the phrase repeated three times (vv. 7, 12, 10): "I am coming soon" (*érchomai tachú*). As we said when interpreting 1:1–3, Jesus is not referring to his second "coming" or glorious manifestation at the end of time (19:11), but rather to his coming now — in the present — to the Christian community struggling in the world and at the present time against the beasts. What must happen soon is this coming of Jesus in the present time; it is Jesus who becomes present within the churches (1:9–3:22). The Parousia is primarily not Jesus' second coming but his triumphant presence in history: in the present time, in the world and the church. It is because of this present manifestation of Jesus that the Spirit, the bride, and the community, say, "Come! Come! Amen! Lord Jesus, Marana tha" (vv. 17, 20). The whole first section in which Jesus is speaking (vv. 6–7) makes sense in the context of this present eschatology. Because Jesus is coming soon, happiness is to be found in keeping the prophetic words of revelation. Verses 8–9 (which refer back to 19:10) show the danger of idolatry in the community. The threat of idolatry was not purely external — from Babylon and the beast — but could also occur within John and the prophets themselves.

In the light of this triumphant presence of Jesus in history we can understand the second section in which Jesus is the speaker (vv. 10–16). This entire section is about present eschatology. Let us begin with v. 10: "Do not seal up the prophetic words of this book, for the appointed time is near." In Daniel (8:26, 10:14) and other apocalyptic books written pseudonymously (identifying with a figure from the past in order to announce a future prophecy), the seer is usually ordered to seal the prophecy, which is to be opened at a future time. Such is not the case here. What Revelation reveals is for now, for the present, for this moment, for the *kairos* that is already here. It is the present time of v. 11, in which the "still" (*eti*) is repeated four times: it is the *kairos* in which there is still time, either to practice injustice and idolatry or to practice justice and be holy.

In vv. 12–14 we find the anticipation of future eschatology in the present of ongoing history, the world, and the community. The basis for making possible this anticipation of history in the present we find in v. 13 where Jesus proclaims himself Lord of history: "I am the Alpha and the Omega, the first and the last, the beginning and the end." Verse 14 exclaims, "Blessed are they who wash their robes." The verb to wash (*pluno*) is found in Revelation only in 7:14 and here, two texts that are clearly parallel. Revelation 7:14 is about the martyrs, "the ones who have survived the time of great distress; they have washed [*éplunan*] their robes. . . . " These are the martyrs who are now in heaven and who washed (aorist past tense of the verb) their robes (we will see the significance of this expression in its proper place). Revelation 22:14, however, refers to the present: those who are washing, those who are now washing their robes (present participle), who "will have the right" in the eschatological future "to the tree of life and to enter the New Jerusalem." The other blessing in v. 7, which parallels this one in v. 14, takes on its full meaning in reference to the present time: now is the *kairos* in which the prophetic words of this book must be observed. Verse 12 likewise stands in this same context of the present: "the recompense I will give to each according to each one's deeds." The word used here is *misthos,* which can mean reward, recompense, or salary, and in Revelation appears only in 11:18 and here in v. 12. In 11:18 it is the recompense that Jesus will give at his glorious manifestation (in 19:11ff.). Here in v. 12 it refers to the reward that Jesus brings, or that he himself is, for those who are struggling now in the present age, reward or recompense in accord with the practice of each one. In 11:18 the recompense is found connected to the judgment after the sounding of the seventh trumpet; here in v. 12 the reward is brought by Jesus who is coming now.

Verse 15 also refers to present eschatology: "Outside are the dogs, the sorcerers, the unchaste, the murderers." If it were about the eschatological future (of the heavens and the new earth and New Jerusalem) nothing could remain outside: there is no longer any inside or outside. Revelation 21:8, which is a parallel text, is clearly about the final eschatology, where the idolaters and murderers are no longer inside, but are hurled into the lake of fire and sulfur, which, as we will see in its proper place, means that they disappear forever. Here in 22:15, however, they do not disappear but are cast out, that is, out of the community. Now, in the present time, there must not be idolaters and murderers in the community. This is the sin of the church of Pergamum (2:12–17), which tolerates the presence of Baalamites and Nicolaitans (who, as we will see, are idolaters) in its midst.

Finally, we are told emphatically in v. 15: "I, Jesus, sent my angel to give you this testimony for the churches." Revelation contains a message to John and to the community of prophets (hence the plural form of "you," about everything related to the churches. The word "church" (*ekklesía*) appears nineteen times in Revelation, but only in chapters 1 to 3 and here in 22:16. The entire message of revelation is therefore for the time of the church, the present time, the *kairos* that is now arriving, the moment in which Jesus says that he is arriving (I am coming soon); what must happen soon means what is going to happen in this present *kairos* of the churches.

The two images that Jesus uses to identify himself confirm this point (v. 16): "I am the root and offspring of David, the bright morning star." Jesus is the root of the people of God; he is the offspring of the true Israel. Jesus is not a shoot (Isa. 11:1ff.) but root and offspring (see John 15: I am the true vine...). Jesus also says he is the morning star. The image refers to the heavenly body (Venus), which announces the end of the night and the proximity of dawn (see Rom. 12:12). Venus is likewise a sign of victory (of light over darkness). This image is familiar in biblical tradition and in apocalyptic: "I see him, though not now; I behold him, though not near: A star shall advance from Jacob, and a staff shall rise from Israel" (Num. 24:17, the source of the idea of the Messiah as a star). See also the Testament of Levi 18:1–5: "The Lord will raise up a new priest, to whom will be revealed all the words of the Lord; he will judge the earth for many days. His star will rise shining like the light of knowledge."

Something similar is found in the Testament of Judah 24:1–5. The image likewise appears in 1 Peter 1:19:

Moreover, we possess the prophetic message that is altogether reliable. You will do well to be attentive to it, as to a lamp shining in a dark place, until day dawns and the morning star [Spanish, *Lucero*] rises in your hearts.

The Spanish word *Lucero* here translates the Greek *phosphóros,* whose Latin form is Lucifer, "he who carries or bears the light."[4] The two Christological images of root and morning star point not so much at something connected to the final eschatology as to the reality of Jesus in the present *kairos,* to the Jesus who with his resurrection sets in motion the triumph of the community in its present struggle (to build the reign on earth and to awaken the dawn, so that light will be victorious over darkness).

In summary, we may say that Revelation 22:10–16 is about present eschatology: God's liberating entry into the present time of Revelation (4:1 to 19:10). This is consistent with the other entry of Jesus in 22:6–7 and with the liturgy found in 22:17, 20. Likewise the imprecation of Jesus in vv. 18–19 only makes sense for the present time. Both the introduction (1:1–8) and the epilogue (22:6–21) frame Revelation in the present *kairos,* in this *kairos* in which Jesus comes. Hence the need to observe all the prophetic words in this book and the happiness that comes from doing so. And woe to anyone who removes anything from these words or adds anything to them! We must live this present time (Rev. 4:1–9, 10) continually repeating "Marana tha Jesus," Come, Lord Jesus! The end-time will come later and it will bring this present time to conclusion (Rev. 19:11–22:5).

---

4. See Franz J. Hinkelammert, *Las armas ideológicas de la muerte,* 2d ed. (San José, Costa Rica: DEI, 1981), 223–27. English translation: *The Ideological Weapons of Death: A Theological Critique of Capitalism* (Maryknoll, N.Y.: Orbis Books, 1986), 183–86.

3

Apocalyptic Vision of the Church

Revelation 1:9–3:22

INTRODUCTION TO THE READING AND STRUCTURE
OF REVELATION 1:9–3:22

Overall Structure of This Section

1. Opening vision: The risen Jesus in the midst of the seven churches: 1:9–20.

2. Seven prophetic messages to the seven churches: 2:1–3:22.

The two sections are very closely connected, in both literary and theological terms. The opening vision provides us with the basis for the seven prophetic messages: Jesus alive in the midst of the churches orders John to write to the seven churches. The seven messages are part of the opening vision. Moreover, the one speaking to each church is Jesus as he has been seen in the opening vision. Almost all the messages read, "The one who . . . says . . ." and some aspect of the opening vision is repeated, thus linking the two parts.

We would also like to draw attention to certain parallels between this first section (1:9–3:22), an apocalyptic vision of the church, and the final section (19:11–22:5), an apocalyptic vision of the future. Both sections begin with an opening vision in which Jesus is the central figure. In the first section Jesus confronts each of the churches: he discerns what is good and evil in each of them and encourages the victor. In the vision of the concluding section, Jesus confronts the beasts and the kings of the earth. Before judging the world Jesus judges the church. There are also numerous parallels between the promises to the victor in each message (2:7, 2:11, 2:17, 2:26–27, 3:5, 3:12, 3:21) and the concluding section (19:11–22:5). Jesus promises the victor that he will eat of the tree of life and will not suffer the second death and that his name will not be erased from the book of life, and so forth, all of which are proper to the last section of Revelation. In the first section, Jesus prepares the church to live the

48

present. In the final section, Jesus ends the present period and transforms history with the destruction of the forces of evil and the building of the reign of God and the new creation. Between these two sections, John places the present time, the *kairos* that is coming, what must soon happen (4:1–19:10).

Structure of the Opening Vision (1:9–20)

1. Context of the vision: vv. 9–10a

    I, John, your brother, who share with you...
    found myself on the island called Patmos
    because I proclaimed God's word and gave testimony to Jesus.
    I was caught up in spirit on the Lord's day...

2. Vision: vv. 10b–19

    hearing (I heard): vv. 10b–11   (v. 11. Write on a scroll what you see and send it to the seven churches)

    sight (I saw): vv. 12–16

    hearing: vv. 17–19   (v. 19: Write down, therefore, what you have seen: what is happening, and what will happen afterward).

3. Explanation of the vision: v. 20

Structure of Each Message to Each Church

Each message has an almost identical structure:

1. Addressee: "To the angel of the church in..."

2. Order to write: "write this..."

3. The one writing: "The one who...says..."

4. Body of the letter: contains almost all the following elements:
    – description of the situation: "I know..."
    – rebuke: "Yet I hold this against you..."
    – order to repent: "Repent..."
    – apocalyptic revelation: "Behold..."
    – promise to visit: "I will come to you...I am coming quickly...."

5. Call to listen: "Whoever has ears ought to hear what..."

6. Eschatological promise to the victor: "To the victor I will give..." (usually points toward the last section of the book: 19:11–22:5).

KEYS FOR INTERPRETATION

Opening Vision (1:9–20)

The context of the vision (vv. 9–10a) provides us with four keys of interpretation. The first is the way John is presented. We do not know the actual identity of this John, the author of Revelation. Check any commentary or introduction for the existing opinions. More important is what John says about himself here and throughout the book. In this passage he introduces himself as "brother and companion" (*adelphós kai synkoinonós*) with the people he is addressing. He thereby rules out any hierarchizing of power within the church. The church of Revelation is a church led primarily by prophets. John is a prophet (see 1:1–3, 10:1–11, 22:6–21) and may be in charge of many communities in Asia Minor, but he does not thereby cease to be a brother and companion. More specifically he shares "in the distress [*thlipsis*], reign [*basileia*], and resistance [*hypomoné*])[1] in Jesus."

John shares with the churches their "distress," meaning persecution and repression. (John is in exile in Patmos and the communities occasionally suffer persecution.) However, the distress mentioned here refers more to the oppression, marginalization, and "ongoing" humiliation that believers must endure in the Roman empire. In positive terms, John also shares in the "reign," the Christian response and alternative to the distress. Christians seek to build the reign of God on earth (20:1–10), and to that end they strive to build the church as a community that is an alternative (14:1–5) to the empire (the beasts and Babylon) and hence they particularly need "resistance," endurance, strength, and struggle. In short, their brother John shares along with the churches their situation of oppression, the alternative within history of the reign of God, and their resistance in building it.

John is in exile on the island of Patmos "for proclaiming God's word and giving testimony to Jesus." This is the entire substance of Revelation (1:2) and the reason for the death of the martyrs (6:9 and 20:4). John is "caught up in the spirit on the Lord's day." He is not dreaming and his visions are not alienating or deceptive. His vision is an act of faith and spirituality; John is transformed by the Spirit so that he may receive a revelation. It is the Lord's day, no doubt Sunday, which by this time Christians have taken as their day. John has this vision during a liturgy, possibly during the Eucharist. That is suggested by the liturgical framework in 1:4–8 and 22:17, 20, on which we have already commented. Revelation 22:17 in particular has eucharistic overtones.

In Revelation vision always seeks to communicate a fundamental certainty. These literary visions are written down; they could scarcely be drawn in picture form. We cannot interpret a vision in the same way that we interpret a theoretical and conceptual text. Both are equally rational and transmit a message, but

---

1. We translate *hypomoné* correctly as "resistance" and not "endurance." *Hypomoné* is an active stance, implying engagement in history.

they must be read differently. Even if it is literary, a vision must be primarily contemplated in an effort to capture the message of the symbols directly. The vision — together with all its component symbols — transmits a certainty, an experience, a spirituality, and a power that cannot be explained conceptually. For example, when John tells us "his eyes were like a fiery flame," he is not expressing an idea but rather a spiritual experience that must be internalized in order to understand the vision's entire message. In transmitting a power or a basic certainty, the vision aims not so much at theorizing as at motivating, convincing, and mobilizing. It seeks to rebuild awareness, or, as we said in the introduction, to rebuild heaven. The vision's purpose is to un-conceal history: it reveals what is not apparent at first glance, even if it is transcendent and foundational. It also serves to critique domination and to preserve historical memory: it helps the community remember fundamental truths that are to be lived.

The basic certainty that this opening vision seeks to transmit is that the risen Jesus is alive bodily within the churches (and therefore within our history), and furthermore that he has power over death and the netherworld (he has power to destroy death and to remove those who have died from the abode of the dead). This message is present not only in the words of v. 18 but in the entire vision. The symbol of the human figure (literally, "like a son of man") is taken from Daniel 7, where it represents the people of the holy ones of the Most High. It is the counter-symbol to the beasts, who represent the empires.[2] In Revelation this symbol clearly represents the risen Jesus (although it does not lose the connotations that it has in Daniel 7). The vision stresses the bodiliness of Jesus: the human figure has clothing, head, hair, feet, voice, hand, mouth, and face. The author expresses symbolically how he experiences each element of Jesus' bodiliness: his garment is a priestly robe; his hair is white; his eyes are like fire; his feet are solid like metal; his hand grasps seven stars (those in charge of each community are held safe in the grip of the risen Christ); from his mouth issues a sharp sword; his face shines like the sun. Finally, John feels the hand of Jesus physically on his body: "he touched me with his right hand."

Jesus twice tells John to write what he is seeing, in vv. 11 and 19, thus establishing an inclusion (a text that repeats at the beginning and at the end, thus framing a section; the device has a special interpretive function). John must write in a book (literally on a scroll) what he has seen and send it to the seven churches. The content of what he sees is "what is happening and what will happen afterward" (v. 19). "What is happening" refers to this bodily and actual presence of the risen Jesus within the churches with everything that such presence means for each community (what the power of his eyes, his face, his mouth transmit, along with the knowledge that the seven angels are in his right hand, and so forth). This presence does not withdraw the churches from ongoing history — for they will suffer persecutions, and they must struggle and be victorious — but it makes them live an eschatological situation, that is, one in which

---

2. Pablo Richard, "El Pueblo de Dios contra el Imperio: Daniel 7 en su contexto literario e histórico," *Revista de Interpretación Bíblica Latinoamericana* (San José, Costa Rica-Santiago de Chile) 7 (1991): 25–46.

this deep and transcendent reality of history counts and is important for the life of the churches. Heaven makes us live differently, transcendently, and spiritually.[3] The existence of the seven churches is different even now, because Christ has risen and the time of resurrection has already begun. "What will happen afterward" is what Revelation presents to us between 4:1 and 19:10, namely, the current history of the churches in the world.

Prophetic Messages to the Seven Churches (2:1–3:22)

Keys to an Overall Interpretation

The first thing that strikes us is the living relationship between the risen Jesus and the churches. Jesus is alive in their midst and holds those in charge of each community (the seven stars) in his right hand (1:16, which is repeated in 2:1). Jesus addresses each church differently and specifically. He is familiar with the life of each one and recognizes what is good, rebukes what is evil, exhorts, calls, threatens, prophesies, and promises a reward to the victor that varies according to the particular church. It is as though Jesus were making a pastoral visit to the churches. The reason that hierarchies and powers cannot be observed in the churches of Revelation may be that Jesus' presence is so real and effective. It is the risen Christ who is personally leading them.

In Revelation the number seven means fullness, and hence many commentators envision an ecclesial fullness and universalize these messages as though they were abstract and addressed to the whole church in all ages. Such a procedure contradicts the meaning of the text. If John chooses seven churches (and not ten or more, which certainly existed in that area) it is in order to give a fullness and a universal character to a specific situation. Universalization does not deny the real and specific character of each community; these communities really exist. The communities in Revelation are like those of today: all are quite different and have specific problems. The community in Smyrna and the one in Philadelphia are wonderful; those in Ephesus and Thyatira have more virtues than failings; the one in Pergamum is both good and bad. Except for a few people, Sardis is seen negatively. Finally, the community at Laodicea is a disaster. Jesus nonetheless addresses all of them with the same pastoral love.

Jesus becomes present in the midst of the churches and addresses a prophetic message to each one in order to change them (he gives them an eschatological existence) and to prepare them to live the *kairos* that is now beginning, the present moment when they will have to face the empire. Jesus is preparing the communities for the present, not for the Parousia at the end of time. Hence he tells the church at Ephesus (2:5) to repent or "otherwise, I will come to you" (*érchomai soi*). Likewise to the church at Pergamum he says: "Therefore, repent. Otherwise I will come to you quickly [*érchomai soi tachú*] and wage war against them [Nicolaitans] with the sword of my mouth" (2:16). To the church

---

3. In the introductory chapter we already saw what "earth and heaven" mean for Revelation: two dimensions of the same history (the empirical dimension that can be experienced and the hidden dimension that is transcendent).

at Philadelphia he says the same thing, "I am coming quickly" (*érchomai tachú*, 3:11). He even tells the vile church in Laodicea: "Behold, I stand at the door and knock. If anyone hears my voice and opens the door, [then] I will enter his house and dine with him, and he with me" (3:20).

All of these expressions have to do with the risen Jesus manifesting himself in the present (which extends from 4:1 to 19:10 in the text); they are not about the final parousia (19:11ff.). The virtues most demanded of the churches are those needed for the distress of the present age: resistance, not weakening or becoming afraid, charity, faith, spirit of service, energy, and so forth. Even in the distress of the present time, it is necessary to struggle and overcome, and hence each message ends with the promise to the victor.

Drawing out who John's *internal adversaries* in the churches are and how he deals with them provides another important key for interpreting the seven messages. These adversaries are those who call themselves apostles but are not (2:2); the Nicolaitans (2:6); some who hold the teaching of Balaam (2:14); the Nicolaitans again (2:15); the prophetess Jezebel and her group (2:20). They are all part of the same current and the names John gives them are typological or symbolic. "Nicolaus" means "he who defeats the people" (*niká-laón*). It is similar to Balaam, which means "he who consumes the people" (*bala-am*), which comes from Numbers 22–24 and is a type of the one who curses and corrupts the people. Jezebel (1 Kings 17–21) is a type of the idolatrous woman who combats the prophets of Yahweh.

What do they do? In 2:14 we find a description in a somewhat obscure reference to the Old Testament. Numbers 25:1–2 narrates the incident of fornication and idolatry in Baal of Peor. According to Numbers 31:16, it came about as the result of the advice of Balaam, who suggested to Balak (Num. 22–24) that he use Moabite women to seduce the Israelites. The meaning is clear: the teaching of Balaam is idolatry. Idolatry takes place in the eating of meat sacrificed to idols and in fornication, which may be actual or may be a symbol for idolatry. In 2:20 what Jezebel does is the same thing as what Balaam does in 2:14; 2:24 says that these adversaries know the so-called "deep secrets of Satan."

Who are all these adversaries: Nicolaitans, Balaamites, false apostles, followers of Jezebel, those familiar with the deep secrets of Satan? They are all the same. They are the same people that Paul fought in 1 Corinthians. These must be people of a gnostic or pre-gnostic tendency who believe that they have a superior knowledge of God and think that they are already saved and look down on more lowly Christians. What prompted the emergence of this tendency? The need on the part of some Christians to modify Christianity so that they could participate in the economic, political, and social life of the empire. Such participation took place in associations and guilds where emperor worship was the common ideology and eating meat sacrificed to idols was a common practice. Christianity is spiritualized in order to allow for participation in these structures with no problems of conscience. It is the rich and powerful who modify Christianity along these lines. Gnosticism arises as an adaptation of Christianity to the empire. In Revelation John takes a radical stance against this tendency. He combats such people with his teaching on testimony and martyrdom: Christian life as a life that runs counter to the Roman empire. One who bears the mark of God cannot buy or sell (chapter 13) and is thus marginalized from the social and business life of the city. Paul similarly combats his enthusiast adversaries with his theology of the cross.

Besides internal adversaries, there are also *outside adversaries.* The all-encompassing outside adversary, omnipresent here and throughout Revelation, is the Roman empire. Jesus tells the church at Smyrna:

> Do not be afraid of anything that you are going to suffer. Indeed the devil will throw some of you into prison, that you may be tested, and you will face an ordeal of ten days. (2:10)

According to chapters 12 and 13 of Revelation, the devil acts in history through the beast, that is, the Roman empire. Here the community is told of a persecution by the empire that will not last long. Jesus tells the church at Pergamum:

> I know that you live where Satan's throne is.... Antipas, my faithful witness... was martyred among you, where Satan lives. (2:13)

Satan here symbolizes the "spiritual" and "supernatural" power of the Roman empire, acting through its structures. In the church in Thyatira Jesus praises those who do not share the teaching of the gnostic enthusiasts (the internal enemies that we have seen). They think that this teaching is about the "deep things of God," but for Jesus it is simply knowing the "deep things of Satan" (2:9, and quite similarly, 3:9). As we saw before, Satan symbolizes the "spiritual" forces of the Roman empire. An assembly or a synagogue of Satan is a synagogue handed over to the empire, politically and spiritually under the sway of the empire. Hence they are no longer Jews, or are Jews in name alone. They are no longer a synagogue of Yahweh but of Satan, who acts in history through the empire.

In short, the risen Jesus bodily alive in the midst of the communities is preparing them to do battle in the present facing their internal and external enemies (pre-gnostic enthusiast Christians and the diabolical forces of the Roman empire).

Keys for Interpreting Each of the Prophetic Messages

Ephesus (2:1–7): This is the most important port in Asia Minor. It is the most populous city and the most important one due to its trade and channels of communication. Even before the arrival of the Greeks the "mother goddess" was adored there. With the Greeks she came to be called Artemis (see chapter 19 of Acts on the practice of magic in the city and worship of Artemis). Worship of the goddess Roma and the god Julius Cesar (Roman imperial worship) was established in 29 B.C.E.

After the church in Jerusalem (destroyed in 70 C.E.) and before the rise of Rome, the most important church during apostolic and post-apostolic periods was that in Ephesus. The church was founded by Paul, and he exercised an important ministry there between December 52 and March 55 (two years and three months). Paul wrote the letter to the Galatians from Ephesus, as well as 1 and 2 Corinthians, and he may have written the letter to the Philippians and the letter to Philemon while in jail there. Chapter 16 of the letter to the Romans is very probably a note to the Ephesians, which provides us with crucial information on that church. The letters of Paul's disciples during the post-apostolic period (after 70) may have been written from there as well, i.e., the pastoral letters and perhaps 2 Thessalonians (which is contemporaneous with Revelation). The tradition of the "Beloved Disciple" (John's Gospel and the three letters of John) was also widely available in Ephesus. Thus we may assume that Revelation was spread from Ephesus. Moreover, the first and most important letter of Ignatius of Antioch is from the church at Ephesus.

Revelation 2:1 again takes up the two elements of the opening vision that refer to the churches in their entirety: "The one who holds the seven stars in his right hand and walks in the midst of the seven gold lampstands says this." The seven stars symbolize the seven angels of the seven churches, who as we noted may be the seven prophets in charge of each of them (see 22:8: the angel is a servant like John and his brothers the prophets who are keeping the words of this book). The seven lampstands are the seven churches. In 2:1 the vision changes in two respects. Jesus now holds the seven stars "with power" (*kratón;* 1:16 simply says that he "holds" them = *echon*); and not only is he in the midst of seven churches but he "walks in their midst" (*peritatón*). With these two changes the author highlights the presence and activity of Jesus in the midst of the churches, and that fact is stated to the prophet of Ephesus, who is probably responsible for the churches, although he can lose that position (v. 5).

The life of the community at Ephesus, with which Jesus says he is familiar, is summed up as "works" (*érga*), "hard work" (*kópon*), and "resistance" (*hypomoné*). Resistance is emphasized: "you have resistance and have suffered for my name, and you have not grown weary." Resistance is the virtue required for building the reign in times of persecution or in a situation of oppression. John is very much a brother and companion of the churches in distress, in the reign, and in resistance (1:9). Resistance takes place in testimony (*martyría*); it is what marks the witness (*martyr*) in his or her struggle against the beasts (empire) and both internal and external adversaries.

More specifically, in its behavior the community at Ephesus is said not to have supported the wicked, to have tested false apostles and discovered that they were impostors, and to have despised the works of the Nicolaitans. These lines refer to different practices of the same internal adversary of the community, symbolically designated Nicolaitans. Would we today not call such an attitude intolerance? Is this a community that has no tolerance for those who think differently? That is not the point. As we have seen, the teaching of the Nicolaitans is a pre-gnostic heresy that seeks to spiritualize Christianity in order to make it compatible with the empire. It stands radically opposed to the ethics and theology of Revelation, in which the life of Christians and the community should be an ongoing witness against the oppression and idolatry of Babylon and its beasts (Roman empire). The Nicolaitans may have been rich Christians who were actively involved in the economic, social, cultural, and unavoidably religious structures of the city, and accordingly sought a teaching that would make Christianity compatible with such involvement.

The eschatological presence of Jesus in the community not only discerns the good that is in it, but also judges what is negative: "I hold this against you: you have lost the love you had at first." The community gave up its first agape (*agápen ten próton*). Agape is the brotherly and sisterly love or the solidarity that holds the community together from the beginning. It has lost this solidarity, perhaps under the influence of the Nicolaitans and as a result of its struggle against them. Jesus accordingly issues three orders to the community: "Realize how far you have fallen. Repent, and do the works you did at first." The first thing to do is to recall the beginning, followed by conversion, meaning a change of behavior. If the community does not change, Jesus declares, "I will come to you" (*érchomai soí*). We have already noted that this coming of Jesus is not the second coming at the end of time, before the last judgment, but rather is about Jesus' coming to the community now, in the present age. It has already been said that Jesus is alive, that he is walking among the communities, that he holds in his right hand his prophets who are in charge, and he sends a prophetic message to the prophet of each community. We now observe something new: a personal visit to the community at Ephesus in order to remove its lampstand. This does not mean possible ranking or position as the mother church or main church, but something much worse: removing it from community with the other churches and from communion with the risen Jesus himself. Without solidarity (*ágape*), there is no communion with Jesus or with the other communities.

Each message to each individual church ends with a call to hear "what the Spirit says to the churches." The one leading the church is the living Jesus. Listening to the living Jesus means listening to the Spirit, the Holy Spirit, who is the prophetic spirit of Jesus dead and risen. At the end of each letter there is also a promise "to the victor" (*tó nikónti*). These are the martyrs who have "won the victory over the beast and its image and the number that signified its name" (15:2). Those who defeat Satan:

> conquered him by the blood of the Lamb
> and by the word of their testimony;
> love for life did not deter them from death. (12:11)

Observe also what the victor inherits in 21:7. The reward for the victor of the community at Ephesus is to be able to eat of the tree of life, that is, to recover immortality through the resurrection of the body. This does not mean the tree of the lost paradise, however, but the tree that abounds in the New Jerusalem. This tree is not subject to the law forbidding anyone from eating of the tree of the knowledge of good and evil. The New Jerusalem is a paradise without law, where God's glory fills all and where all see God face to face.

Smyrna (2:8–11):   Smyrna is a prosperous port city, rivaling Ephesus, and maintains a special loyalty to Rome. It built a temple to the goddess Roma in 195 B.C.E. and one to the emperor Tiberius in 26 C.E. This Christian community may have been founded by Paul (Acts 19:10). Ignatius of Antioch wrote a letter to this church and another to its bishop, Polycarp. The church in Smyrna was the author of the story of the martyrdom of Polycarp,[4] which took place in the year 155. Jewish and pagan collaborators with the empire conspired to have him killed. He was probably important in the church when Revelation was written, since at the time of his death he said he had served the Lord for eighty-six years.

Jesus does not reproach the church community in Smyrna in the least. This church is suffering "tribulation and poverty." Its poverty may be the result of distress that can be momentary (persecution, see v. 10) or systematic (oppression and exclusion). The Christians in Revelation do not bear the mark of the beast and hence can neither buy nor sell (chapter 3); they are marginalized and therefore are impoverished. Besides suffering distress and poverty, the community suffers the "calumnies" of the Jews, who, as we have explained above, are Jews allied to the empire, collaborators who bear the mark of the beast.

The entire prophetic message to the community at Smyrna is stamped with the paired terms "life" and "death." Jesus, who writes the message, is said to "have died once but to have come back to life." The exhortation bears the same key: "Remain faithful until death, and I will give you the crown of life." The victor is also promised that he "shall not be harmed by the second death." This second death is mentioned in the last part of Revelation, where definitive death (complete annihilation forever) is also mentioned.

Pergamum (2:12–17):   Starting in 133 B.C.E. this city is the capital of the Roman province of Asia. It is the center of imperial worship for the whole region, and John therefore describes it as "where Satan's throne" is and "where Satan lives." Satan is the symbol of the "supernatural" strength of the beast. Standing over the city is a great acropolis, the site of numerous temples. In the midst of the acropolis stands an altar to Zeus. This is the first city in Asia to have a temple dedicated to Augustus and to Rome (29 B.C.E.). Asclepius, very popular god of health, is also venerated in Pergamum.

The community has undergone a persecution and now has a martyr named Antipas. Jesus therefore praises its faithfulness and the fact that it has not denied the faith. Nevertheless, the community has committed the sin of tolerating the adversaries of Revelation: those who hold the teaching of Balaam and of the Nicolaitans. As we have seen, these adversaries engage in idolatry, which is here expressed in eating meat sacrificed to idols and in sexual immorality. Such practices are idolatrous because they were the normal practice in the city's official institutions, where those powerful Christians who fit into the empire also participated. John calls for noninvolvement, for a rejection of any idolatrous practice that might compromise the churches with the empire and its spirituality. John's

---

4. Daniel Ruiz Bueno, "Martirio de San Policarpo, obispo de Esmirna," *Actas de los mártires,* bilingual text, 9th ed. Madrid: BAC, 1987, 263ff.

critique is aimed not only at the religious life of the empire, but also at the economic and social life of which such idolatry is part and parcel.

Jesus calls the community to conversion. If that does not happen, he says, "I will come to you quickly" (*érchomai soi tachú*). Just as in the community at Ephesus, the passage is about the coming of Jesus in the present time of the community, in the *kairos* that the community is now living, in which it must give testimony against the oppressive idolatry of the Roman empire. In this message Jesus is presented with the power of his word: "the one with the sharp two-edged sword" (v. 12), and he who "wages war against [the idolaters of the community] with the sword of his mouth" (v. 16).

To "the victor" is promised something mysterious: "some of the hidden manna...[and] a white amulet upon which is inscribed a new name, which no one knows except the one who receives it." The manna is that hidden by Jeremiah at the destruction of the temple, which now appears in the messianic temple. This is a meal of community life, which stands poles apart from the meal of death, of meat sacrificed to idols. This may be an allusion to the Eucharist. The hidden manna would be the bread of God, life of the people; one who eats it will never die (see John 6:31ff.). It is quite possible that the white amulet was something Christians wore to set themselves apart. It is a sign of victory when history is judged.

Thyatira (2:18–29): This city is not important either administratively or militarily, but is rather a city of traders and artisans, who are organized into guilds and associations. The community has a "practice" (works): of "solidarity" (*agape*), "faith" (*pistis*), "service" (*diakonía*), and "resistance" (*hypomoné*). These latter works are better than the former (contrary to the community at Ephesus). The behavior of the adversary group led by Jezebel is the same as that of the Nicolaitans and Balaamites. John applies the symbolic name Jezebel, taken from the Old Testament figure (2 Kings 9:22) to the prophetess who is corrupting the community. Jezebel leads the prophets of Baal with whom Elijah is engaged in combat. John is now the new Elijah who is doing battle with this false prophetess and her followers. Jezebel is dragging the community away to participate in the idolatrous practices of their oppressors. To that end she employs a theology that claims to be deep, high-minded, and spiritual, but that John labels the "deep secrets of Satan." Jesus makes a discernment between the satanic oppressive theology of the followers of Jezebel and the liberating apocalyptic theology of John: "I am the searcher of hearts and minds." That is why at the beginning of the message to Thyatira he is represented as having "eyes like a fiery flame," precisely in order to discern. Although the prophetess Jezebel is seen negatively here, her presence provides positive testimony to the existence of women prophets. Hence whenever we speak of prophets in Revelation, we must be thinking of both men and women.

The most beautiful thing about this letter is the promise to the victor: "I will give [him] authority over the nations...and to him I will give the morning star." The theology underlying this promise takes its inspiration from Psalm 2 (a political psalm powerfully present throughout Revelation), in which the Messiah is presented as Son of God (the reason that Jesus is presented as Son of God at the beginning of the message in 2:18) and as the one who receives power over the nations and the kings of the earth. Jesus now promises this power to the victor in the community of Thyatira. Jesus, the risen Messiah, hands over his messianic power to the community; it is an eschatological and political power over nations and kings. Jesus likewise gives the victory to the "morning star." In 22:16 Jesus himself says he is the radiant light of dawn. This star is Venus, sign of victory, which announces the end of night and the approach of dawn. This sign is now handed over to the community: it also must defeat the darkness and announce that the light of dawn is near.

This theme is very common in apocalyptic, in Daniel 7, for example, where the people of the holy ones of the Most High receive the kingdom and power. This is the exaltation of the holy ones, of the just and the oppressed. The victors over the beast, over his image, and over the number that signifies his name (15:2) now receive power over the kings and nations that make up the Roman empire. "He has thrown down the rulers from their thrones but lifted up the lowly" (Luke 1:52). What kind of power is this? It is obviously not the same power as that of the empire, a murderous and idolatrous power. This is not simply turning everything upside down. It means messianic or eschatological power, that is, the power of solidarity, faith, service, and resistance (which are the works of the community of Thyatira in v. 19), as well as the power of truth (14:5) and testimony (12:11). This is the power of the holy ones, of the poor and the oppressed. For its part the community, like the morning star, must announce the end of darkness and the approach of dawn. Paul proclaimed:

> the night is advanced, the day is at hand. Let us then throw off the works
> of darkness [and] put on the armor of light. (Rom. 13:12)

Sardis (3:1–6):   This city's former magnificence has declined, thus making it analogous to the community. Its economy is based on the production of cotton goods and the art of dyeing. The city has twice been taken in a sneak attack (for failure to be on the lookout).

The church is dead — its life is only apparent. Only a few have not soiled their garments. This clearly means behavior uncontaminated with the idolatry of the empire. We may assume that what killed the church was the idolatry spread by the Nicolaitans, the Balaamites, and gnostic groups. Since it is stated that only a few are not idolaters, presumably most of the church was idolatrous. Jesus stirs up the community with five imperatives:

> ... wake up ... strengthen what remains before it dies.... Call to mind how
> you accepted what you heard ... keep to it, and repent.

Jesus sketches for the community a whole strategy for recovering the life that they have lost. If the community does not respond, Jesus tells it, "I will come like a thief in the night." The expression is used here for Jesus' coming to the community in the present (see 16:15) and is parallel to the expression "I will come to you soon" (*érchomai soi tachú;* see 2:5, 2:16, 3:11).

Clothing is an important matter in this community, and it is mentioned three times here. The white garment unstained by idolatry is that of the martyrs, those who overcome the beast, his image, and his mark. Jesus is also a martyr and is dressed like the martyrs. These may be the witnesses who are still alive or those who have given their lives in testimony. All are wearing white garments. The same expression is used in 4:4 for the twenty-four ancients dressed in white in heaven alongside God's throne. Another term (*stolé* = clothing) is used for the white garments of the martyrs in 6:11 and 7:9, 13, or the garments washed (bleached) in 7:14 and 22:14. Yet another term (*byssinos* = linen) is used in 19:8 and 19:14. The garment symbolizes people's behavior or practice (see 19:8).

The Greek word *ónoma* (name) appears four times in this message to the community of Sardis, and it means that persons are being identified precisely: the community is identified as such (its name, its reputation of being alive); there are few names of people who are not idolatrous; the name of the victor will not be erased from the book of life; and Jesus will acknowledge his name before the Father. It is striking how many echoes of the synoptic Gospels are found in this message to Sardis.

Philadelphia (3:7–13):   There is not much to say about this city. It is the newest of the cities, has been destroyed by earthquakes several times, and is very Romanized. In 17 C.E. it was completely destroyed by an earthquake and was rebuilt by Tiberius and accordingly called Neocaesarea. Under Vespasian it was called Flavia.

The church in Philadelphia has much in common with that of Smyrna. Jesus does not reprehend either of them. The Smyrna community is poor, and the one in Philadelphia is powerless. Both have problems with "Satan's assembly," and both are expecting an impending crisis.

Jesus is presented to the church with divine authority as "the holy One, the true" (titles applied to God in 6:10). Jesus likewise has the power to open and close access to the reign of God (here symbolized as the kingdom of David). With this power Jesus says to the community, "I have left an open door before you": in other words, to the community he opens access or a direct entrance to the reign of God. It may be that the synagogue was closing its doors to Christians and thereby excluding them from God's reign. Jesus steps in as the one who wields David's key, as the only one who can close or open the gates to the reign. Paul of Tarsus speaks of a door being "opened" as a missionary opportunity (1 Cor. 16:9, 2 Cor. 2:12, Col. 4:3). The reference here is rather to the reign, the ultimate reason for mission. Jesus opens a door for the community, which means this opportunity to build the reign, because the community in Philadelphia "has held fast to Jesus' word and has not denied his name." The community has little economic, political, social, or institutional power, but it is very faithful to what Jesus comes to do (his word and his name). This is a community that finds its only strength in holding fast to his word.

As we saw with regard to the Smyrna community, "Satan's assembly" is the synagogue of those Jews who are integrated into the empire, who are subjected to Babylon, the beast, the image of the beast, and its mark. This expression is not aimed at Jews. It is not anti-Semitic but anti-empire: all who follow the empire are of Satan, for he is the one who gives the empire its power. This assembly closes the door to Christians who are apocalyptic and stand up to the empire, but Jesus, who owns the keys to the reign, opens a door for them. The power-less and the poor are those who now have access to the reign thanks to Jesus. Jesus says that he is going to bring low these Jewish collaborators. The issue is not that they should be converted — that they cease being Jews — but that they should cease being pro-imperial idolaters. The powerful and pro-Roman institu-tional community is going to fall down at the feet of this apocalyptic powerless community and learn how much Jesus loves it.

Jesus tells the community that "a time of trial" (*he hora tou peirasmou*) is coming over "the whole inhabited world" (*he oikoumene*). The inhabited world, or *oikoumene,* is not all the earth, but the world that is organized and controlled by the Roman empire. Everything else is the world of the barbarians. The trial (*peirasmós*) is intended to test (*peirasai*) "all men on earth." In Revelation the expression "all men on earth" is a technical term for the wicked, those who follow the beast. What is the test? It is not the final judgment (19:11–22:5), but the historical judgment that takes place in the present (4:1–19:10). Those to be tested are the wicked who follow the beast; it is the crisis of judgment on the empire, prompted now in the present by Jesus' coming (*érchomai tachú*) and the testimony of Christians. Christians will be persecuted and oppressed for their testimony at this moment, but Jesus nevertheless promises that the community will be safe for "it has kept the word of the resistance of Jesus" (*ho lógos tes hypomones*). At this moment Christians must "hold fast to what they have lest someone rob them of their crown."

In the message to the church in Philadelphia the promise to the victor is quite developed. As is the case with all the other promises to the victor, there is an allusion to the last part of the book (19:11–22:5): the community is struggling in the present period of history while keeping in mind the ultimate reality of God in history: the new creation and the new Jerusalem. Jesus will "make the victor a pillar in the temple of God." What temple is this? In Galatians 2:9, Paul calls James, Cephas, and John pillars of the church in Jerusalem. The text here is not referring to the present church, since this is a promise for the future. Nor is it referring to the future church, since there is no temple in the New Jerusalem (21:2), for the Lord is its temple since his glory fills the entire city. Every victor in the struggle against the empire will be a pillar in the new Jerusalem (and not just the outstanding figures as in the old Jerusalem). Jesus will write three names over the victor: that of God, that of the new Jerusalem, and the new name of Jesus. The inscribing of the name indicates belonging to God, to the new Jerusalem, and to Jesus (it is they who appear in 14:1–5, where those who follow the Lamb here on earth have inscribed on their forehead the name of the Lamb and of his Father; they are also those who are marked in 7:1–8). Those who adore the beast bear the anti-sign of the mark of the beast. Only the holy ones know the new name of Jesus, which will be revealed at the end (19:11 ff.).

Laodicea (3:14–22):   This was the richest city in Phrygia, known for its banks, its linen and cotton industry, and its medical school and pharmacies. As is the case with the other messages, in writing to the community, John invokes the characteristic features of the city.

Jesus is presented under three titles: "the Amen," "the faithful Witness and true," "the Source of God's creation." John draws inspiration from 1:4–8 more than from the opening vision. The Amen expresses firmness and assurance in testimony, and hence Jesus is the faithful witness. In 1:5 Jesus is the ruler (*ho árchon*) of the princes of the earth; here he is the source (*he arché*) of God's creation. In Revelation history is made by the cosmos as well as humankind. Jesus has both cosmic and political primacy. We find this representation of Christ relating to both cosmos and history also in the Christological hymn of Colossians 1:15–20. The cosmic reinforces the historical.

Contrary to the communities in Smyrna and Philadelphia, which are entirely positive, the community in Laodicea is seen in an entirely negative light. This community is "neither hot nor cold" and hence Jesus "spews it out of his mouth." The cold-hot dichotomy is not expressing merely a psychological attitude of indifference or enthusiasm, but rather two opposed historical categories. The cold symbolizes the indifference of the pagan and rich world toward Christians. The hot symbolizes the apocalyptic indignation of poor Christians toward the oppressive structures of the Roman empire. The Laodiceans want to be both rich (cold) and Christian (hot) and thereby end up lukewarm. They want to live simultaneously as rich Romans and as Christians, and in the end they are neither one nor the other. They are like the Nicolaitans (gnostics), who seek to live a spiritualistic, individualistic, and ahistorical Christianity apt for living as part of the Roman empire. They seek to "inculturate" Christianity into the oppressive structures of the empire and end up being neither true followers of the beast nor true followers of Jesus. They are lukewarm, and Jesus vomits them out of his mouth.

Let us consider what the Christian of this lukewarm community is saying: "I am rich, I have become rich, and I have no need of anything." Each phrase says something different: first the fact that they are rich now, and then the process of becoming rich (which in the light of the parallel text in Hosea 12:8–9 connotes corruption and exploitation of others), and finally the subjective attitude of self-sufficiency and pride. Jesus reproves the person with five adjectives: you are "wretched, pitiable, poor, blind, and naked." He then says,

> Take my advice. Buy from me gold refined by fire if you would be truly rich. Buy white garments in which to be clothed, if the shame of your nakedness is to be covered. Buy ointment to smear on your eyes, if you would see once more.

A very common but false interpretation of this text is that the church in Laodicea is materially rich but spiritually poor and that Jesus is advising it to be also spiritually rich. This interpretation falls into the very teaching that Revelation is striving to correct: it is a gnostic, Nicolaitan, and lukewarm interpretation. In this false interpretation the important thing is spiritual poverty or wealth, and material poverty or wealth means nothing. What Revelation is really demanding of the church in Laodicea is that it stop being lukewarm, gnostic, and Nicolaitan, that is, that it stop being rich like the idolatrous and oppressive Romans, that it not become rich by exploiting others, and that it cease being haughty and self-sufficient. If it is rich in this fashion it will be (materially and spiritually) wretched, pitiable, poor, blind, and naked. Jesus is not simply urging it to be spiritually rich, but to strive (materially and spiritually) for a wealth that is not acquired by exploiting others (gold refined by fire, a rich life shared by all), that its behavior not be idolatrous (white garments), and that its conscience be clean (ointment for restoring its sight). The language is of course symbolic, but the underlying contradiction is not the material (visible, external) as opposed to the spiritual (invisible, interior); it is rather what is of life (material and spiritual) in opposition to what is of death (material and spiritual), what is pure in opposition to what is idolatrous.

In v. 18 Jesus says, "Take my advice" (*sym-bouleuo*), which indicates a degree of distance from the community, but in v. 19 he explains: "Whoever is dear to me I reprove and chastise." The community must change its behavior in order to be dear to Jesus who reproves and chastises. In v. 20, Jesus proposes that a community be formed:

Here I stand, knocking at the door. If anyone hears me calling and opens the door, I will enter his house and have supper with him, and he with me.

The meaning is not individualistic and about internal feelings (Jesus knocking at the door of the soul), but related to community. It is about forming a household or local community; a community leader hears Jesus' voice and opens the door, and then Jesus has supper (possibly the Eucharist) with the community.

The promise to the victor is almost a conclusion to all the messages and serves as a transition to the next section (4:1–8:1). The linking word here is "throne" (3:21 and 4:2). Jesus promises to bring the victor (over the beast, his image, and his mark) to share in his power, as he shares in his Father's power.

4

Prophetic Vision of History

Revelation 4:1–8:1

INTRODUCTION TO THE READING AND STRUCTURE
OF REVELATION 4:1–8:1

Introduction

Structurally we find two sections in Revelation 4:1–8:1: a liturgy in heaven (in two scenes, chapters 4 and 5), followed by an arrangement into seven parts, as the seven seals are opened. The first four seals form a single unit. The sixth seal is the most fully developed, since the author sees himself as standing between the sixth and seventh seals. In this vision of history the pairing of heaven and earth plays an especially important role in the structure of the text. As we have already explained "heaven and earth" is a mythical symbol for expressing theologically the transcendent and empirical dimensions of history. We find the same structure (opening vision + seven parts) in Revelation 1:9–3:22. In that case it was seven messages to the seven churches; here it is seven seals. Outwardly the structure is the same, but the literary genre and theology of the two sections are very different.

Overall Structure of the Text

    a. Opening vision: liturgy in *heaven:* chapters 4 and 5

    b. The seven seals: 6:1–8:1

    From the first seal to the fourth: on *earth:* lethal reality of the empire: 6:1–8

    Fifth seal: in *heaven:* the martyrs cry out, "How long ... ?" 6:9–11

    Sixth seal: on *earth:* 6:12–7:8

                    judgment on oppressors: 6:12–17
                      protection of God's people: 7:1–8

in *heaven:* 7:9–17
    liturgy of the martyrs: 7:9–15a
    reality of life with God: 7:15b–17

Seventh seal: in *heaven:* silence for a half hour: 8:1

KEYS FOR INTERPRETATION

Opening Vision: Chapters 4 and 5

Every vision in Revelation seeks to transmit a basic conviction. As we have stressed, these are visions, not theoretical texts about ideas. The vision must first be contemplated, then we must absorb the power of its symbols, and finally must use that power to transform our situation. The vision is a reconstruction of the community's collective awareness. Moreover, this vision in chapters 4 and 5 depicts a liturgy. It is a community moment of prayer, praise, and spiritual transformation.

This opening vision directly introduces the section that we have titled "Prophetic vision of history" (4:1–8:1), but it also introduces section 4:1–19:10, which in our structure represents the present moment of history before the beginning of the eschatological reality at the end of time (19:11–22:5). We also discover that this present moment begins with a liturgy (chapters 5 and 6) and closes with another liturgy (19:1–10). In these liturgies John seeks to transmit directly the power and the spirituality with which the community of the holy ones and witnesses must live this historical present.

Chapters 4 and 5 are a striking refashioning of heaven. In the introduction we saw what the expression "heaven and earth" symbolizes. It is a symbolic or mythical expression to designate the two dimensions of history: that of appearance and that of the depths. Earth is where the wicked, the idolatrous, and the oppressors are in control. Heaven is the transcendent world of God within history; it is the world of the holy ones, of those who are not oppressors and idolaters. To refashion heaven means to reconstruct this world of the holy ones, of the poor, of the oppressed. It is a world that is not visible amid the ostentatious life of the empire and of the city, but it is nevertheless real and becomes visible through the un-concealing effected by Revelation. The refashioning of heaven takes place in a liturgy: it is the feast of the holy ones and of the poor, in which they celebrate their faith, their deep convictions, their hope, and their utopia with joy and shouts of praise. Let us now examine the key elements in the refashioning of heaven, which likewise means the refashioning of the collective consciousness of the Christian community at a moment when it is confronting present history.

There is "an open door to heaven," that is, a chance to enter into this deep dimension of history. In 19:11 it will be said that "the heavens [are] opened," that is, the moment of complete revelation arrives. Apocalyptic states that "the heavens are closed" when there is no revelation, when nothing is understood, and there is no hope, no utopia. Here we have an open door: it is an opportunity, a beginning. The voice that calls to John is the voice of the risen Jesus, the very one who has earlier appeared to John and has sent seven prophetic messages to the churches (1:9–3:22). Jesus is going to show John "what must take place in time to come" (*ha dei genésthai meta tauta*). Like 1:1 ("what must happen very soon") and 1:19 ("Write down whatever you see in visions — what you see now and will see in time to come"), this passage clearly refers to what is going to happen soon, when the vision or initial liturgy is over.[1] It may refer directly to the seven seals (6:1–8:1) or to the whole section about the historical present before the final judgment (6:1–19:10).

The other central element in the vision in chapter 4 is the "throne... standing there in heaven." God's throne is a symbol of God's power. On earth, in the world organized and controlled by the Roman empire, the emperor's throne holds sway. Christians are familiar with this power and endure it. The great hope that the apocalyptic vision transmits is that in heaven God's power holds sway. That is the basis for Christian hope and what makes it possible to resist the empire.

In the vision there are also "twenty-four elders and four living creatures." In general terms, these elders symbolize liberated humankind: holy humankind, humankind that is not idolatrous and has made an option for life. More specifically, they represent the people of God, the people of the martyrs who receive the power to set up God's reign and who are priests for God (1:6 and 5:10). The number twenty-four represents the people in its perfection: the people of the twelve tribes of Israel and the people of the twelve apostles. The "four living creatures" symbolize the cosmos. In Revelation the number four suggests the four cardinal points or the four ends of the earth (thus in 6:1–8 and 7:1). The author highlights the positive qualities of the cosmos: its power, strength, wisdom, and majesty (v. 7: symbol of the animals: lion, lamb, eagle, and human face) and God's presence and wisdom in it (v. 8: symbol of wings full of eyes). In Revelation the moving force of history is not simply humankind (the twenty-four elders) but also the cosmos (the four living creatures). Liberated humankind and the cosmos alike participate in the liturgy of heaven and sing to the creator God.

The fundamental elements of the vision in chapter 5 are the scroll sealed with seven seals in God's right hand, and the risen Jesus who is worthy to take the scroll and open its seven seals. The chapter is dramatic in character: the events take place there, one after another, as in a socio-drama. The sealed book symbolizes human history. The point is not that everything that is going to transpire is written there, but rather that it contains the mystery or secret of history: the revelation of God's mystery that makes history intelligible and gives it meaning. The problem, however, is that no one can open the scroll and read it. Seeing this, John "weeps bitterly." As depicted dramatically in the liturgy, his weeping symbolizes the anguish of the Christian community, which does not understand history and does not understand why there is persecution and oppression. At that

---

1. The same literary form is found in 17:1, where an angel is going to show John the trial of the famous harlot, except that here the judgment comes after the opening vision.

very moment, the risen Jesus appears. We have the impression that Jesus has just risen: he has "won the right by his victory [*eníkesen*]...to open the scroll with the seven seals." Jesus appears as the lion of Judah and the root of David,[2] in triumph (standing up), bearing the marks of his martyrdom (like a lamb that had been slain), with fullness of power (seven horns) and the fullness of the Spirit and of the Wisdom of God (seven eyes). The anguish that had overwhelmed the community disappears and once more the holy ones break forth into praise and joy: "This is the new hymn they sang" (vv. 9–14).

The hymns in Revelation are especially important. First, they express the joy and hope of the poor. All of Revelation is full of this joy and hope. Second, the hymns have a hermeneutic function: they explain and interpret for their audience what is happening or is being revealed. Finally, and for those two reasons, hymns are generally packed with political meaning. They represent an alternative consciousness. We have already seen the liturgical nature of the prologue (1:1–8) and of the epilogue (22:6–21). Chapters 4 and 5 are full of hymns. We likewise find such hymns of hope and political utopia in 7:10–12, 11:15–18, 12:10–12, 14:2–3, 15:3–4, 16:5–7, and 19:1–8.

The hymn in 5:9–15 has all these features of the hymns in Revelation. It is a song to Jesus who is worthy to interpret history (take the scroll and open its seals) for three reasons, which are expressed in three parallel verbs: because you were slain (*espháges*), you purchased for God (*egórasas*)...and you made (*epoíesas*) a kingdom. Jesus can interpret history because he was slain, that is, because of the witness of his death. He is the faithful witness (*martus,* 1:5); he is the community's first martyr, murdered by the empire.

John then employs an economic expression ("to purchase") and another that is political ("kingdom"). Jesus "with his blood purchased for God men of every race and tongue, of every people and nation." The politico-theological meaning of the hymn is that Jesus has set up here on earth a community that is an alternative to the empire.[3] This community is powerful and rules over the earth. "Buying" has the sense of liberating. With his blood Jesus has liberated persons from the whole world; it is a universal community from every race, tongue, people, and nation. This community has been constituted by the witness of Jesus, by his surrendering of his life (of his blood); hence it is a community or people of priests. This expression is taken from Exodus 19:5–6: the people of God is a people of priests, for it is a holy nation that hears the word of Yahweh and keeps his covenant. According to Isaiah 61 the people will be called "priests of the Lord," for the Spirit of the Lord is upon the people so that it may announce good news to the poor, heal the brokenhearted, proclaim liberty to the captives and release to the prisoners. The community set up by Jesus is thus a universal community and has the power to rule over the earth; it is not, however, a community of emperors, senators, nobles, and the powerful, but rather a

---

2. A strange Christology: Christ is lion (v. 5) and lamb (v. 6). This shows the author's free use of symbols. It does not follow a Western rationality, but a symbolic logic taken primarily from the Old Testament. Here the lion refers to Genesis 49:9–10 and the root to Isaiah 11:4.

3. Elisabeth Schüssler Fiorenza, *The Book of Revelation: Justice and Judgment* (Philadelphia: Fortress Press, 1985), chapter 2.

community of priests, a holy community that listens to God's word, and a community that liberates the poor. This community is an *alternative* to the empire. It rules over the earth, but it does so with its witness, its hope, its utopia, its joy, and its spirituality.

The Seven Seals: 6:1–8:1

The opening vision (chapters 4 and 5) and the passage on the seven seals (6:1–8:1) are closely connected, just as we saw that the opening vision in 1:9–20 and the messages to the seven churches (chapters 2 and 3) were closely connected. In this passage about the seven seals, John offers us a prophetic and apocalyptic vision and interpretation of history, that is, he reveals to us the hidden meaning of history, the meaning of what happens on earth by taking into account what is happening in heaven. Today we would say that John is engaging in an analysis of the situation or of the historical conjuncture — except that he is doing so with an apocalyptic (socio-theological) method, by encompassing in his analysis not only the empirical reality (what can be seen and touched) but also spiritual realities, which are present and at work within ongoing history. The fashioning of heaven, or the building of the collective consciousness of the community, in chapters 4 and 5 provides him with the basis for this apocalyptic analysis of current history. Each seal opened reveals an aspect of history to us. Jesus himself opens them one by one.

The First Four Seals: 6:1–8

The first four seals — four horses with four riders — symbolically represent the death of the Roman empire. In the structure of the book they correspond to the beast ridden by the prostitute in 17:1–7, which is likewise a representation of the Roman empire, headed by Rome — that is, Babylon, the idolatrous and murderous city. When presenting the overall structure of Revelation, we pointed out the relationship between sections 4:1–8 and 17:1–19. In both we find a prophetic vision of history opening and closing the present age (4:1 to 19:10). The four horses and riders of Revelation are mythical and symbolic in nature and represent four aspects of the Roman empire.

It is both false and muddled to set up a parallelism between the seven seals, the seven trumpets (8:2–11:19), and the seven bowls (15:5–16:21). These latter passages are in another literary genre, and the underlying theological idea is a rereading of Exodus in the context of the Roman empire. In those passages (trumpets and bowls) we find successive plagues against the Roman empire, whereas here the seals present the oppression of the empire over the people and the community. The four living creatures call forth each of the four horses. The four living creatures represent the cosmos, the four corners of the earth. Here the reality of the empire in all its geographical extension is being examined. Each corner of the earth has something to say about the bestial nature of the Roman empire.

The first horse is white (6:1–2). The color white and the rider's crown are tokens of victory. The rider is a warrior carrying a bow, a typical weapon of a barbarian people (possibly the Parthians, who live to the east of the empire). The warrior "rode forth victorious to further his victories" (*nicon hina nikese*). This is the first and most terrible thing about the empire: it is a victorious empire that continues to enjoy victory. Such is the tragic reality for those oppressed by the empire. John, however, makes a critical observation: the empire is victorious like the barbarians (the rider is carrying a bow), and its victory is ultimately the victory of political violence (red horse), economic oppression (black horse), and death (pale green horse).

A false interpretation identifies the rider of the white horse as Jesus, by seeing a parallel in 19:11ff., where Jesus appears on a white horse. Parallelism does not necessarily mean that things are synonymous; they may even be antithetical. Jesus on the white horse in 19:11ff. defeating the imperial beast and its false prophet is the counter-symbol of the empire. Furthermore, we saw that the four beasts in 6:1–8 stand parallel to the beast of 17:1–7. Revelation 19:11 signals the beginning of the final eschatological reality, after the end of the present time. Furthermore, in 6:1 it is Jesus who opens the seal: it is very unlikely that Jesus would simultaneously be the rider on the first horse, called forth by the first living creature. In short, the white horse is a symbol of the victorious nature of the Roman empire, which achieves victory as a barbarian does, by killing and oppressing.

The second horse is red (6:3–4). Its rider's mission is "to take peace away from the earth, so that people would slaughter one another. And it was given a huge sword." This horse symbolizes the political violence of the Roman empire. The so-called *Pax Romana* means political violence for the poor and oppressed. The verb "slaughter" or "slay" (*sphazzo*) denotes an extreme level of violence. In Revelation it is applied to Jesus slain (5:6, 9, 12; 13:8) and to the martyrs who are slain (6:9; 18:24). The empire slays and likewise sows violence among the oppressed.

The third horse is black (6:5–6). The rider "holds a balance in his hand," a symbol of economic power. A voice is announcing an economic disaster: "A ration of wheat costs a denarius, and three rations of barley cost a denarius." A denarius is a day's pay, and with it formerly one could buy eight or ten times as much wheat or barley. A terrible inflation is raging and it affects what people buy and leads to hunger among the poor. By contrast, the price of luxury goods, oil and wine, does not change. The black horse symbolizes the economic oppression of the Roman empire. Only the wealthy enjoy the economic prosperity for which the empire is known, just as only they enjoy the *Pax Romana*.

The fourth horse is pale green (6:7–8). For the first time we learn the name of the rider, Thanatos, which means death. He is accompanied by Hades (the ruler of the dead). This rider has been given authority over a quarter of the earth to kill with the sword, famine, plague, and wild beasts. This horse and rider symbolize the overall reality of the empire, and in a way sum up the three previous horses. The Roman empire is an empire of death. It kills with political repression and economic oppression. Plague and wild beasts are symbols of death: they are the lethal forces of nature unleashed as a result of the empire's repression and oppression.

The Fifth Seal (6:9–11)

After revealing and interpreting the lethal reality of the Roman empire on earth, John now peers into the depths of heaven, the concealed and transcendent reality of history. In this heaven John "sees alive those slaughtered because of the witness they bore to the word of God." The expression "I saw alive" (*eidon tas psychas*) is usually translated literally and falsely as "I saw the souls." Besides the fact that souls cannot be seen, the Greek term denotes the soul insofar as it gives life to the body.[4] What is extraordinary here is that in heaven the martyrs are alive. The martyrs are also seen alive in 7:9–17 ("a great multitude... standing before the throne and before the Lamb,... cried out in a loud voice..."), in 15:2–4 ("those who had won the victory over the beast and its image and the number that signified its name... standing... they sang..."), in 19:1–4 ("liturgy of the martyrs in heaven... they shout Alleluia"), and in 20:4–6 ("I saw alive those beheaded for their witness to Jesus and for the word of God and who had not worshiped the beast.... They came to life and they reigned over the earth"). All these texts are parallel, although the first refer to the present time and 20:4–6 to the first resurrection that leads to the thousand-year reign in the history that is to come. For the Christian community persecuted by the empire it was a joy to know that its assassinated martyrs were alive in heaven, that is, in that transcendent dimension of history.

The martyrs alive in heaven "cried out in a loud voice." The verb "to cry out" (*krazo*) is strong; it recalls the cry (*kraugé*) of the Israelites oppressed in Egypt before the Exodus. It is the cry of all those assassinated throughout history; it is the despairing and demanding cry of the prayer of the outcast, as found very often in the Psalms (see Psalm 5, for example). The martyrs who are alive cry:

> How long will it be, holy and true master, before you sit in judgment and avenge our blood on the inhabitants of the earth?

In short, they cry: justice and vengeance. That is the cry heard in heaven. A curious parallel is found in Luke 18:7–8a: "Will not God then secure the rights of his chosen ones who call out to him day and night: Will he be slow to answer them? I tell you, he will see to it that justice is done for them speedily" (see also Sir. 35:11–24). The verb avenge (*ek-dikeo*) appears in Revelation only here, in 6:10, and in 19:2, where the martyrs in heaven sing that God has already judged Rome, the great harlot, and thus "has avenged" on her the blood of his servants.

The answer given to the martyrs is first the acknowledgement of their works, their faithfulness, their testimony ("Each of them was given a white robe"). Then they are told that the number of martyrs who are to die like them is not yet complete. In other words, they are told that the justice and vengeance for which they plead will only be given at the end of time, that there is still more time to come before this end, and that the present time of resistance and martyrdom still continues. As we would say today: The struggle goes on!

---

4. *Nueva Biblia Española*, L. Alonso S. and J. Mateos, eds. The same thing is true of the parallel text, 20:4.

The Sixth Seal (6:12–7:8)

In the first four seals John examined the lethal reality of the Roman empire on earth, which arouses in heaven the anguished and pressing cry of the martyrs, "How long...?" They demand justice and vengeance. They want God to intervene in history and terminate the situation of injustice and impunity in the Roman empire. They are told, however, that there is still time remaining before the end and that the present time of oppression, persecution, and resistance continues. The martyrs want the last judgment now but they are asked "to be patient a little while longer," and told that God still offers a *kairos,* an opportunity for grace and conversion. The times are going to be terrible and many holy ones will have to suffer martyrdom, but they must not worry, for during this period the Lamb's anger will flare out against oppressors and idolaters, and the people of God marked with the seal of the living God will be saved. This present time of oppression, judgment, resistance, and martyrdom is what will be revealed with the opening of the sixth seal.

Because it is about the present time, the sixth seal has a more complex structure. Let us recall this structure (which we have already presented along with the overall structure of this section):

what happens *on earth:* 6:12–7:8
    judgment on oppressors: 6:12–17
    protection of God's people: 7:1–8
what is happening *in heaven:* 7:9–17
    liturgy of the martyrs: 7:9–15a
    life with God: 7:15b–17

What Happens on *Earth:* 6:12–7:8: A frightful cosmic cataclysm is first described (vv. 12–14):

> ...there was a great earthquake; the sun turned as black as dark sackcloth and the whole moon became like blood. The stars in the sky fell to the earth....Then the sky was divided like a torn scroll curling up, and every mountain and island was moved from its place.

This is not the absolute end of the cosmos before the last judgment spoken of in 20:11 ("The earth and the sky fled from his presence and there was no place for them") and in 21:1 ("The former heaven and the former earth had passed away, and the sea was no more"). Here the cosmos goes on: the wicked hide in caves, and in 7:1–3 the earth still exists. Cosmic catastrophe is a way of dramatizing a human catastrophe within history. The text is not to be interpreted literally, but as a mythical-symbolic figure. Such a practice is very common in late prophetic literature and in apocalyptic. As an example, we may cite Isaiah 34:2–4:

> The Lord is angry with all the nations...he has doomed them and given them over to slaughter. Their slain shall be cast out. The mountains shall

run with their blood. The heavens shall be rolled up like a scroll, and all their host shall wither away.

Here is text from Isaiah 24:17, 19–21:

Terror, pit, and trap are upon you, inhabitant of the earth.... The earth will burst asunder, the earth will be shaken apart, the earth will be convulsed. The earth will reel like a drunkard, and it will sway like a hut. Its rebellion will weigh it down, until it falls, never to rise again. On that day the Lord will punish the host of the heavens in the heavens, and the kings of the earth on the earth.

These are catastrophes within history, dramatized by cosmic and mythical symbols.

The empire now suffers cataclysm because "the great day of the wrath of God and of the Lamb has come." On that day the wicked "will seek to hide from the face of the one who sits on the throne and from the wrath of the Lamb," thus prompting the great question: "Who can withstand it?" (*tis dynatai stathenai*). The answer is given further on in 7:9 (as well as in 15:2): the martyrs stand before the throne of the Lamb, ... singing. The wicked, however, try to hide from God and the Lamb and are unable to remain standing. In v. 15 we have a detailed list of who they are, in five social categories:

1. the kings of the earth (*hoi basileis tes ges*)

2. the nobles (*hoi megistantes*)

3. the tribunes (*hoi chiliarchoi*)

4. the rich (*hoi plousioi*)

5. the powerful (*hoi íschyroi*)

6. (added on) every slave and free person, which amounts to an "etc."

These are well-defined social categories. The kings of the earth are the local kings who are vassals of Rome (such as the Herods). The nobles may be ministers or important political figures in the Roman provinces (they also appear in 18:23). The tribunes are military leaders (each commanding a thousand soldiers). The rich, in the plural and with the article, point to a social class: they are against the poor. The powerful are "those up above," those who wield a great deal of power. They stand over against the lowly. All of them are wicked, since by their power or wealth they are structurally integrated into the Roman empire, thus inevitably entailing complicity with imperial idolatry. All are followers of the beast and of its image, and they bear its mark on their right hand.

What can all this mean in historical terms? Did the cosmic and historical crisis described here take place on a particular date, or is it rather a deep and extended crisis of the Roman empire? The text does not make it clear, but from

Revelation as a whole we may assume that it is a prolonged crisis or historical judgment on the empire and its oppressive groups that takes place in the present and is effected by the power of God's word and the testimony of Jesus. This is what Revelation is all about (1:2) and why John is exiled on Patmos (1:9), the reason why Christians are persecuted (12:17) and martyrs are slain (6:9 and 20:4). These are those who have triumphed (actually, not just rhetorically) over the beast, his image, and the number signifying his name (15:2 and 20:4). The author of Revelation believes that it is such power in God's word and in the testimony of Jesus that produces this cataclysm within history so that the wicked are seized with terror and must conclude that no one can stand in the presence of God and of the Lamb, that all stability is lost, and that everything is tumbling down. The author reveals how powerful is this strength of the word and testimony so that Christians may resist and have hope.

The cataclysm that shakes the Roman empire — mythically expressed in the form of a cosmic disaster — is threatening to all the inhabitants of the earth. Even the Christian community is afraid of this cataclysm. The poor and the oppressed are usually the first to suffer from such disasters. Hence in the midst of the catastrophe it must be announced that God will protect the people of the holy ones, and an alternative community must be organized. This is the ultimate meaning of the passage in 7:1–8, which is the counter-image to 6:12–17. In 7:1–8 we see the community of witnesses (living martyrs) who are resisting on earth. The word "earth" or "land" appears five times to place the community clearly on the earth. This community will be marked with the seal of the living God. This seal is what protects the holy ones from the catastrophe threatening the empire. See the parallel text 9:4. The idea is taken from Exodus (Exod. 12:7, 13), where the houses marked are saved as the exterminating angel passes by. The same thing happens in Ezekiel (Ezek. 9:4–7), where all are annihilated except those who are marked on the forehead. This seal (*sphragis*) parallels the mark (*cháragma*) in 13:16–17, which is the mark of the beast. In 14:1 those who follow the Lamb are said to have written on their forehead the name of the Lamb and the name of his Father. To be sealed, to be marked, to bear the name on the forehead expresses a similar idea: it indicates belonging to something or someone and symbolizes a behavior, a practice, and a way of being. Some are holy ones, some are idolaters; some follow the Lamb, others the beast. The seal here does not refer to baptism but to a way of living within history.

These marked and saved holy ones are now organized into a people of 144,000 (twelve thousand for each tribe of Israel). The figure of the tribes of Israel is plainly a symbol, and the number signifies perfection. The people of God is thus complete, perfect, and well organized. This is the people of the holy ones who here "on earth" make up the people or the community that is an alternative to the empire; it is the people who keep the word of God and the testimony of Jesus. It is the people who triumph over the beast, his image, and his mark. It is the people who bring about the calamitous downfall of the empire, its shame, and its inability to stand before God and the Lamb. It is the same people that appears in 14:1–5.

What Is Happening in Heaven: 7:9–17:   History is not simply what can be seen in the world of appearance, the empirical world. It also has a deep, transcendent, hidden dimension. Christians live history in accord with what Revelation makes known about what is happening in heaven (the hidden deep dimension). History involves heaven and earth alike. In 6:12–7:8 John shows us what is happening on earth, now in the present age. These are historical events that the reader and listeners of Revelation discover. Ordinary inhabitants of the Roman empire are scarcely aware of these events (judgment of oppressors and protection of the holy ones), which almost escape their notice. They grasp something of it because the testimony of Christians is public and the formation of the community of the holy ones as an alternative community takes place on earth and is something visible that poses a challenge. Nevertheless, the powerful are unaware of what happens "among the poor," although John believes that the faith of the holy ones is what is going to make the empire tremble. However, a deep understanding of history can be obtained only by knowing what Revelation unveils about what is happening in heaven.

There are two moments to what is happening in heaven: a present liturgical moment (7:9–15a) and a future utopian moment (7:15b–17). John receives this revelation through a vision in heaven. In the vision there appears "a great multitude, which no one could count." This multitude is in heaven and does not bear a seal, and hence it cannot be counted like the 144,000 on earth. It goes beyond all numerical limit, and it breaks the organizational patterns of the church on earth. It is moreover, a universal multitude surpassing any limit of "nation, race, people, and tongue." In heaven religious, racial, national, and cultural barriers are shattered. This multitude "stands before the throne and before the Lamb," in contrast to the wicked who cannot stand on the great day of the Lamb's wrath (6:17). They are wearing the "white robes" of the martyrs, those who are not stained with the idolatry of the empire, and the palm branches in their hands are tokens of victory. They are the ones who have triumphed over the beast, his image, and the number of his name. They are the same ones who sing in 15:1–4 and 19:1–4. The martyrs cry out as did those of the fifth seal. There they cried for justice and vengeance; now they cry: "Salvation comes from our God, who is seated on the throne, and from the Lamb." Within the Roman empire the term "salvation" (*sotería*) is political: it designates the peace, security, and welfare that the empire provides. Now the martyrs recognize that salvation comes from God and from the Lamb. They are in effect saying that it does not come from the Roman emperor and his empire. Nor is it an individual salvation affecting the soul; it is social and bodily, although the personal and spiritual are not excluded. The martyrs now receive from God in heaven the salvation that the empire denies to the holy ones here on earth. The praises of the twenty-four elders and the four living creatures are combined with the cry of the martyrs, thus returning to the opening liturgy of chapters 4 and 5.

In 7:13–14 the question arises over the identity of this universal multitude dressed in white robes. One of the elders answers, "These are the ones who have survived the time of great distress; they have washed their robes and made them white in the blood of the Lamb." Many interpret "the great distress" (*thlipsis*) as persecution, thereby raising the question of what great persecution produced this throng of martyrs. Some think it must be Nero's persecution in Rome during in the decade of the 60s C.E. However, I do not believe that the distress here means something so restricted and distant. The distress refers to the ongoing oppression of the empire, which is economic, political, social, cultural, and religious, which is endured by those who are not willing to be integrated into it and to take part in its oppressive and idolatrous structures. It is not a the distress of a particular moment like persecutions but rather an everyday and continual oppression. It is the great distress suffered for following the Lamb wherever he goes, and it is suffered for the sake of the word of God and the testimony of Jesus. The multitude in heaven may not correspond exactly to the church organized on earth, symbolically represented by the one hundred and forty-four thousand people sealed. About this multitude the author stresses that it is beyond calculation and is universal, more so than the people. The point is that the triumph of the martyrs goes beyond the visible limits of the organized church.

The end of the sixth seal (7:15b–17), coming after the liturgy of the martyrs, points toward a utopian future. It describes the life of the martyrs in heaven with God, a life that contrasts with the lethal reality of the Roman empire depicted in the first four seals (6:1–8). Christians know that if they have to suffer the death meted out by the empire on earth, they are already enjoying God's life in the dimension of heaven present in history. This life is described with seven verbs whose accent is very much bodily and historical: God "will shelter them [as a sign of welcoming and protection]. They will not hunger or thirst any more, nor will the sun ... strike them; For the Lamb ... will shepherd them and lead them to springs of life-giving water [symbol of bodily and spiritual immortality], and God will wipe away every tear from their eyes." We have noted that in Revelation heaven is not another life but the transcendent depths of our history that make us lead this present life differently. In chapter 21 and in 22:1–5 heaven will be construed in a far more developed fashion. What we have here is a mere hint of that future of history that all the outcasts of the empire for the sake of God's word and the testimony of Jesus are already enjoying in heaven.

The Seventh Seal (8:1)

"When [the Lamb] broke open the seventh seal, there was silence in heaven for about half an hour." This mysterious verse, which closes the apocalyptic vision of history begun in 4:1, is quite polysemic — in other words, it has many meanings. I think we must respect that polysemia, as long as consistency with the whole section is maintained. In a way this silence in heaven concludes what begins with the opening liturgy in chapters 4 and 5, where heaven is full of songs, hymns, and shouts. In the two visions of heaven, 6:9–11 and 7:9–17, we also feel the cries of the martyrs. Now there is silence in heaven. In literary terms, this silence serves as a transition to the next section, that of the seven trumpets (8:2–11:19), and particularly to the opening liturgy in 8:2–5. Silence in heaven may likewise let the reader know that the moment of earth has arrived. From heaven we now come down to earth. Silence in heaven now impels us to look for God on earth. Indeed, the next section on the seven trumpets will be a frightful and yet hope-inspiring apocalyptic struggle on earth. Silence in heaven focuses our attention on earth.

5

The Seven Trumpets and the Seven Bowls

Revelation 8:2–11:19; 15:5–16:21

In presenting Revelation's overall structure we indicated that the sections on the seven trumpets (8:2–11:19) and the seven bowls (15:5–16:21) are related to one another. In this chapter we are going to demonstrate in detail the deep parallelism between these two sections and how this parallelism provides us with an important key for interpreting them. The central theme of these two sections is a rereading of the Exodus, now being experienced not in Egypt but in the heart of the Roman empire. We also said in the introduction that the earlier section on the seven seals (4:1–8:1) is different in nature and is parallel to 17:1–19:10. The title we applied to these two sections was "prophetic vision of history." Many writers place the sections on the seven churches, seven seals, seven trumpets, and seven bowls all in parallel, thereby confusing the interpretation. It is important to understand the content and different nature of the section on the seven seals as well as the section containing the seven letters to the seven churches (chapters 2–3). The fact that sections are divided into seven parts (seven letters, seals, trumpets, or bowls) is not enough to establish a parallelism. The content, nature, and literary genre of each section must be examined. Finally, we also said that the parallel sections of the seven trumpets and the seven bowls constitute a framework for the central section of Revelation: 12:1–15:4.

The overall pattern thus becomes:

A. Prophetic vision of history: 4:1–8:1

    B. The seven trumpets: 8:2–11:19

        Center of Revelation: 12:1–15:4

    B'. The seven bowls: 15:5–16:21

A'. Prophetic vision of history: 17:1–19:10

INTRODUCTION TO THE READING AND STRUCTURE
OF THE TEXTS

Structure of Revelation 8:2–11:19 (The Seven Trumpets)

Vision in heaven: 8:2–6

First trumpet: 8:7
  – hail, fire mixed with blood on the *earth*
  – result: a third of the land burned up

Second trumpet: 8:8–9
  – large burning mountain on the *sea*
  – result: a third of the sea turned to blood

Third trumpet: 8:10–11
  – large star burning on *rivers and springs of water*
  – result: a third of the water turned to wormwood

Fourth trumpet: 8:12
  – a third *of the sun, of the moon, and of the stars* struck
  – result: a third of them become dark

(Woe! Woe! Woe! to the inhabitants of the earth from the rest of the trumpet blasts that the three angels are about to blow!)

Fifth trumpet: 9:1–11
(First woe)
A star fallen from the sky opened the passage to the abyss, and locusts came out and tormented the people who did not have the seal of God on their foreheads; the locusts were like horses ready for battle; their king is the angel of the abyss.

(The first woe has passed, but there are two more to come: 9:12)

Sixth trumpet: 9:13–11:13
(Second woe)
The four angels of the Euphrates river are released to kill a third of the human race; the number of cavalry troops is two hundred million; out of their mouths come fire, smoke, and sulfur; those who are not killed are not converted from their idolatry and murder: 9:13–21

Prophetic movement: 10:1–11:13

  a. Vision of the angel and revelation to the prophets: 10:1–7

  b. John's prophetic calling: 10:8–11:2

  c. The prophetic church (the two witnesses-prophets): 11:3–13

The second woe has passed but the third is coming soon: 11:14

Seventh trumpet: 11:15–19
(Third woe)

> – The seventh angel blows the trumpet... loud voices say, "God's reign over the world has arrived...": v. 15

> – The twenty-four elders... adore God, and say "We give thanks to you,... God,... who are and who were
> For you have assumed your great power...
> and have established your reign;
> The nations raged
> but your wrath has come,
> and the time for the dead to be judged
> and to recompense your servants... and the holy ones
> and to destroy those who destroy the earth...": vv. 16–18.
> The temple in heaven was opened... and the ark of
> the covenant could be seen
> There were flashes of lightning, rumblings, and peals
> of thunder, an earthquake, and a violent hailstorm: v. 19.

The Structure of Revelation 15:5–16:21 (The Seven Bowls)

Vision in heaven:[1] 15:5–16:1

First bowl: 16:2
– bowl on the *earth*
– festering sore on those who bear the mark of the beast or worship
  its image

Second bowl: 16:3
– bowl on the *sea*
– the sea turned to blood; every living creature in the sea dies

Third bowl: 16:4–7
– bowl on the *rivers* and *springs of water*
– the water turned to blood

Liturgy of God's justice:
I heard the angel in charge of the waters say:
  "you are just... in passing this sentence...
  For they have shed the blood of the holy ones and the prophets
  and you have given them blood to drink;
  it is what they deserve."
I heard the altar cry out, "... your judgments are true and just."

---

1. Verse 1 is here shifted to connect the section on the bowls (15:5–16:21) to the previous section (12:1–15:4). The words "seven angels, seven plagues, filled with the fury of God" are taken up again at 15:5ff.

Fourth bowl: 16:8–9
- bowl on the *sun,* to burn all with fire
- all were burned by the scorching heat
- but they nevertheless blasphemed, and did not repent.

Fifth bowl: 16:10–11
- bowl poured on the throne of the beast
- its kingdom plunged into darkness and all bit their tongues
  in pain
- but they nevertheless blasphemed, and did not repent.

Sixth bowl: 16:12–16
- bowl emptied on the great river Euphrates
- its waters dried up to prepare the way for the kings of the East.

Anti-prophetic movement: 16:13–16
  a. Vision of the false prophets (v. 13)
  b. Revelation about the false prophets and their mission
     (vv. 14–16)

Seventh bowl: 16:17–21
- bowl poured into the air
- A loud voice came out of the temple saying: It is done.
- And there were lightning flashes, rumblings,
    and peals of thunder and a great earthquake
    the great city was split into three parts
    the gentile cities fell
    and God remembered great Babylon
       giving it the cup filled with the wine of his fury and wrath
    Every island fled, and mountains disappeared.
- Large hailstones came down from the sky on people,
- but they blasphemed for the plague of hail.

Comparison of the Structure of the Seven Trumpets (8:2–11:19) with That of the Seven Bowls (15:5–16:21)

This comparison is going to provide us with the basic key for interpreting these two sections. The two parts are complementary and help explain one another.

The section on the seven trumpets begins with the vision in heaven (8:2–6):

1. The seven angels receive seven trumpets

2. An altar in heaven (three times)

3. Smoke (incense with the prayers of the holy ones)

4. Burning coals from the altar hurled down to the earth. (10:7: "At the time when you hear the seventh angel blow his trumpet, the mysterious plan of God *shall be fulfilled*")

5. Thunder, rumblings, flashings of lightning, and earthquakes (8:5 paired with 11:19).

The section of the seven bowls also begins with a vision in heaven containing the same elements (15:5–16:1):

1. The seven angels receive seven bowls.

2. The temple of the tent of testimony is opened in heaven (the temple is mentioned four times)

3. Smoke (God's glory)

4. Seven bowls of God's fury poured over the earth. God's fury *is consumed* with the seven plagues.

5. (Here there are no peals of thunder, rumblings, and so forth, but they appear at the end at 16:18 and in parallel with 11:19).

First trumpet (8:7): over the earth.
First bowl (16:2): over the earth.

Second trumpet (8:8–9): over the sea.
Second bowl (16:3): over the sea.

Third trumpet (8:10–11): over rivers and springs of water.
Third bowl (16:4–7): over rivers and springs of water

The liturgy of God's justice, which does not have any parallel in the section on the trumpets, is placed after the third bowl (16:5–7). This liturgy resembles very closely the one found in 19:1–10.

Fourth trumpet (8:12): over the sun, moon, and stars.
Fourth bowl (16:8–9): over the sun.

Fifth trumpet (9:1–11): the sun and the air were darkened.
Fifth bowl (16:10–11): the kingdom of the beast plunged
    into darkness.

Sixth trumpet (9:13–11:13): Four angels of the river Euphrates
        released.
    Their cavalry troops number 200 million.
Sixth bowl (16:12–16): the waters of the river Euphrates[2]
        dried up.
    The waters dried up to prepare the way for the kings of the East.

---

2. In the New Testament the Euphrates is mentioned only in Revelation 9:14 and 16:12.

After the sixth trumpet
  prophetic movement (10:1–11:13).
After the sixth bowl
  anti-prophetic movement (16:13–16)

Seventh trumpet (11:15–19)
  Introduction: 11:15a
  The reign has arrived: 11:15b–19a (*egéneto he basileia*)
  Cosmic cataclysm: 16:18–21 (expands what is found at 11:19b).
Seventh bowl (16:17–21)
  Introduction: 16:17a
  It is finished: 16:17b (*gégonen:* summarizes 11:15b–19a)
  Cosmic cataclysm: 16:18–21 (enlarges upon 11:19b)

KEYS FOR INTERPRETING THE TWO TEXTS
(THE SEVEN TRUMPETS AND THE SEVEN BOWLS)

Opening Vision in Heaven

Both sections open in heaven with a liturgy in which angels appear to be the main protagonists. In the section about the trumpets, an altar appears in heaven, and on it the incense and prayers of the saints are offered. The smoke of the incense rises to heaven with the prayers. An angel hurls the coals from the altar over the earth. In the bowls section, the temple of the tent of testimony is seen in heaven. The seven angels receive the seven plagues, which are seven bowls filled with God's fury. The temple fills with the smoke of God's glory. The angels receive the order to pour the seven bowls of God's fury over the earth. In the first section the accent falls on the active role of the holy ones through their prayers; it is they who cause fire to be cast over the earth. In the second section it is God's fury that is highlighted.

As we have said, heaven is the depth of history. In this heaven John finds God's revelation: the deepest reasons for what happens on earth, that is, what is visible and empirical in history. This heaven is experienced in the liturgy of the Christian community, and the faith and consciousness of the community are expressed in its symbols and rites. It is the prayers of the holy ones in the community that will prompt God to intervene in history, thus renewing the Exodus, this time in the heart of the Roman empire. These prayers parallel the cry of the people in the Exodus (Exod. 2:23 and 3:7–8).

In both sections, we find a very important verb, *teléo* (= to consummate, finish, accomplish). In Revelation this verb is used only in 10:7; 11:7; 15:1, 8; 17:17; and 20:3, 5, 7. It means to consummate, to be accomplished, to fulfill. In 11:7 and 17:17 the verb has a neutral meaning, whereas in the other passages it has an important theological meaning. In 10:7 with the seventh trumpet the mysterious plan of God is consummated (is accomplished); in 15:1 with the seven bowls, God's fury is consummated (is accomplished); in 15:8 the seven plagues are consummated (are accomplished). The meaning is the same: the present time, when God's mysterious plan — or the time of God's fury (against oppressors) — is being played out, comes to an end with the seventh trumpet or the seventh bowl. Now is the time of exodus when repentance is still possible. The other passages, 20:3, 5, 7, are about the consummation of the thousand-year reign, when the present period comes to an end. Hence we find in Revelation two consummations or two final moments (when something is completed): at the end of the present time, when the seventh trumpet sounds (or when the seventh bowl is poured out), and the end of the thousand-year reign. After the thousand-year reign comes the last judgment and the new creation. Hence the pattern is:

> present time — *end* (*télos*)
>
> thousand-year reign — *end* (*télos*)
>
> last judgment — new creation (without *end*).

The First Four Trumpets and the First Four Bowls

This section is in line with the characteristically Jewish framework for understanding the world, which divides the cosmos into earth, sea, rivers-watersprings, and sun-moon-stars (only the sun is mentioned in the fourth bowl). Cosmic language is uppermost in the section on the trumpets. The only direct allusion to history is found in 8:9, which tells of a third of the ships being wrecked. There is also an indirect allusion to history in Revelation 8:8, where we find a reference to Jeremiah 51:25: the "large burning mountain" points to Babylon. The same is true of Revelation 8:10 with the reference to Isaiah 14:12: the "large star burning like a torch [that] fell from the sky" is a reference to the death of the tyrant. The tyrant's fall turns the waters bitter. This fallen star reappears in 9:1. History becomes more explicit in the bowls, however: the sores break out only on those who bear the mark of the beast; only those who have poured out the blood of the holy ones and prophets are given water turned into blood to drink; with its fire the sun burns only the blasphemers.

A liturgy is placed after the third bowl: 16:5–7. Its theme is God's justice. This liturgy is like those in 15:3–4 and 19:1–10.[3] This liturgy breaks in at this point so that the community may be actively present; indeed, whenever the liturgy appears in the text, the community is making an appearance. Far from being a spectator to the exodus that God is bringing about in the Roman empire, the community is involved in it, as expressed symbolically in the liturgy.

---

3. The term "just" (*díkaios*) appears in Revelation only in 15:3; 16:5, 7; and 19:2 (and also in 22:11 within another context); the two terms "to pass sentence" (*krino*) and "judgment" (*krisis*) appear in 16:5 and 19:2.

The Fifth and Sixth Trumpets (9:1–21)
and the Fifth and Sixth Bowls (16:10–12)

Here the language is heavily apocalyptic and difficult to interpret. Let us begin with the clearest elements. Obviously, both sections are about "plagues sent against the wicked": in 8:13 it is said that the next three trumpets (from 9:1 to 11:19) are a threefold woe for "the inhabitants of the earth," which in Revelation is a technical term to designate the wicked (those who are of the beast and bear its mark). Moreover, 9:4 explicitly says that the plague of locusts is "only for those people who did not have the seal of God on their foreheads." Likewise in the sixth trumpet in 9:20–21, it is clear that those being punished are idolaters and murders. The parallel text on the bowls, as we have already stressed, also makes it quite clear that the plagues are against those who follow the beast. The fifth bowl is poured over the throne of the beast, and the ones who bite their tongue in pain are those who blaspheme against the God of heaven. The sixth bowl dries up the Euphrates, the eastern boundary of the Roman empire, thus enabling the kings of the east who are enemies of the empire to invade. Thus it is not a universal punishment of all humankind but is aimed at the beast and its wicked and blasphemous followers.

When the fifth trumpet blew, says John, "I saw a star that had fallen from the sky to the earth" (9:1). The biblical background to this line is Isaiah 14:3–15, where we find the fall of the tyrant, the king of Babylon (possibly Nebuchadnezzar) ridiculed. In his arrogance the king wanted to make his throne higher than God and hence he was thrown to the bottom of the pit:

> How you have fallen from the heavens,
>> O morning star, son of the dawn!
> How are you cut down to the ground,
>> you who mowed down the nations! (Isa. 14:12)

The fallen star is now the emperor of Rome. The apocalyptic tradition gave this prophetic oracle a mythical meaning: the fallen star is a fallen angel, now become a devil. He has power over the abyss, the dwelling place of the devils. The fall of this satan-emperor causes the plague of locusts (inspired by Exod. 10:1–20 and Joel 1–2), which is the prototype of terror. Here the locusts take on a satanic character: they emerge from the smoke of the abyss of the devils. They do not eat the grass or the trees, like real locusts, but attack "those people who do not have the seal of God on their foreheads." They had as their king (*basileus*) "the angel of the abyss, whose name in Hebrew is Abaddon and in Greek Apollyon" (which mean "destruction" and "destroyer," respectively). The Greek name Apollyon for this angel of death mimics that of the god Apollo, with whom the emperor (at this point Domitian) identified himself. This demoniacal plague does not kill but rather torments the wicked for a period. The consequences of the plague are a wave of wars, cruelty, torment, deceit, and so forth (the general meaning of 9:7–10).

The fifth trumpet (9:1–11) refers not to any historical fact at the time of Revelation nor to any fact that was to take place in the future, but in a general way to God's action punishing the arrogance of the tyrant. The imperial power is a fallen star, a demon, chief of the devils, who instills demonic terror in the wicked, those who bear the mark of the beast. This terror does not affect those who bear God's seal on their forehead (9:4). We find a clearer symbolic explanation of this in the parallel text of the fifth bowl: the fifth angel poured his bowl out over the throne of the beast, his kingdom was plunged into darkness, and people bit their tongues in pain (16:10). The darkness also appears in the fifth trumpet: "the sun and the air were darkened" (9:2). Thus is expressed the terror that the Roman empire experiences when God humbles the pride of the tyrant and unleashes his fury over the tyrant's throne.

The sixth trumpet and the sixth bowl refer specifically to the river Euphrates (9:14 and 16:2), the eastern boundary of the empire and a bulwark against invasions by the eastern barbarian kings (the Parthians). In the sixth trumpet, like the fifth, the text takes on a mythical and demonic connotation. In the bowls section the text is more geographical and historical. God's action announcing the sixth trumpet signals the release of the four angels of the Euphrates river, who are unleashed to kill a third of the empire's population. The killer angels lead an infernal cavalry with two hundred million horses, whose mouths spew forth fire, smoke, and sulfur. Once again we should say that we do not have here any reference to specific historical events. The invasion of the Parthians is used to stir the imagination. The deep meaning of the sixth trumpet and the sixth bowl is God's action that is capable of punishing the Roman empire from its weakest flank, the eastern border. This political action against the empire is presented in mythical terms as an invasion by demonic forces. At this point the devils are foreign. In the fifth trumpet and fifth bowl, it was the attack of the empire's own internal devils, unleashed when God punishes the pride of the beast. In both cases (fifth and sixth trumpet) the Roman empire endures terror and undergoes brutal and massive attack by demons, its own as well as those from outside.

After the sixth trumpet (9:20–21) we find a passage on those who survive the plagues, which also has its parallel after the fifth bowl (16:11). It is said that they did not repent, that they continued to be idolaters and murderers; that they blasphemed the God of heaven and did not repent of their works. Note the connection here between idolatry (presented symbolically also as sorcery and fornication) and murder. One who distorts God's image or replaces it with an idol is capable of murdering a sibling (idolatry as the root of social sin).[4] Likewise note Revelation's pessimism over the possibility of conversion within the Roman empire and of those who bear the mark of the beast.

What is the overall meaning of the plagues that John sees after each of the six trumpet blasts and that take place after the six bowls of God's fury? As already noted, we find the meaning in the Exodus tradition: God hears the cry of his people, decides to liberate them, and to do so sends plagues and unleashes

---

4. Pablo Richard, *La fuerza espiritual de la Iglesia de los Pobres* (San José, Costa Rica: DEI, 1988).

divine fury on Pharaoh and the Egyptians. This is not the last judgment, but God's judgment in history to save the people. God's judgment is God's liberating action in history: God does justice to the poor by liberating them from the oppressor and from their poverty. God's judgment is now being rendered not in Egypt but in the Roman empire. In visions, symbols, and myths, John portrays for us God's liberating action on behalf of Christian communities at the very heart of the empire. These are actions in history, presented in a cosmic and mythical manner. God's plagues or punishments do not mean total or final destruction, but a partisan action by God carried out at the present moment of history. That is why the section on the four trumpets is so insistent that only a third of everything is destroyed. Two-thirds remains untouched, thus leaving room for conversion and repentance. The demonic locusts do not kill but torment for only five months. The four murderous angels kill scarcely a third of the idolaters in order to see whether the other two-thirds change their behavior. In the bowls there is a special insistence that those punished by God's fury are specifically those who bear the mark of the beast, those who spilled the blood of the holy ones and of the prophets, those who blaspheme the God of the heavens. All God's fury and the destructive terror of the devils — those from within (as in the fifth trumpet and bowl) and those from outside (sixth trumpet and bowl) — fall on those who belong to and adore the beast, the Roman empire. The aim of this judgment of God in history, or the realization of the Exodus in the bosom of the Roman empire, is the conversion of the oppressors and idolaters and the liberation of the holy ones. Repeating the Exodus, God attempts to rein in the Roman empire's rush to destroy the world and itself. Hence the Exodus is the good news of God's judgment (see 10:7 and 14:6–7).

It is impossible to identify in history all the plagues and punishments found in Revelation. All efforts to decipher these texts historically in order to discover in them historical events at that time or in the future end in bizarre conclusions and textual manipulation. What is most important is to interpret these two sections (the trumpets and the bowls) in the spirit of the Exodus, as a liberating intervention of God in history against the oppressors and on the side of the oppressed. These are not natural disasters (earthquakes, volcanic explosions, floods, droughts, cyclones, hurricanes, plagues), since such disasters fall not on the empire and its partisans but basically on the poor. Cosmic agonies of this kind, however, are not "natural" disasters but rather direct consequences of the structure of domination and oppression: the poor die in floods because they are pushed out of safe places and forced to live alongside rivers; in earthquakes and hurricanes the poor lose their flimsy houses because they are poor and cannot build better ones; plagues, such as cholera and tuberculosis, fall primarily on the poor who are malnourished, uneducated, and lacking in sanitation infrastructure. Hence the plagues of the trumpets and bowls in Revelation refer not to "natural" disasters, but to the agonies of history that the empire itself causes and suffers; they are agonies of the beast caused by its very idolatry and lawlessness. Today the plagues of Revelation are rather the disastrous results of ecological destruction, the arms race, irrational consumerism, the idolatrous logic of the market, and the irrational use of technology and of natural resources.

Prophetic Movement (10:1–11:13) and Anti-prophetic Movement (16:13–16)

Structured Reading of Both Passages

Prophetic movement: 10:1–11:13

a. Vision of the angel and revelation to the prophets: vv. 1–7
   – Vision of the mighty angel with the small scroll opened: vv. 1–2
   – Cry of the angel as a roaring lion: not written down: vv. 3–4
   – Angel swears: the good news of the *end*: vv. 5–7.

b. John's prophetic calling: 10:8–11:2
   – John ordered to eat the opened scroll: 10:8–10
   – John ordered to prophesy again: 10:11
   – John ordered to measure the temple: 11:1–2

c. The prophetic church (the two witnesses/prophets): 11:3–13
   – Powerful action of the two witnesses/prophets: vv. 3–5
   – Triumph of the beast and the inhabitants of the earth: vv. 7–10
   – Final triumph of the prophets: vv. 11–13

Anti-prophetic movement: 16:13–16

a. Vision of false prophets (v. 13): "I saw three unclean spirits like frogs come from the mouth of the dragon, from the mouth of the beast, and from the mouth of the false prophet."

b. Revelation on the false prophets and their mission (vv. 14–16): "These were demonic spirits who performed signs. They went out to the kings of the whole world [*oikoumene*] to assemble them for the battle on the great day of God the almighty. (Behold I am coming like a thief. Blessed is the one who watches and keeps his clothes ready ...). They then assembled the kings in the place that is named Armageddon in Hebrew."

What we have in these two sections (prophetic movement and anti-prophetic movement) takes place after the sixth trumpet and the sixth bowl. It is the present moment in which the author of Revelation and the Christian community are situated. Next to come are the seventh trumpet and the seventh bowl, when the present time comes to its end. Between the sixth and seventh seals the author also reveals to us the historical situation of the church at the present moment, both on earth (7:1–8) and in heaven (7:9–17). This section is not an interruption or a hiatus but is rather the center of everything and that which gives meaning to everything. It is basic to the structure of the whole section of the seven trumpets and of the seven bowls. In Revelation the center of attention is always on the present; that is the location of the community that is resisting and testifying against the empire (see the overall structure of Revelation whose center is found at 12:1–15:4). This present has a part that has already occurred (the first six trumpets and the first six bowls) and has an end that is soon to come (the seventh trumpet and the seventh bowl). The author stands between what has already occurred and the coming end; it is the present moment which defines everything and in which everything finds meaning. In the section of the trumpets the central challenge of the present moment, which gives meaning to what has happened previously (first six trumpets) and to what is coming (seventh trumpet), is the prophetic movement (10:1–11:13). In the bowls section the central challenge to the community is the anti-prophetic movement of the three beasts (16:13–16). This prophetic and anti-prophetic movement in the present time represents the activity of the holy ones and of the wicked in this exodus of God within the Roman empire. It is the struggle between the prophets of the Lamb and the prophets of the beast. God intervenes in history, although the community is also active in this judgment of God.

Prophetic Movement: 10:1–11:13

Vision of the Angel and Revelation to the Prophets: 10:1–7:   The central figure in 10:1–7 is the mighty angel who announces the good news of the end, which is already revealed to the prophets; in 10:8–11:2 the central figure is John the prophet who receives three precise instructions (to eat, to prophesy, and to measure), while in 11:3–13 the protagonist is the church in its entirety in its prophetic mission. 10:1 (where the angel comes down from heaven wrapped in a cloud) and 11:12 (where the two prophet martyrs rise up to heaven on a cloud) mark off one section.[5] Everything happens on earth between these two movements. The center of the section is 10:11, where John is ordered to prophesy.

In 10:1–7 we have the vision of the angel coming down from heaven. First the vision of the angel is described (vv. 1–2), followed by his cry as a roaring lion, and finally his oath. This is an astonishing vision. The angel has the features of Yahweh in the Old Testament (Job 37, Ps. 18:7–15, Amos 3:8): he has a rainbow over his head (like Yahweh in 4:3) and holds a scroll in his hand (like Yahweh in 5:1). He likewise has features of the risen Jesus (his face like the sun: 1:16). God, Christ, and the angel thus appear in a single figure, as it were. The angel's first revelation is a sealed revelation (cry-rumble, thundering) which is not made known; then comes the solemn oath revealed by John. This sequence of concealment and revelation makes the scene more dramatic, and it also lets us know that what is being revealed is not everything but is simply one aspect of a much greater revelation that remains for the end. Understanding Revelation 10:1–7 requires a very careful reading of Daniel 12:1–13. Here the angel is called by his name, Michael (which is to appear in Rev. 12:7). A time of anguish is mentioned, but it is also proclaimed that "at that time your people shall escape." There is also an extraordinary oath announcing what will happen when "the power of the destroyer of the holy people [is] brought to an end." Many other details are likewise in agreement and the underlying meaning is the same.

The solemn oath in 10:5–7 provides us with the meaning of the whole section 10:1–11:13 (that is why the oath is so dramatic). We are told, "There shall

---

5. The word "cloud" (*nephele*) appears in Revelation only in 1:7, 14:14, 15:16, where it refers to Jesus and the background is Daniel 7:13, and in this passage (10:1 and 11:12 mark off the section).

be no more delay" (*chronos oukete estai*); that is, the time is up. This time is the present, the now when God is bringing about the exodus that the first six trumpets and bowls describe for us. It is the time when conversion is still possible. But now we are told that this time is going to end: "At the time when you hear the seventh angel blow his trumpet, the mysterious plan of God shall be fulfilled" (*etelesthe to mysterion tou theou*). The verb to "come to the end," "consummate," and "fulfill" (*teleo*) as we said, here refers to the end of the present time. It has the same meaning in 15:1, which it parallels exactly (with the seven bowls the time of the plagues, the time of God's fury, concludes). Here the word "mystery" designates God's action in history, God's plan that gives meaning to history. This is what had been "promised to his servants the prophets." It is found with the same meaning in three parallel places in the synoptics, Matthew 13:11, Mark 4:11, and Luke 8:10: "... knowledge of the mysteries of the kingdom of heaven has been granted to you" (see also in the same sense 1 Cor. 2:1; 4:1; Eph. 3:4; Col. 2:2; 4:3). In Revelation 1:20 and 17:5, 7, "mystery" points to the meaning of a vision or symbol.

John's Call to Be a Prophet: 10:8–11:2: In 10:8–11:2 (which is a single unit that should not be split up) John is given three orders: to swallow the scroll, to prophesy again, and to measure the temple. The word for scroll appears twice in the diminutive form (10:2, 10: *biblarídion*) and once in the normal form (10:8: *biblíon*). The accent is not on the size of the scroll, but on the fact that it is an *open* scroll (vv. 2 and 8). The contrast is clearly with the scroll in chapter 5, the *sealed* scroll bearing seven seals that is in God's hand and that the risen Christ is going to open and interpret. The scroll containing the revelation of the meaning of history is now open: its content is known and has been interpreted. The point now is to read it and put it into practice. The idea is presented with the image of eating the scroll. That is why John is given the order to eat the open scroll. The author is clearly drawing inspiration from Ezekiel 2:8–3:3 (which we suggest should be read). John must not only read or interpret God's revelation, but swallow it, that is, internalize it, nourish himself and be satiated with it; God's word must come to be flesh and blood of his own body. This revelation or word is sweet to the taste, even though it turns his stomach "sour": our first contact with it is pleasing and makes us enthusiastic, but when we internalize it, we are obligated to endure suffering and persecution for its sake.

The second order that John is given is to prophesy: "You must prophesy again about many peoples, nations, tongues, and kings." The order is presented as a necessity (*dei se propheteusai*): it is a part of God's plan. The text draws inspiration from Jeremiah 1:9–10, where God places his words in Jeremiah's mouth and gives him authority over nations and kingdoms. Revelation always mentions tribe, tongue, people, and nation together (5:9; 7:9; 13:7; 14:6). Perhaps under the influence of Jeremiah "tribe" (*phyle*) is here replaced by "kings" (*basileusin*), which gives a more political character to John's calling. He is ordered to prophesy "again" (*palin*). This is not a second prophecy, but rather a new prophecy: Revelation is a prophetic book in a new time (after the resurrection of Jesus).

The third order given to John (11:1–2) is to measure: "Come and measure the temple of God and the altar, and count those who are worshiping in it." The outer court of the temple is not to be measured, but it will be handed over to the Gentiles who will trample the holy city for forty-two months. Here measuring has the sense of rebuilding, restoring, and protecting. The temple and the altar are symbols of the Christian church. When Revelation was written (90–96 C.E.) the historical Jerusalem had been destroyed by the Roman empire. Jerusalem is mentioned in 3:12 and 21:2, 10 as a utopian symbol of the future society that God is building in these new heavens and new earth. John thus situates himself between the historical Jerusalem, now destroyed by the Romans, and the celestial Jerusalem, which has still not come. Here John is taking as symbols elements of the Jerusalem of history (altar, temple, outer courtyard, city); utopian Jerusalem has no temple (21:22). John depicts the Roman empire's domination over the people of God, taking as symbol the destruction of the Jerusalem of history. Rome's war against the Jewish people symbolizes the empire's war against the people of the holy ones. Nevertheless, John is now going to save what was not saved in the destruction of Jerusalem in history: the temple and the altar. The rest of the city is not saved. Revelation thereby shows the historical efficacy of John's prophetic mission. After eating the open scroll and being given the order to prophesy again, he now carries out his prophetic mission under the protection of the Christian community. The prophet John is able to do what the Jewish leaders during the Jewish war were not able to do: save the community. John's prophetic action of protecting the community is not different from God's action of sealing the elect in 7:1–8.

The current war in which the community is saved through John's prophetic action is going to last forty-two months more. This mysterious number is repeated in 11:3 and 12:6, translated into 1,260 days (42 times 30 days), and more vaguely in 12:14: a year, two years, and a half year (taken from Dan. 7:25). Forty-two months, or 1,260 days, is half of seven years (seven years = eighty-four months = 2,520 days), which symbolically represents the present time. The present is the time of persecution and martyrdom, of conversion and struggle; it is the time of exodus, of the church, and of Christian prophets like John. Using Daniel's symbolic framework, it is the last week before the end (Dan. 9).[6] We would therefore now be in the middle of this present time, of this last time before the end, before the last trumpet sounds and the last bowl of God's fury is poured out. It is for this time that John has been called to be a prophet. The Angel's oath has to do with this time period (10:1–7; Dan. 12).[7]

---

6. Pablo Richard, "El Pueblo de Dios contra el Imperio: Daniel 7 en su contexto literario e histórico," *Revista de Interpretación Bíblica Latinoamericana* (San José, Costa Rica-Santiago de Chile) 7 (1991): 25–46.

7. If we take the related words "prophet," "prophecy," and "prophesy" (eighteen times), we see that they are used most frequently (seven times) at the beginning of Revelation (1:1–3), in the epilogue (22:6–21), and in 10:1–11, 13 (five times). The prophetic character of the book of Revelation is defined in these three sections. 16:6, 18:20, and 18:24 recall the murdered prophets.

The Prophetic Church (the Two Witnesses/Prophets) 11:3–13: After presenting John's calling to prophesy (10:8–11:2), the text continues with the prophetic testimony of the whole church: 11:3–13. We have here a narrative or symbolic representation of the church in this present time (between Christ's resurrection and the end, when the last trumpet sounds and the seventh bowl is poured out). It is not an allegory, but a drama or sociodrama. We find here two figures who are called simultaneously witnesses (v. 3) and prophets (v. 10); they prophesy (v. 3) and give testimony (v. 7). In 19:10 this relationship between testimony and prophecy is summed up in the phrase: *"Witness* to Jesus is the spirit of *prophecy."* Prophets are martyrs and martyrs are prophets.[8] Why are there two witnesses (martyrs)? Because for every valid testimony there must always be two witnesses. However, the background here is also made up of Zechariah 4, where the two olive trees are Joshua and Zorobabel (the political and religious leaders in the restoration of the temple); there is likewise an allusion to Moses and to Elijah (political and prophetic power), and perhaps there is some thought of Peter and Paul as well.[9] In any case the two witnesses-prophets represent the church. The whole community is called to be prophet and witness (martyr) in the present time.

We first encounter a symbolic description of these two witnesses-prophets (vv. 3–6): they are covered with sackcloth, for they are poor and are preaching repentance and conversion, which is what God's activity seeks during this exodus time. Their presence is humble, but their power is tremendous. If anyone seeks to do them evil (this is mentioned twice) fire comes out of their mouth, devouring and killing their enemies. The background is Jeremiah 5:14: "Behold I make my words in your mouth, a fire" (likewise those of Elijah in Sir. 48:1). Verse 6 specifies the power of this prophetic community: they have the power of Elijah (to close up heaven) and the power of Moses (to turn water into blood and to wound the earth with all kinds of plagues). This is the prophetic power of Elijah and the political power of Moses. (In 13:13 the false prophet also has this power). The plagues described in the first six trumpets and first six bowls are carried out by God against the wicked, but likewise by the prophetic community which has the power to bring about these plagues. We see here the active role of the Christian community in carrying out the exodus in the very bosom of the Roman empire. There is no passivity and fatalism in Revelation.

In 11:7–13 we find the passover of the prophetic community: its passion, death, resurrection, and ascension. Martyrdom begins when the community "has finished [has brought to the end: *telésosin*] its testimony [*martyrian*]." Only then will "the beast that comes up from the abyss wage war against them and conquer

---

8. In Greek "witness" means "martyr"; the word is the same. In modern languages we have given it the connotation of death: martyrs are those who with their death truly give witness or who are ready to die for what they believe in and what they hope for, even if that death does not really take place. In this sense there is no difference between a living and a dead martyr. The living martyr is continually threatened with death, and the dead martyr remains alive in the community.

9. In rereading the text we could also legitimately regard the two witnesses as man and woman.

them and kill them." This is the first appearance of the beast in Revelation, antic-
ipating what will be described in detail in chapter 13. The corpses of the martyr
prophets lie out in the open in the main street of the "great city." Throughout
Revelation, the great city is Rome, which is also called Babylon. Here it is also
compared symbolically (*pneumatikós*) to Sodom (the idolatrous city), to Egypt
(taken as a city and type of the oppressor country), and to Jerusalem (mentioned
indirectly as the type of the city that kills prophets: where the Lord was crucified). We have here a concentration of the symbolism of evil: Rome = Babylon
= Egypt = Jerusalem. The death of the martyr prophets is known internation-
ally (v. 9) and unleashes an equally international celebration among the wicked
and the idolaters in the empire (v. 10). These wicked are called the "inhabitants
of the earth" (*hoi katoikountes epi tes ges*).[10] The international celebration over
the death of the prophets lasts only a short time (three and a half days), for "a
breath of life from God entered them [and they] stood on their feet" (the reviv-
ifying of the dead bones in Ezek. 37 is reenacted). They then rose to heaven on
the cloud (enclosing the section beginning with 10:1: the angel who comes down
from heaven wrapped in a cloud). We have here an "abduction" that symbolically expresses the exaltation or glorification of the prophet martyrs, after they
have given their prophetic testimony and have suffered martyrdom for the sake
of their testimony. The abduction is not an escapist and alienating vision (as we
find in the discourse of many fundamentalist sects) to escape from martyrdom,
but the recognition of that martyrdom.

We are told that everyone gazes on the martyrs' corpses and sees their resurrection and their exaltation. This is therefore a historical, visible, and public
event. These events are presented symbolically in Revelation, but their meaning
is nonetheless related to ongoing history: the glorious passover of the martyrs
murdered for the prophetic testimony is an event that is known publicly. The
passover of the martyrs triggered "a great earthquake, and a tenth of the city fell
in ruins. Seven thousand people were killed during the earthquake" (v. 13).

As in all apocalyptic literature, the cosmic earthquake is mythical and symbolic in nature. It represents the disturbance and historical subversion brought
about by the testimony of the martyrs and prophets (a true *pachakuti*, according
to the Aymara conception of history). The martyrs bring about true social, political, spiritual, and ecclesiological earthquakes at the heart of empires. A tenth
of Rome falls in ruins, and seven thousand people are killed in the earthquake.
However, the testimony of the martyrs and prophets brings about a massive conversion: "the rest were terrified and gave glory to the God of heaven" (v. 13).
This is the only place in Revelation where John is optimistic about the possibility that idolaters might be converted (the optimism is rooted in the prophetic
power of the martyrs).

As we come to the end of this overall interpretation of the prophetic movement (10:1–11:13) which takes place in the present between the sixth and

---

10. Throughout Revelation this is a technical term for those who follow the beast, idolaters,
murderers, and enemies (Rev. 3:10; 6:10; 8:13; 11:10; 13:8, 14; 17:2, 8 — eleven times in all).
When the inhabitants of the earth are named in a neutral sense another verb is used: those who
"dwell on the earth" (*skenoo:* 12:12) or those who "sit" over the earth (*kathemai:* 14:6).

seventh trumpets, we understand that what we have here is not a hiatus but a narration that fits perfectly into the seven trumpets section (8:2–11:19). More specifically, the prophetic movement described here (10:1–11:13) is part of the threefold "Woe!" announced in 8:13. The fifth trumpet is the first woe (9:12). The sixth trumpet is the second woe, which includes this present time between the sixth and seventh trumpets in which the prophetic movement takes place (10:1–11:13). In 11:10 it is said that the prophets had "tormented the inhabitants of the earth," which explicitly refers back to what is said in 8:13, "Woe! Woe! Woe! to the inhabitants of the earth." The prophets are certainly a woe or a torment to the wicked. The text of 11:14, when the prophetic movement ends, before the seventh trumpet, is also consonant with the overall account: "The second woe has passed, but the third is coming soon." It is precisely the sounding of the seventh trumpet that brings about the third woe. Here the woe over the wicked refers to the coming of the end, the coming of the kingdom. We are about to examine this matter, but first let us look at the anti-prophetic movement (16:13–16), which is the section parallel to the prophetic movement that we have just seen.

Anti-prophetic Movement (16:13–16)

In the present period, between the seventh trumpet and the seventh bowl, we find not only the activity of John the prophet and the prophetic community, but likewise the action of the demonic spirits who come "from the mouth of the dragon, from the mouth of the beast, and from the mouth of the false prophet." These three beasts are described in chapters 12 and 13 (which we are about to examine). What is new here is that the beast who comes out of the earth (13:11–18) is called false prophet (also in 19:20). The power of the three beasts is in their mouths, from which come "demonic spirits": it is a "spiritual" power. We are thus prompted to think about the demonic power of the ideologies of the empire and of its ideological apparatus (schools, means of communications, imperial religions). It reminds us of the apocalyptic text in Ephesians 6:12:

> For our struggle is not with flesh and blood but with the principalities, with the powers, with the world rulers of this present darkness, with the *evil spirits in the heavens.*

The empire's demonic spirits produce signs (*semeia*) and have an enormous political power to draw together the kings of all the earth (the *oikoumene*). They assemble them for "the battle on the great day of God the almighty." This battle is the one that takes place in 19:11–21, where Jesus faces the beast, the false prophet, and the kings of the earth. The battle site will be a place called in Hebrew Armageddon. It may refer to Mount Carmel next to Megiddo, the mountain where the prophet Elijah overcame the prophets of Baal (1 Kings 18).[11] This battle of Armageddon between Jesus and the beasts is the one preceding the thousand-year reign (which we will examine further on).

---

11. See also 2 Kings 23:29 on the defeat of King Josiah and also Zechariah 12:11.

In this climate of spiritual confrontation between the prophets of Jesus and the demonic spirits of the Roman empire, soon there is heard the cry of the risen Jesus himself saying: "Behold I am coming [*érchomai*] like a thief. Blessed is the one who watches and keeps his clothes ready" (v. 15). In 22:7 Jesus also says, "Behold, I am coming soon. Blessed is the one who keeps the prophetic message of this book." We have already emphasized that the risen Jesus stands in the midst of the communities (1:9–3:22) and interprets history (5–7). Christians want Jesus to be made manifest in this present moment of resistance and confrontation. Jesus is going to manifest himself in the resistance of the community and, finally, by putting an end to the beast, to the false prophet, and to the kings of the earth (19:11–21), and then during the thousand-year reign (20:4–6) before the last judgment. The statement in v. 15 recalls Matthew 24:42–43.

The Seventh Trumpet (11:15–19) and the Seventh Bowl (16:17–21)

We again return to the text and its structure. We have already seen that these two texts (seventh trumpet and seventh bowl) are parallel and have the same structure, which very briefly is as follows:

Seventh trumpet		Seventh bowl
11:15a	introduction	16:17a
11:15b–19a	The reign has arrived. "It is done."	16:17b
11:19b	cosmic cataclysm	16:18–21

Let us likewise recall that with the seventh trumpet time concludes and the mysterious plan of God is fulfilled (arrives at its end = *etelesthe*, 10:6–7). Likewise it is said that when the seven bowls are finished God's fury is done (arrives at its end = *etelesthe*, 15:1, 8). We said that this is not the end of the world but the end of the present age when God's action or judgment is taking place in history as the Exodus is being renewed within the Roman empire. It is not the end, but it brings to an end persecution and suffering in this present age. With the seventh trumpet God's reign arrives. This is not yet the end point of history but the reign of God in history.

Introduction (11:15a and 16:17a)

The seventh trumpet sounds, the seventh bowl is poured out. This bowl does not yet spill out over land, sea, rivers, the sun, the throne of the beast or the river Euphrates, but "into the air." The air is a dimension of the earth, but it is that invisible dimension where the spirits dwell. Ephesians 2:2 mentions "the ruler of the power of the air." God's action with the seventh bowl is therefore over this invisible, spiritual, supernatural (ideological) dimension of the Roman empire. At the sound of the last trumpet, "there were loud voices in heaven" (11:15). Likewise at the seventh bowl "a loud voice came out of the temple" (16:17). This is the voice of God (one variant text accentuates the point by saying that the voice comes "from the throne"). This is the same voice as that in 16:1. We now find not plagues and punishments, but a solemn announcement in heaven. It is voice, word, communication that is uppermost here.

The Proclamation (11:15b-19a and 16:17b): The Reign Has Come – "It Is Done"

The proclamation in heaven is well developed in the passage on the seventh trumpet, and it has an extraordinary theological and prophetic weight. With the seventh trumpet, however, the proclamation comes down to a single word: *gégonen,* "It is done." Let us examine in detail the proclamation in 11:15b–19a:

> There were loud voices in heaven, saying,
> "The kingdom of the world now belongs
> to our Lord and to his Anointed,
> and he will reign forever and ever."
> The twenty-four elders . . . said:
> "We give thanks to you, Lord God almighty,
> who are and who were.
> For you have assumed your great power
> and have established your reign."

Throughout Revelation the noun "reign" (*basileia*), referring to God, appears only in 11:15 and 12:10. The verb "to reign" (*basileuo*), with God as subject, appears only in 11:15, 17, and 19:6. All the terms appear in a liturgical song: here after the seventh trumpet (11:15b–19a), after the defeat of the monster in heaven (12:10–12), and in the liturgy at the end of the present age (19:1–10). These are parallel texts. The closest is 12:10–12:

> Now have salvation and power come
> and the kingdom of our God
> and the authority of his Anointed (Christ).

The words "salvation" (*soterίa*), "force" (*dynamis*), "reign" (*basileia*), and "power" (*exousίa*) are political terms and take their inspiration from Psalm 2, that is also a political psalm (a psalm which also stands in the background of all these parallel texts and many places in Revelation).

The fundamental content of these proclamations is "the coming of the kingdom of God." In our text, the kingdom comes when the seventh trumpet is blown; in chapter 12 it is when Satan is defeated in heaven and hurled down to earth. The kingdom comes through God's power, but also by the prophetic testimony of the Lamb and of the martyrs (10:1–11, 13, and 12:11). The kingdom comes over the earth, over the world in present history.

This coming of the kingdom now, on the earth, is good news for the holy ones, but it is tragic for the wicked. Hence in 11:14 the coming of the kingdom is presented as the third woe that falls on idolaters and murderers. The positive aspect of thanksgiving for the coming of the kingdom is found in the hymn of the twenty-four elders (11:17–18), but so is the negative part: the coming of the kingdom unleashes the anger of the nations and the response of God's judgment:

> The nations raged,
> but your wrath has come,
>> and the time for the dead to be judged,
>> and to recompense your servants, the prophets,
>> and the holy ones...
> and to destroy those who destroy the earth.

Again Psalm 2 stands in the background. The coming of the kingdom on the earth has a visible, historical, and political dimension, and hence it arouses the "rage of the nations" (the kings of the earth, enemies of God). Nevertheless, the response is "God's wrath" against them. In the text this wrath of God occurs in three divine actions (three verbs in the infinitive: *krithenai, dounai, diph-theirai*): judge, recompense, and destroy. The verb "judge" (*krino*) means "to do justice." In this passage God does justice to the dead: God gives recompense to the prophets and to the holy ones and destroys those who destroy the earth. In the Bible, God's judgment and action of judging do not have a forensic or legal sense, but rather denote God's action in history: God does justice for the oppressed and liberates them; God does justice to the oppressors and destroys them. The Exodus is God's great judgment. This is bad news for sinners, but good news for the holy ones (hence 14:6–7 speaks of the good news of God's judgment). This judgment of God is not reduced to God's last and final judgment; on the contrary, God's justice or liberating action in history is occurring especially now, in the present age. In this passage the judgment takes place with the arrival of the kingdom.

The coming of the reign, the wrath of the nations, and God's judgment take place on earth even though the proclamation and thanksgiving take place in heaven. In 11:19a we have the vision of the opening of "God's temple in heaven" and the appearance within it of the "ark of the covenant." The historical Jerusalem temple was razed by the Romans in the year 70 C.E. In the Jerusalem to come there is no temple (21:22). Here the temple in heaven symbolizes the Christian community (as in 11:1). The historical ark of the covenant was kept in the Holy of Holies in the Jerusalem temple. When the temple was destroyed in 586 B.C.E. the ark was lost or destroyed. It was the symbol of the covenant and constituted the deepest identity of the tradition of the people of God, of the Exodus and the events experienced in the desert. Now this cherished symbol is seen to be within the Christian community. With the coming of the kingdom and God's judgment in history, the community recovers its identity.

This passage of 11:15b–19a, which is so profound and meaningful, has its parallel after the seventh bowl (16:17b) in the form of a single word (*gégonen,* it is done). The one seated on the throne in 21:6 says the same thing. Given the very close parallelism between the seventh trumpets and seven bowls, we may assume that this mysterious "it is done" points back toward, and summarizes, what was said in 11:15b–19a.

The Cosmic-Historical Cataclysm: 11:19b and 16:18–21

In 11:19b this cataclysm appears summed up in an expression that has already been used: "There were flashings of lightning, rumblings, and peals of thunder, an earthquake, and a violent hailstorm." The same line (without the hailstorm) appears in 8:5 (thus enclosing a section). In the parallel text after the seventh bowl (16:18–21), this expression is taken up again and developed. In v. 18 we see the flashings of lightning, the rumblings, the peals of thunder, the violent earthquake, and then at the end the hailstorm (*chálaza*) in v. 21. Between vv. 18 and 21 the theme of the earthquake is developed. It is a disaster: the great city, the great Babylon (Rome) split into three parts. The cities of the nations come tumbling down. The islands flee, and mountains disappear. In the prophetic and apocalyptic tradition, these disasters have a cosmic-mythical nature: they express symbolically a disaster in history. The author here is not referring to a specific earthquake (there were such, and perhaps the author is taking them as a reference point), but to a great disaster of a historical nature: the collapse of the Roman empire and all its allies. This collapse is occurring with the arrival of the kingdom of God and God's judgment over the earth. The kingdom of God and the Roman empire are contrary and contending realities. The arrival of one means the collapse of the other. This collapse of Rome and of the empire is going to be described in chapter 7 below.

6

Center of Revelation —
Center of History

*The Christian Community
Confronting the Beasts*

Revelation 12:1–15:4

We are standing at the center of the book of Revelation. Everything previous converges toward this center, and this point sheds light on everything to follow. We stand not only at the literary center of the book, but also at the center of the present time. This is the community's now — and also God's: it is the time of conversion and action. We stand between the sixth and seventh trumpets and between the sixth and seventh bowls (see above). We also stand at the heart of the community (14:1–5) at its highest level of consciousness and within its crucial situation, as it stands between the beasts (12:1–13:18) and God's judgment (14:6–15:4).

INTRODUCTION TO THE READING AND STRUCTURE
OF REVELATION 12:1–15:4

General Structure of the Text

    A. From heaven to earth: 12:1–18

        a. confrontation in *heaven:* a woman and a red dragon: vv. 1–6

           b. war in heaven: Satan is thrown down to earth: vv. 7–9

             center: victory hymn: Now has salvation come: vv. 10–11

           b. consequences of the war: joy in heaven — terror on
              earth: v. 12

        a. persecution on *earth:* the dragon pursues the woman: vv. 13–18

B. On earth: the two beasts: 13:1–18

    a. the beast that comes out of the sea: vv. 1–10

    b. the beast that comes up out of the earth: vv. 11–18

    Center: the community following the Lamb: 14:1–5

    (while on earth it hears singing from heaven)

B'. On earth: God's judgment: 14:6–20

    a. Three angels *announce* the judgment on earth: vv. 6–13

    center: the son of man: v. 14

    b. Three angels *carry out* the judgment on earth: vv. 15–20

A'. From earth to heaven: 15:1–4

    a. Another sign in heaven: seven angels carry the seven bowls (which are to be poured out over the *earth:* next section announced): v. 1

    b. Those who had triumphed over the beast, his image, and the number that signified his name sing in *heaven* the hymn of Moses and of the Lamb: vv. 2–4.

The structure here is concentric. The action begins in heaven, unfolds on earth, and ends in heaven. The beginning is centered on the victory hymn of the martyrs in heaven (12:10–11) who conquered (*enikesan*) the devil by the blood of the Lamb and by the word of testimony that they gave. Likewise at the end in heaven we find the hymn of those who defeated (*nikontas*) the beast, his image, and the number that signifies his name, and who sing the hymn of the Lamb (15:2–4). At the center as well (14:3) the community following the Lamb hears a hymn in heaven that only the community may learn. These three hymns endow the whole section with a triumphal liturgical character: they express the Christian community's awareness that it is struggling on earth against the devil and the beasts. The Lamb's presence throughout the section is likewise noteworthy. He is mentioned seven times: in the hymn at the beginning (12:11), at the end (15:3), and three times in the middle, as well as in 13:8 (the book of life of the Lamb who was slain) and in 14:10 (the torment of the follower of the beast before the Lamb). The beasts even seek to imitate the Lamb: one of the heads (an emperor) of the beast imitates the Lamb (13:3, 12, 14: to be discussed later), and the false prophet has two horns like a lamb (13:11).

The internal structure of this section is like that of Daniel 7, where the central conflict takes place between the four beasts and the son of man. In Revelation as well we find opposition between the two beasts (chapter 13) and the son of man (14:6–20). Both are mythical representations to express the confrontation between the empire (the Babylonian, Median, Persian, and Hellenistic empires in Daniel; the Roman empire in Revelation) and the people of God. It is the confrontation between what is bestial and what is human in history. In both books there is likewise a judgment: in Daniel we find the annihilation of the beasts and in Revelation judgment over the beast's followers (the annihilation of the beasts takes place later, in 19:11–21). In Daniel the people of the holy ones of the Most High receives the kingdom (Dan. 7:27). In Revelation, the kingdom comes through the blood of the Lamb and the testimony of the martyrs (12:10–11); the risen Jesus is identified with the figure of the son of man (here in Revelation and in the entire synoptic tradition). Nevertheless the human figure (as son of man) remains the symbol of the people of God, standing up to the beast, symbol of empires. In Daniel it is God who carries out the judgment (the Ancient One: Dan. 7:9); in Revelation it is Jesus who does so directly, carrying out an order from God (14:5). In both Daniel 7 and Revelation 12:1–15:4 we have a theology of history and a powerful message of hope for God's people.[1] We will later examine the points of contact with Daniel 10–12.

Revelation 12:1–15:4 is presented in its relationship with the previous and following sections. The beast that comes out of the sea (13:1–10) has already appeared in 11:7. The same is true of the forty-two months that symbolize the time of the Gentiles in 11:2 and the time of the beast in 13:5, and the 1,260 days, which in 11:3 designate the time of the witnesses-prophets and in 12:6 the time of the woman in the desert. The verb *ophthe* ("could be seen") in 11:19 is taken up again in 12:1, 3. The connection with the following section is made explicitly in 15:1 and in 16:13–14. Hence it is clear that 12:1–15:4, which is by itself a very tight and independent section, is very much connected to the preceding section on the seven trumpets and to the subsequent one on the seven bowls. As we have already said, this placement of 12:1–15:4 at the center of Revelation, between the sections on the trumpets and the bowls, situates this section within the theology of Exodus. It also situates us within the historical time designed by the author of Revelation, at the present moment, between the sixth and seventh trumpets (the age when the prophetic movement takes place) or between the sixth and seventh bowls (age of the anti-prophetic movement). We have explained all of this in the previous chapter.

KEYS FOR INTERPRETING THE TEXTS

Revelation 12:1–18

A Woman – a Red Dragon: 12:1–6

Chapter 12 of Revelation is emphatically mythical in character, but that does not make it unrelated to history. Myth is simply another way of conceptualizing processes within history. Furthermore, myth is not a simple reproduction of reality, but a way of organizing and processing reality in the mind. Myth organizes the collective awareness of being a people. Hence it expresses a social practice, a hope, a utopia. Myths, and the visions that appear in myths, serve not only

1. Pablo Richard, "El Pueblo de Dios contra el Imperio: Daniel 7 en su contexto literario e histórico," *Revista de Interpretación Bíblica Latinoamericana* (San José, Costa Rica-Santiago de Chile) 7 (1991): 25–46.

for contemplation, but are primarily for taking action.[2] Myth expresses a fundamental conviction and transmits a special energy for acting and for transforming history. Sometimes a myth is proclamation, protest, or proposal; there are myths that seek to rebuild the hope of a people or also to delegitimize or destroy their enemies. At the center of chapter 12 of Revelation (vv. 10–11) we have a liturgical hymn that is not expressed mythically and that provides us with the key for interpreting the myths that precede and follow this nonmythical core.

In this chapter we have two fundamental and diametrically opposed myths: a woman and a dragon. Both appear as signs in heaven. The signs send a message and guide our activity. The first great sign in heaven is a beautiful woman: she appears clothed with the sun, with the moon under her feet and with twelve stars over her head. The other sign is a horrible dragon: it is huge and red and has seven heads and ten horns. The woman is seen as a sign of life: she is pregnant and about to give birth, and she then gives birth to a male child. The dragon is a sign of death: it is there to kill the woman's son; with its tail it also sweeps away a third of the stars. Thus the basic meaning of these two myths is the confrontation between life and death. Life appears to be beautiful, but weak and frail; death seems like a frightful and powerful force. Nevertheless, in the confrontation between life and death, it is life that is victorious. Hence the basic message mythically represented here is a one of hope.

This myth of the cosmic clash in heaven between a woman and a monster was very well known in antiquity. In Egypt we have the case of the goddess Isis, or Hathor (wife of Osiris), mother of Horus. A red dragon called Set or Typhon seeks to kill Horus, but in the end Horus kills the dragon. In Greece we have the goddess Lethe (wife of Zeus), mother of Apollo. The dragon Python seeks to kill Apollo, but Lethe flees to Delos and saves Apollo from the dragon's pursuit. There is likewise an Akkadian myth in which Tiamat, a seven-headed monster, attacks the gods of heaven. The young god Marduk kills Tiamat, who sweeps away a third of the stars. In these myths, the societal language of that era, there is always an effort to represent the struggle of God versus evil, heaven versus chaos, life versus death. They all have a political meaning. In the Roman empire in particular, Caesar was often represented as Apollo, as were Augustus, Nero, and others. The goddess Roma was the mother of the gods. All this can be seen on coins from that period, which were the most effective political propaganda.[3]

The author of Revelation may be familiar with these myths, but he uses them with a new meaning. In the particular context of the Roman empire he is going to undermine the dominant myth: the empire is not divine, but satanic; the emperors are not the incarnation of Apollo, but heads on a monster that is indeed satanic. Rome is a prostitute rather than a goddess; it is the new Babylon, mother of all prostitutes on earth (chapter 17). Furthermore, the mother is now neither Isis, Lethe, or Roma, but the people of God, from whom the Messiah Jesus is

---

2. Xavier Pikaza, "Apocalipsis de Juan: Origen y fin de la violencia," *Carthaginensia* 8, nos. 13–14 (January–December 1992): 609–39.

3. G. B. Caird, *A Commentary on the Revelation of St. John the Divine,* Harper's New Testament Commentary (San Francisco: Harper & Row, 1966).

born. The Roman empire kills Jesus, but even so, his blood and the testimony of the martyrs are able to defeat Satan, which is the force that endows the empire with power. This empire is represented as a beast in chapter 13, with the same features as those of the satanic monster. This undermining of myths by Revelation has an impact on the minds of Christians by creating a new consciousness and a new praxis in history. Myth is power.

The author builds chapter 12 of Revelation on Old Testament foundations. The people of God is often represented as a woman: a woman giving birth to a new people (Isa. 66:5–9: "Zion is scarcely in labor when she gives birth to her children"). The resurrection of a people is like a birth (Isa. 26:17–19). The Old Testament also speaks of mythical monsters: Leviathan (Isa. 27:1), Behemoth (Job 40:15), Rahab (Ps. 89:11), the sea serpent (Amos 9:3). Likewise myth becomes political: Antiochus IV Epiphanes is called beast (Ps. 74:19); the Egyptian pharaoh is Rahab, the dragon (Isa. 51:9–10); the king of Babylon is a dragon (Jer. 51:34). Genesis 3:15 speaks of enmity between the serpent and the woman and tells how the woman's descendants will crush the serpent's head. Revelation sees this fulfilled with the Messiah's birth from a woman and Satan's defeat by the Messiah.

Revelation 12:5 says that "she gave birth to a son, a male child." Some think that the text is referring to the birth of the Messiah in Bethlehem. The problem, however, lies in the fact that the newborn is taken away to God. The life of Jesus would then be presented through his birth in Bethlehem and his ascension into heaven (the two extremes of his life), with no mention of the cross and resurrection (we have something similar in 1 Tim. 3:16). Here it is preferable to think of Golgotha rather than Bethlehem: these are the sufferings and torment of the birth of the Messiah on the cross; it is the birth of the New Human on the cross. Jesus himself compares his cross and resurrection to a woman who suffers birth pangs and rejoices in the birth of a child (John 16:20–22). Jesus is "established as Son of God in power... through resurrection from the dead" (Rom. 1:4). We find an application of Psalm 2:7, where the consecration of the messiah (king) is like a birth: "You are my son; this day I have begotten you." This same text is applied to the resurrection of Jesus in Acts 13:33. Verse 9 of Psalm 2 is quoted in Revelation 12:5: he is "destined to rule all the nations with an iron rod." Psalm 2 is a political psalm, and Christians used it to proclaim the Messiah's power over the people (likewise in 19:5). The Hebrew text says "shatter," and the Septuagint translates it "to pastor." The Christian victor, like the Messiah, receives the same power to rule the nations (2:26–27). Jesus' suffering on the cross and the sufferings of Christians are sufferings not of death but of birth: something new is born. Likewise, the agonies of history (earthquakes, famine, and the like) are not the sufferings of the end of the world, but the labor pains of a new world (Mark 13:8). The kingdom of God will prevail over the powers of the world. The verb "to be born" (*tekein*) is used four times in 12:1–6 and the noun "son" (*teknon*) is used twice to indicate the newness of the Messiah's project in history. This project is born from the people of God (the woman clothed with the son) confronting the satanic force of the empires (monsters).

War in Heaven: 12:7–9, 12

Satan is thrown down from heaven to earth: 12:7–9

Consequences of the war:

joy in heaven — terror on earth: 12:12

Another myth is now used in 12:7–9 and its continuation in v. 12: the war between Michael and his angels and the dragon and his angels. The figure of Michael is taken from Daniel 10:13, 21, and especially from 12:1: "At that time there shall arise Michael, the great prince, guardian of your people." Michael offers assurance that in the time of tribulation "your people shall escape." Etymologically, Michael means "who is like God?" (*mi-qui-el*). Michael together with his angels is a mythical figure representing the transcendent and spiritual force of the people of God (see Exod. 23:20–21), which is now going to confront the spiritual and transcendent force of the empire, represented by the dragon and his angels. The passage speaks of a war in heaven. Revelation 11:7, 12:17, 13:4, and 13:7 speak of a "real war" on earth between the beast and the Christian community. Revelation 16:14, 17:14, and 19:11, 19, speak of the "final [eschatological] war" of Jesus against the beasts and the kings of the earth; 20:8 speaks of the "final war" of the devil and his allies, Gog and Magog against the holy ones. Revelation 12:7–9 speaks literally: "war broke out in heaven" (*egéneto pólemos en to ouranó*). The noun "war" is used once and the verb "to make war" is used twice. In heaven we usually find a liturgy (chapters 4 and 5, 7:10–12, 11:15–18, and so forth). We have already said that heaven represents this transcendent and hidden dimension of history; earth, on the other hand, represents the visible and empirical dimension of history. The war on earth between the empire and the Christian community is simply the visible part of history; parallel to this visible war is another transcendental and spiritual war (in heaven) between the transcendent and spiritual force of the people of God (Michael) and the "spiritual" force itself of the empire (dragon). It is a transcendent and spiritual war that is played out and decided in the depths of history. It is the spiritual combat that is also described wonderfully in Ephesians 6:10–20, especially in v. 12:

> Our struggle is not against human forces, but against the Rulers and Authorities who lead this world and their dark forces. We are confronting the spirits and the supernatural forces of evil. (As translated in the *Biblia Latinoamericana*)

Revelation tells us that Michael and his angels won this war, that the dragon and his angels did not prevail, and that there was no longer any place for them in heaven. This represents the transcendent (in heaven) defeat of the supernatural forces of evil, personified in the figure of the ancient serpent, the devil, or Satan. The devil is thrown down (*eblethe* is used five times, three times in v. 9 and then in vv. 10 and 13) to earth where it makes war on the community. Nevertheless this devil is already spiritually defeated and no longer has transcendent force.

Heaven is now cleared of dark forces, of the supernatural forces of evil, thus giving Christians a reason for tremendous hope. The beast (the Roman empire) has power, will make war and will defeat Christians, but it is already defeated in heaven — in other words it is spiritually defeated. We find the best parallels to this passage in John 12:31: "Now is the time of judgment on this world; now the ruler of this world will be driven out," and in Luke 10:18: "I have observed Satan fall like lightning."

Who is this "devil" or "Satan"? It is clearly a mythical personification of evil, of iniquity, of lawlessness, of sin. "Devil" is the Greek translation in the Septuagint of the Hebrew term "Satan." Its general meaning is adversary, accuser, calumniator. It does not mean an eternal or absolute personal agent existing forever just like God (as in eastern Manichean mythologies). God created all things and everything created by God was good. There is no such thing as the devil as an absolute personal agent. It is a myth to personify evil. Evil certainly exists but it is created by human beings; it is produced socially, it is (personal or social) sin; it does not come from, nor was it created by, God. As evil personified, the devil is a myth, which does not mean that it is a deception or a lie. It is something real in history: it expresses the supernatural forces of evil (see Eph. 6:12). What does not exist is the devil as a person, as absolute subject, but these supernatural powers of evil certainly exist. The devil myth simply serves to personify these dark forces and to make them more real and dramatic. Where do such "supernatural forces of evil" come from? They come from the historical accumulation of sin, personal as well as social, but they come especially from the capacity of the human being to build idols. Idolatry is the perverse spiritual world created by human beings themselves. They are capable of distorting the image of God or of displacing God with false idols, by absolutizing earthly realities. Such idolatry (by distortion or displacement) is the mystery of iniquity or the supernatural force of evil created by human beings themselves; it is the root of social evil that makes it powerful and effective.[4] This is the force personified in the mythical figure of the devil, or Satan.

Revelation 12:9 lists the known mythical personifications of evil. The author does so to concentrate his hearers' minds and so that no myth will be absent from people's minds. It becomes necessary to unify the myth in order to endow it with greater force (similarly in 20:2). The dragon is identified with the devil and Satan but also with the "ancient serpent." This is a clear reference to Genesis 3. In the original Genesis account (Yahwist tradition) the serpent symbolizes the city-state that deceives the peasant tribes in order that they may doubt and betray their historical memory and their faith in Yahweh. The serpent symbolizes the Egyptian pharaoh, but likewise all the kings of Israel and Judah who oppress the people in the name of Baal (god of the city-state). It therefore symbolizes the spiritual force of the oppression that the city exercises over the countryside in the tributary mode of production. The description of the devil as

---

4. Pablo Richard, "Teología en la teología de la liberación," *Mysterium liberationis: Conceptos fundamentales de la teología de la liberación* (San Salvador: UCA, 1990), 1:201–222; English translation: "Theology in the Theology of Liberation," *Mysterium Liberationis: Fundamental Concepts of Liberation Theology* (Maryknoll, N.Y.: Orbis Books, 1993), 150–67.

he who deceives the entire inhabited earth (*ho planon ten oikoumenen*) exactly fits the idolatrous nature of the supernatural forces personified in the devil.

Persecution on Earth: The Dragon Pursues the Woman: 12:13–18

In 12:13–17 we have another mythical account that this time unfolds on earth. It corresponds to the clash in heaven already described in 12:1–6. The monster who has now been hurled down from heaven to earth — whose supernatural force has been taken away — pursues the woman on earth. In 12:14 the woman saves herself in the desert as she did in 12:6. Here the desert is a symbol of the Exodus, the place where the people of God wins its liberation and saves its identity. The two wings of eagles with which the woman saves herself are likewise a symbol of the Exodus (Exod. 19:4; see Deut. 32:11 and Ezek. 17:7). It represents God's power helping the community. This is not from outside, but rather the community itself which with God's help flies away to the desert. God empowers the community for its liberation. The earth also comes to the community's aid. The earth is here personified as something opposed to the dragon, to the ancient serpent. Perhaps it points toward the aspiration of tribal peoples, the people of the earth (*am ha aretz*), who have always found their liberation in the land.

Center: Victory Hymn: 12:10–11

We finally come to 12:10–11, which constitutes the center of the chapter. It is the only nonmythical part of the account, and it provides us with the key for interpreting the whole of chapter 12 from a historical and theological perspective. It is a liturgical hymn that places us at the heart of the Christian community and makes its thought clear to us.[5] Literally, the text says:

Now have come [*arti egéneto*]
the salvation and the power and the kingdom of our God
and the authority of his Christ
For the accuser of our brothers is cast out. . . . (v. 10)

We have a parallel text in 11:15 (when the last trumpet sounds):

The kingdom of the world of our Lord
and of his Christ
has come [*egéneto*] (see whole text 11:15–18).

What is central to both texts is that the kingdom of God has now arrived. The terms "salvation" (*sotería*), "power" (*dynamis*), "kingdom" (*basileia*), and

---

5. The hymns in Revelation always play this hermeneutical (interpretive) role in relation to the account or the text. Being a liturgical hymn, it places us at the heart of the community, at its very core, where the historical consciousness of the Christian community of that time becomes clear. Hence the hymns are by no means decorative, but are of the utmost hermeneutical and theological intensity throughout Revelation.

"authority" (*exousía*) are strikingly political. The coming of the kingdom is a social, public, and visible event in history here on earth. The coming of the kingdom of God is caused by Satan's defeat in heaven; he has been hurled down to earth from heaven. Satan has been spiritually defeated. As we have noted, Satan has lost his power in the transcendent and spiritual realm. It is the martyrs who bring about Satan's defeat.

> They [*autoi*] conquered him [Satan]
> by the blood of the Lamb and
> by the word of their testimony,
> love for life did not deter them from death.

Why does this defeat of Satan make possible the coming of God's kingdom? How have the martyrs been able to defeat Satan? The kingdom certainly comes by God's power and grace, but it becomes visible and public here on earth when the supernatural forces of evil, the religious perversion of idolatry, and the mystery of iniquity disappear. This is the spiritual defeat of Satan that makes it possible to discover by the light of faith the kingdom of God and of the Messiah as a project in history that is liberating and powerful and has authority. It is the martyrs who bring about this spiritual defeat of Satan that makes possible the manifestation of God's kingdom. Revelation makes this spiritual power of the martyrs very clear. They are capable of casting the devil out of heaven, of stripping him of all his transcendent and spiritual power; they are capable of destroying the supernatural forces of evil, of destroying all idolatry and religious falsehood. However, the martyrs are powerful "by the blood of the Lamb." This is not a sacrificial blood, but the blood of the faithful martyr (1:5), who gave testimony of the kingdom even to the cross (read the beautiful passage of Heb. 12:1–4, which illustrates the meaning of the blood of the Messiah Jesus). The death and resurrection of Jesus is what enables the martyrs to defeat Satan and manifest the kingdom of God. However, we are also told that the martyrs defeat Satan "by the word of their testimony" (*logos tes martyrías*). Testimony is not just any word, but only that public word that commits one in the face of the powers, that word that cannot be retracted.[6] The testimony of the martyrs has this anti-idolatrous force, and it strips Satan of all spiritual and transcendent power. In 15:2 the martyrs appear in heaven as victorious, although by that point matters have advanced: not only have they defeated Satan in heaven but they have also been able to triumph over the beast, his image, and the number of his name on earth.

In 12:13–18 the Christian community is represented by the woman being pursued by Satan on earth; at the same time in 12:10–11 the martyrs are singing victory in heaven. We have the same picture in 14:1–5, where the Christian

---

6. Testimony (*martyria*) is a word pronounced in a trial that can be used for or against the accused. It is a public word that remains in effect, that commits us, and that we cannot retract. Today we use the word "testimony" in a sense that is more commonplace and trivial (José Comblin, *Cristo en el Apocalipsis* [Barcelona: Herder, 1969]).

community is seen on earth following the Lamb wherever he goes; but the community hears the new hymn coming from heaven, and in 15:2 the victors in this community sing the hymn of Moses and of the Lamb in heaven. We also had this same twofold reality in chapter 7: in 7:1–9 the church is on earth and in 7:9–17 the martyrs are singing in heaven. The community is on earth facing the beasts; it is persecuted and sometimes defeated by the beasts (Rev. 13), but it nonetheless keeps alive its faith in the efficacious power of the blood of Jesus and of the martyrs' word of testimony that defeats Satan: it makes possible the manifestation of the kingdom (12:10–11) that in the end defeats the beasts, their image, and the number that signifies their name (15:2–4).

Revelation 13:1–18

Chapter 12 is written from heaven. It begins with two signs counterpoised: there is a war in heaven, Satan is thrown down to earth, the martyrs sing victory in heaven, and in the end Satan pursues the Christian community on earth. By contrast, chapter 13 unfolds entirely on earth; it is now the beasts who prevail and Christians are defeated. Chapter 12 expresses the community's faith and theological vision; chapter 13 expresses what actually happens in history. The two beasts in chapter 13 are active on the earth: we stand in real, visible, empirical history. This chapter is realistic and tragic, but it must be read in the light of chapter 12, for in chapter 13 the victory of the holy ones is already implicit. Likewise without chapter 13, chapter 12 could lead us to an illusory and frustrating vision of reality.

Chapter 13 is clearly divided into two parts: 13:1–10, the beast that comes out of the sea, and 13:11–18, the beast that comes up out of the earth (except that here it is called beast: whenever it is mentioned anywhere else it is called "false prophet": 16:13, 19:20, 20:10). The beast that comes out of the sea is the dominant figure throughout chapter 13. It is mentioned fifteen times (see vv. 1, 2, 3, 4, 12, 14, 15, 17, 18). It is just as central in chapter 17, where it appears nine times (in the whole of Revelation it is mentioned thirty-six times). This chapter offers us a striking analysis of the structure of power in the Roman empire. We will first explain some key elements for reading and understanding the text, and then we will make an overall interpretation of the chapter.

The Beast That Comes Up out of the Sea: 13:1–10

The beast comes up out of the sea, the symbol of chaos, the source of evil, but for the churches of Asia Minor it is also geographically the western sea over which come the Romans. The beast has "ten horns and seven heads," the very way Satan appears in chapter 12. What is new is that the diadems sit on the horns, and "blasphemous names" appear over the seven heads. The horns, heads, diadems, and names express symbolically the complexity of the Roman empire's apparatus of domination (economic, political, ideological, and religious power). Revelation 17:9 explains that the seven heads are seven hills and seven emperors, and 17:12 explains that the ten horns are ten kings.

The beast has features of a leopard, bear, and lion: these are the beasts in Daniel 7:3–7, which likewise come up out of the sea and represent the empires that have oppressed God's people in a bestial manner. The Roman empire is regarded as having the features of all the previous beasts. This reference to Daniel 7 provides us with a key for interpreting Revelation 13: we are dealing with the same historical framework, along with the same theology and hope.

The dragon (Satan, or the devil, in chapter 12) gave the beast his power (*dynamin*), his throne (*thronon*), and his great authority (*exousían megálen*). This is an extremely important statement of political theology: the Roman empire has no power or authority of its own, but a power and authority given by Satan. Satan stands behind the Roman empire. This belief is quite common throughout all apocalyptic literature (see 1 Thess. 2:18, Eph. 6:12, 2 Thess. 2:9). This idea is repeated here in v. 4. In vv. 5 and 7 the beast's authority is mentioned again, but this time the verb is in the passive voice: it was granted authority (*edothe*). This verb is repeated four times in vv. 5–7, where its implicit subject is God. The meaning is that whatever the beast does is ultimately under God's control. The beast's power is not absolute, even though it comes from Satan. Moreover, Satan has already been defeated in heaven.

According to v. 3, one of the beast's heads "seemed to have been mortally wounded" (*hos esphagmenen*), and its mortal wound was healed. The same expression is used with reference to Christ: a Lamb that seemed to have been slain (5:6). Those slain in Revelation are Christ (5:6, 9, 12 and 13:8), the martyrs (6:9 and 18:24), and the head of the beast here in 12:3. In v. 12 the beast is identified as the one whose mortal wound was healed and in v. 14 similarly as the one that had been wounded by the sword and revived. This threefold use of the word can have various meanings that are not mutually exclusive: the expression "seemed to have been mortally wounded" may be ridicule or parody of Christ: one of the beast's heads (an emperor) imitates the Lamb dead (slain) and risen. It may also be a way of making a personal identification: it would then be referring to the myth of Nero resurrected (*Nero redivivus:* Nero would be regarded as having miraculously escaped his death in the year 68, and after being abducted would have returned to earth to wreak vengeance on his enemies). Nero is seen to be the prototype of the emperor who persecutes Christians and is identified as the "anti-Christ" who returns in every persecuting emperor. Nevertheless, all three verses stress the beast's "mortal wound," which may refer to its basic and transcendental "wound": the empire is mortally wounded because Satan, its father, has already been defeated in heaven (12:7–11).

Satan (the dragon) is seen to be worshiped in v. 4 because it gave its authority (*exousía*) to the beast, and the beast itself is also worshiped. Worship of the beast reappears in vv. 8 and 12, with the further note that those worshiping are the "inhabitants of the earth," which in Revelation is a technical term for the wicked and idolaters; in v. 15 the image of the beast is also adored (the verb "worship" = *proskuneo* appears four times). Worship of the beast is expressed in two rhetorical questions asked by those who adore it: "Who can compare with the beast or who can fight against it?" "No one" is the implicit answer. The beast is a unique and absolute subject; no other subject exists. The logical consequence is total submission to it. Resistance and struggle against the beast is ruled out. Idolaters actually must have said, "What is there like the Roman empire? Nothing. Who can struggle against it? No one." Worship of the empire thus consists in absolutizing it completely, leading to complete subjection. In the Bible the claim that Yahweh is the only God is made in similar terms:

> Who is like to you among the gods, O Lord?
>
> (Exod. 15:11–13; cf. Deut. 3:24).

> Thus says the Lord...
> I am the first and I am the last;
> there is no God but me.
> Who is like me? Let him stand up and speak.
>
> (Isa. 44:6–7; cf. Isa. 40:12–31)

All these texts entail a critique of idolatry that Christians use precisely to stand up to the conversion of the Roman empire into an idol. In a complementary tradition in the Bible the expected answer to the question "Who is like God?" is "everyone." Jesus defends himself by using this tradition to claim that he is Son of God (John 10:34–38). To those who receive the word, "he gave power to become children of God" (John 1:12). Jesus used to say, "So be perfect just as your heavenly Father is perfect" (Matt. 5:48). In Revelation, Jesus acts along the lines of this tradition, the opposite of the beast: he promises to give the victor the power that he himself has received from the Father (Rev. 2:26–28). The Father hands power to Jesus who hands it to the faithful believer. By contrast the beast receives power from Satan and dominates with an absolute power, stripping his worshipers of all power and identity.[7]

From vv. 5 to 8 the verb "was given" is used four times to describe the beast's powers. The implicit subject of the passive verb form (was given = *edothe*) is God. The idea is that all the beast's powers are under God's control. The beast's power is not absolute. Another idea latent in the passive form "was given" is that all power comes from God and hence in itself is good. This power coming from God is given to the Roman empire. When the empire becomes beast by reason of its idolatrous and criminal character, the beast transforms this power that comes from God into a power that is perverse. Revelation makes a discernment between the power that comes from God and the power that becomes criminal

---

7. In Revelation 2:28 Jesus also promises to give the victor the morning star. In 22:16 he is presented as the bright morning star. Second Peter 1:10 speaks of the morning star rising in the heart of believers. However, when the king of Babylon in his arrogance is made an idol, the prophet says to him, "How have you fallen from the heavens, O morning star, son of the dawn. How are you cut down to the ground, you who mowed down the nations!" (Isa. 14:12). The glorification of the believer who recognizes God as the only true God is something positive; making an idol of the tyrant who wants to be like God and who rebels against God is quite different. In the extrabiblical tradition the archangel Michael confronts the devils, the tyrants, and the powers that want to be like God (the name Michael means "Who is like God?"). This tradition is the anti-idolatry tradition in the Bible itself. See Franz Hinkelammert, *Sacrificios humanos y sociedad occidental: Lucifer y la Bestia* (San José, Costa Rica: DEI, 1991).

and blasphemous in the hands of the beast. There is no contradiction between Romans 13 and Revelation 13. Romans 13 says that all power comes from God, and that is why revelation says that the beast "was given power to act" (13:5). Revelation also reveals to us how the beast perverts this power that comes from God into criminal power.

The text first tells us that the beast was given "a mouth" for uttering "proud boasts and blasphemies" (see Dan. 7:8, 20, 25). To utter proud boasts is to speak insolently, arrogantly, and with an overbearing attitude, which always leads to a blasphemous and idolatrous way of speaking. The word to "blaspheme" is derived from a Greek word that means to speak evil of someone, to destroy with the tongue. Oppressors and tyrants typically have a grandiose, arrogant, and ultimately blasphemous way of speaking. We are told explicitly in v. 6 that the beast

> . . . opened its mouth to utter blasphemies against God, blaspheming his name and his dwelling and those who dwell in heaven.

The beast perverts three things with its idolatrous and blasphemous speech: God's name, that is, God's essence, what God is; God's dwelling, that is, God's presence in history and in the community (it is not about the temple, but God's presence in history that will reach fulfillment in 21:3); and finally it perverts those who dwell in heaven, that is, believers and the holy ones. Hence we see that the beast's "theological" discourse is extremely dangerous and destructive of the whole spiritual reality of the people of God. Second, the beast was allowed "to wage war against the holy ones and conquer them." This line concisely expresses the actual situation as it must have been: Christians were defeated by the Roman empire. As we have already said, chapter 12 presents a different perspective: the martyrs defeat Satan. Further on we will see that Satan's defeat in heaven likewise permits the defeat of the beast on earth (chapters 14ff.). Nevertheless, here it is the holy ones who are overcome and defeated. Finally the beast was granted "authority [*exousía*] over every tribe [*phylén*], people [*laón*], tongue [*glossan*], and nation" [*ethnos*]. In 5:9 the Lamb buys with his blood persons from every tribe, tongue, people, and nation. Jesus' power is universal; Jesus acquires it on the cross and it means liberation. The beast receives its universal power from Satan and it is oppressive. The four terms utilized, besides expressing the universal character of the power of the empire, likewise express the all-encompassing nature of this domination: it is a political power but it is also patriarchal, ethnocentric, and cultural. The beast was given "power to act for forty-two months." This is the time of the beast that has been set by God. It does not have control over time in an absolute and unlimited form. In 11:2 the Gentiles (Romans) have the same amount of time to trample the outer court of the temple (that is, outside of the Christian community). Seven years make up eighty-four months, half of which is forty-two (three and a half years). It means that we now stand in the middle of the present age, which is described as a week of years, the last week before the end (see Dan. 9).

Verses 9–10 present an exhortation to resistance and to faith, in order to face persecution and martyrdom. The text draws inspiration from Jeremiah 15:2 and 43:11. The intention is not to discourage Christians with inevitable punishment, but to forewarn them of the risks of resistance and of witness against the beast: some are going to be imprisoned and others will be slain by the sword. One variation turns the text into a warning against the persecutors: "he who kills with the sword will be killed by the sword." This variant does not fit into the context, which presents a clear exhortation to resistance and to martyrdom. The word "resistance" (*hupomoné*) is often incorrectly translated as "patience." Faith-based resistance is crucial throughout Revelation: see 1:9; 2:2, 3, 19; 3:10 and the parallel text 14:12 (see the beautiful passage on Christian resistance in Heb. 12:1–4). There are four parallel phrases in Revelation that begin with the word "here" (*hode*) and that have the same structure and exhortatory function: 13:10 (calling for resistance and faith), 13:18 (wisdom), 14:12 (resistance), and 17:9 (wisdom). The ethic at work in Revelation is revealed in these lines (an ethic of resistance, which demands faith, wisdom, and intelligence), which today we would call the practice of liberation. It is simply not true that Revelation presents us with passivity and no praxis (we will return to this point later on).

The False Prophet: 13:11–18

In vv. 11 and 12 we are told of the nature and mission of the false prophet — except that here he is called "beast," while in 16:13, 19:20, and 20:10 he is called "false prophet." He looks like a lamb but speaks like the dragon. If it is Satan who assures the beast's power and authority, Satan is now the one speaking through the false prophet, who exercises all the beast's power in its service. Its mission is to lead all the inhabitants of the earth (the wicked) to adore the beast, who is again identified as the one that is mortally wounded and was healed. The dragon, the beast, and the false prophet constitute a perverse Trinity. The relationship between the three is like that of the Father, the Son, and the Holy Spirit. Satan is the anti-Father, the beast is the anti-Son, and the false prophet is the anti-Holy Spirit. At the center of this perverse Trinity stands the beast. Just as all of Revelation is Christocentric, the oppressive structures are similarly bestiocentric. This perverse trinity is united and structured in 16:13–14:

> I saw [coming from ...] the mouth of the dragon, from the mouth of the beast, and from the mouth of the false prophet ... demonic spirits who performed signs. They went out to the kings of the whole world to assemble them for the battle on the great day of God the almighty.

In vv. 13–17 we have a description of the false prophet's "mechanisms of ideological domination." First, he performs "great signs" (*semeia megala*). He performs the prophetic miracle par excellence, the one performed by the prophet Elijah (1 Kings 18:38–39): making fire come down from heaven to earth before the people. Second, with the signs that he performs he deceives (verb *planao*, like Satan in 12:9) the inhabitants of the earth (the wicked) to make "an image for the beast." Here also for the third time the beast is identified as the one who had been wounded by the sword and has revived. Verse 14 speaks of making an image for the beast, although v. 15 twice speaks of an image of the beast. The reference may be to the image on coins in circulation in the Roman empire, on which the emperors were depicted as having divine features. It may also refer to the statues of the emperors that were set up in markets, temples, and guilds (professional associations). The Greek word *eikon* means image or statue. Third, the false prophet was permitted "to breathe life into the beast's image." Literally, it is said that he gave the image spirit (*pneuma*). It is an image with spirit, with life. Fourth, the beast's image was given life "so that it could speak and have anyone who did not worship it put to death." The image's life is made manifest in its ability to speak and to kill. The image of the beast has been transformed so that it is actually a living agent that can speak and kill. The signs that the false prophet performs and the life that is in the image — as expressed in its ability to speak and kill — is not an illusion. These are not tricks or magical acts, but things that really happen. In the overall interpretation below we will explain what all this is and what it means. The false prophet likewise has power to force all "to be given a stamped image [*cháragma*] on their right hands or their foreheads." The text specifies that "all the people" are included: "small and great, rich and poor, free and slave." The meaning is that all groups or social classes are included. The stamped image is for all, without regard for group or social class. Sixth, "no one could buy or sell except one who had the stamped image of the beast's name or the number that stood for its name." Only those stamped can participate in the market (buy and sell); those not stamped are left out. The stamp may be a name or the number that stands for that name. It may be that this is not a physical stamp on the hand or forehead, like those put on animals or slaves, but is instead symbolic in nature; but it must in some fashion be something visible and recognizable, social and public, that allows for actually identifying all those who are intended to be included in the market.

In v. 18 the author of Revelation challenges his hearers directly and exhorts them to "have wisdom" in order to "calculate" the number of the beast. "It is a number that stands for a person. His number is 666." Letters can be used as numbers in both Hebrew and Greek and hence people's names can also be written with numbers. In this case the author is not exhorting people to decipher the number in order to know the name, since his hearers already know the name of the beast. Moreover v. 17 says that the beast's stamped image is expressed with both the name and the number that stands for the name. Both of these are known. The author is urging the deciphering not of the number but of the meaning of the number. The verb used is *psephidso*, which means to calculate (to count with pebbles = *psephos*). The author wants his hearers to have understanding (*nous*) to capture the meaning, what the number of the beast known to everyone means. The aim is to interpret the meaning of the number, not to decipher the name that the number expresses. Since the number six means imperfection or lack and seven expresses perfection or fullness, 666 would accordingly mean utter imperfection or lack. Six is repeated three times because it is an asymptotic number, it is ever imperfect, to the infinite (666666666666...)[8] When seven is mentioned it is mentioned only once for it is a perfect number. The name of the beast, which everyone knows, when put in number form expresses this utter imperfection or lack. In 13:10 the author of Revelation exhorted his hearers to resistance and faith. Now in 13:18 he is exhorting them to be intelligent in order to understand that the beast's name expresses utter imperfection or lack. The beast's entire system of domination is not so perfect and powerful as it may seem, but is quite flawed. As we would say today, the beast is a paper tiger. In 17:8–11 the author is going to express with other images what he is expressing here with the 666: the beast was but is no longer; it is coming up but is heading toward its destruction. The beast has seven heads, which mean seven kings, that is, the fullness of power. That seven, however, is an illusion: five are fallen, the sixth is now in place, and the seventh will not last long. The beast makes an eighth, but as one of the seven this eighth destroys the perfection, and so everything is heading toward destruction.

Overall Interpretation of Chapter 13

This whole chapter is a critical analysis of the Roman empire's structure of oppression. The author engages in a theological critique of the empire. The depth and complexity of the analysis is quite striking. This chapter expresses the life and consciousness of the Christian community oppressed by the empire; when we read it we know how Christians lived, felt, and thought of the Roman empire. They lived in the empire but were excluded from its life (they could not buy and sell); they lived as people sentenced to death for not adoring the empire turned into an idol. The Christian community represents resistance to the empire; it was a community of faith that discovered Satan's presence in the empire; it also had the intelligence to understand (calculate) the frailty of the empire. It is out of this situation of exclusion, resistance, and faith that the author engages in this theological critique of the Roman empire. He is writing for the churches of Asia Minor at the close of the first century. Revelation must be interpreted from within this historical context. This vision becomes a paradigm and criterion of interpretation for us as well.

The beast is the central figure in chapter 13, although it is also prominent in chapter 17 (it is likewise mentioned in 11:7; 14:9, 11; 16:2, 10, 13; 19:19, 20; 20:4, 10). It is mentioned a total of thirty-six times in Revelation. The beast is unquestionably a symbol or myth used to identify, think about, and critique the Roman empire. When John or the community call the empire the beast, they are giving voice to a way of living and thinking about the reality of the empire and also reflecting a particular practice at the heart of the empire. John calls it the beast, following the apocalyptic tradition in general and Daniel in particular. Chapter 7 of Daniel represents four specific empires with the symbol of four different beasts. The beast is the symbol with which the empire is represented in the mind; likewise the human figure (like a son of man) is a mental representa-

---

8. "Asymptotic" comes from *asymptote* (*a*, negative, and *sympiptein*, which means to unite). A line extending indefinitely and approaching a curve but never touching it is asymptotic.

tion of the people of the holy ones of the Most High. The empire represents what is bestial in history, and the people of God represent what is human. In chapter 17 of Revelation the beast is clearly identified with the Roman empire, and the harlot riding on the beast is identified as Rome, which is called "Babylon the Great." The beast represents not any one Roman emperor or another but the emperors in their entirety (seven heads = seven kings), and likewise represents the entire imperial structure. The beast is a whole system, one that is universal and total (it has power over every tribe, people, tongue, and nation). The beast is the entire empire, in its economic, political, social dimension, and especially its religious, theological, and spiritual dimension. It must be understood in its complexity and profundity and in its own historical context in order to avoid falling into facile and superficial kinds of concordism.

Chapter 13 emphasizes that the beast receives its power, throne, and authority from Satan. The spirit of the institution and the institution itself must be distinguished from one another. Satan is the spirit that endows the empire with its drive and power as institution and as system. Behind the empire stand the supernatural powers of evil. In chapter 12 John offers us a mythical representation of Satan's defeat: by the blood of the Lamb and the testimony they gave, the martyrs threw Satan down from heaven to earth. Satan accordingly no longer has an absolute power, but has power on earth only through the beast. The beast consequently bears a mortal wound, although it has now recovered from that wound, which was caused by Christ's death and resurrection. John analyzes the Roman empire from the standpoint of Christ risen.

A central feature in the chapter is worship of the beast. The Roman empire has been turned into an idol; it is an idol like Baal (Canaanite god) or Moloch (Ammonite god). It is an idolatrous system. John analyzes very well this absolutizing or idolizing of the empire in v. 4 (as we have already explained). Although it is a structure within history, the empire has been transformed into an absolute subject (Who is like the beast?) and the worshipers of the beast have become objects (who can struggle against it?). This is precisely what fetishization or idolization is all about: structures become subjects and human subjects become things. Those worshiping the beast (denoted by the technical term "the inhabitants of the earth") surrender their subjectivity and their life to the beast and become objects in thrall to the beast, which it can stamp (we will soon see the meaning of the stamp). Not only do people surrender their subjectivity and life to the beast but even the kings of the earth worship it, as expressed in 17:13: the kings "are of one mind and will give their power and authority to the beast."

Revelation very much emphasizes the beast's ability to destroy spiritual things. John expresses it with the notion of blasphemy, as we have explained. Grandiose and blasphemous statements come from the mouth of the beast, thus denoting the beast's spiritual pride. With his arrogant and blasphemous way of speaking, he destroys God's name (his essence), God's dwelling (his presence in history), and the holy ones. This is the most dangerous feature of idolatry: its ability to destroy the spiritual. The beast likewise has power to defeat and physically kill the holy ones. John's concern is nonetheless for the capacity of the beast to spiritually destroy the reality of the God of life and the reality of the holy ones who believe in the God of life, and who accordingly resist the beast, Baal, and Moloch.

The sophisticated and complex mechanisms and structures of the worship of the beast are analyzed in the section devoted to the false prophet (vv. 11–18). This false prophet looks something like a lamb, perhaps in imitation of Jesus, but its way of speaking is satanic. It does not have power of its own, but receives its power from the beast and is in the service of the beast. Its basic mission is to organize worship of the beast within the empire. In Revelation the false prophet symbolizes the entire ideological structure of the empire: its priests, philosophers, teachers, magistrates; its worship, its huge celebrations, the circus; its cultural activities in the theater, concert hall, and racetrack; its gymnasiums and youth activities, sports and their olympics; Roman law and Greco-Roman philosophy; the imperial insignia in the army, the imperial images on coins; the organization of the market and of trade; and international relations. Idolatry permeates everything, and everything is at the service of the idolatry of the empire. The issue goes beyond emperor worship, that is merely one dimension of the imperial idolatry which is absolute, universal, systemic, and institutional.

John describes for us some of the ideological mechanisms of the idolatrous system (vv. 13–17), among which the prophetic signs are the most noteworthy. Revelation presents the false prophet as an Elijah performing extraordinary miracles. I think that these miracles or signs are real; they are not merely magic or deceit. These signs appear throughout the apocalyptic tradition:

> False messiahs and false prophets will arise, and they will perform signs and wonders so great as to deceive, if that were possible even the elect. (Matt. 24:24, par. Mark 13:22)

> [the lawless one]...whose coming springs from the power of Satan in every mighty deed and in signs and wonders that lie, and in every wicked deceit for those who are perishing because they have not accepted the love of truth. (2 Thess. 2:9–10)

One possible interpretation would be that these signs are the empire's works or achievements that are then presented in an idolatrous fashion as miracles. The Roman empire really did do wonders: in technology, communications, construction, art, law, and philosophy. These works were presented as the work of the gods, extraordinary works, true miracles of the empire (today we also speak of the miracles of technology, various economic miracles, medical miracles, and so forth).

The ideological mechanism that John captures most profoundly is that of the image of the beast. We have already explained that this image has spirit (*pneuma*), that is, it has life as evidenced in the fact that it can speak and kill. We noted that John may be referring to the image of the emperors on Roman coins, where they were usually depicted with divine features. John takes this depiction as something that typifies a much more complex and universal idolatrous structure. How are we to explain that the image of the beast has spirit, is alive, speaks and kills? We already said that we must make a distinction between institutions and their spirit. John makes this distinction when he speaks of the beast and of Satan as the power of the beast. All the institutions of the Roman empire are in place, but there are also the supernatural forces of evil (to use the images in Eph. 6). The image of the beast is simply the visible representation of that spirit that lies invisible in the empire. The image is the body of the fetish or idol. Although it is a dead object, the image of the beast has spirit and life when it becomes the visible symbolic representation of the spirit or supernatural force of the Roman empire. If the image of the beast is really the depiction of the empire on Roman coins, the meaning would be that Roman money is the visible representation of the empire's spirit. Money is fetishized and becomes an active subject: it has spirit and life, and it speaks and kills. Money becomes the image of the beast being worshiped, the idol being worshiped, the divinity being worshiped. Money becomes, in Jesus' words, Mammon, the God of this world, Lord of the world. Money is something inert that the false prophet turns into a living subject. What speaks and kills is not money as a thing in itself, but rather the spirit of the empire; nevertheless, money now takes on the qualities of a subject and appears as the visible body of the empire's invisible spirit, and as such it is alive, speaks, and kills. In Revelation is the one who gives life and power to the Roman empire; money now becomes the body of Satan.

If money becomes an active subject, the worshipers of the beast become an object. As we have said, fetishism turns things into persons and persons into things. We earlier spoke of the beast as subject. Now the false prophet organizes worship of the beast by using the emperor's image on coins and transforming money into an active subject. The false prophet organizes worship of the beast on a universal and all-encompassing level by making coins fetishized money, money that is worshiped, the visible manifestation of the divinity, a living subject speaking and killing. This transformation of money into a subject transforms the worshipers of the beast into objects, and hence they can be stamped. Subjects again surrender their subjectivity to the image of the beast, to the idol of money, and become objects. This is what the mark of the beast means. The beast's worshipers are stamped by it: they bear the beast's name on their foreheads (in their minds) and on their right hand (in their work). The stamp expresses the logic or rationality of the empire. Those who adore it have this logic and hence they are able to participate successfully and happily in the life of the empire. To describe this integration into the life of the empire John uses the economic image of selling and buying.

This economic integration into the market, however, is in turn a symbol of integration into all the empire's structures. Since Christians reject the idolatry of the beast and of money, they do not have the stamp of the beast, are not identified as belonging to the empire, and so are made outcasts and ultimately murdered. They are sentenced to death economically by being excluded from the market, and they are sentenced to death politically, culturally, and spiritually for not acknowledging the beast as a god. Christians refuse to be turned into objects of Baal (the empire-god) and into objects of Mammon (the money-god). Satan is the power of the beast and of the image of the beast; he is the supernatural force of evil that Christ and the martyrs have defeated. That is why Christians understand that the Roman empire is not an absolute subject that no one can resist. The empire is not 7 but 666; it is an empire that is spiritually defeated, and hence resistance is meaningful, even though the empire may still have the power to go on blaspheming, defeating, and killing. It is this community of Christians who resist the idolatry of the beast and his image and who reject his stamp, which now comes into view in Revelation 14:1–5, which we are now going to interpret.[9]

Revelation 14:1–5

This section, 14:1–5, is the center of the larger section 12:1–15:4, which in turn is the center of the whole of Revelation. We therefore stand at the "center of the center" of Revelation. It is not only a literary center (in the book's structure) but also a center in salvation history: the present, between past and future, the *kairos* in which the fate of humankind is at stake and on which Revelation focuses its attention. At this center of the center the people of God stands on earth, alongside the Lamb; this people refuses to worship the Roman empire and follows Jesus wherever he goes. Even though it is short, this section is the most brightly lit point in Revelation. John depicts for us the people of God gathered with the Lamb on Mount Zion (14:1–5), after having pictured for us the perverse trinity — Satan, the beast, and the false prophet (chapters 12 and 13) — and before the judgment over those who worship the beast (14:6–20). The sight of the community following the Lamb wherever he goes in the midst of fierce beasts as well as a dramatic judgment constitutes an impressive and very meaningful picture.

As we have noted, this vision of the community on earth alongside the Lamb has its parallel in the community in heaven of those who are victorious over Satan (at the beginning and 12:10–11) and in the community of those who are victorious over the beast (at the end and in 15:2–4), which is likewise in heaven. In this fashion the community resisting on earth is identified with the community singing victory in heaven.

The text is composed of two parts, a vision (vv. 1–3) and its explanation (vv. 4–5). In v. 1 we have the vision as such, and in vv. 2 and 3, something heard: a new hymn. What John sees in v. 1 and then explains in vv. 4–5 takes place on earth. The hymn heard, on the other hand, comes from heaven (*ouk tou ouranou*). Thus we have two levels: a community on earth and a hymn in heaven that is heard on earth and that can be learned only by those who belong to the community on earth. Let us now interpret the key elements in this passage.

The first thing John sees is the "Lamb standing on Mount Zion." Here in 14:1 Mount Zion does not refer to the Jerusalem of history built on Mount Zion, nor

---

9. Hugo Assmann and Franz Hinkelammert, *A idolatria do mercado: Ensaio sobre economia e teologia* (São Paulo: Vozes, 1989), and Enrique Dussel, *Las metáforas teológicas de Marx* (Estella, Spain: Verbo Divino, 1993).

to the heavenly Jerusalem (chapters 21–22). Zion is here a symbol to designate the meeting place of the new people of God that now gathers alongside the risen Jesus. The symbol certainly evokes the old Jerusalem and anticipates the vision of the New Jerusalem. Nevertheless, the 144,000 are not physically in Jerusalem, which by now the Romans have razed to the ground, nor are they in the heavenly Jerusalem, which has not yet arrived (or better, has not come down). Even in the Old Testament Mount Zion had this symbolic character, as the eschatological place for the Messiah to meet his people. In Psalm 2, as interpreted messianically — as is so common throughout the Christian tradition and particularly in Revelation — the Messiah is consecrated on Mount Zion and from there he shepherds (according to the Septuagint) the nations. Other texts to read are Joel 3:1–5 and Zephaniah 3:11–13. The best parallel within Revelation is 11:1–2, where the temple in the holy city is also used as a symbol of the community (see commentary on that section).

The people of God alongside the Lamb are presented as a people of "144,000 who had his name and his Father's name written on their foreheads." One hundred and forty-four thousand is clearly a symbolic number to indicate the people of God, whose model is the people of the twelve tribes. While the number seven indicates totality in general, the number twelve designates a social whole (an entire people). This is a perfect people: twelve tribes of twelve thousand members each = 144,000 (12 x 12 x 1000). The people of God is here gathered in perfect form, as a whole, alongside the risen Christ. Besides totality and perfection, the number 144,000 expresses organization. The people resisting the beast is well organized. "People of God" here means something more complex than the church. When John refers to the church, he speaks rather of "the churches," for example the seven churches in chapters 1–3. The image here is also an anticipation (the first fruits) of the heavenly Jerusalem (21–22), where it is explicitly stated that there is no temple, because the Lamb is its temple (21:22). These 144,000 appear twice: in 14:1–5 and in the parallel text of 7:1–8. They are the same people, and in both cases they are on earth. In chapter 7 the 144,000 are marked with the seal of the living God on their foreheads; in chapter 14 they have the Lamb's name and his Father's name written on their foreheads. In chapter 7 the seal is to protect them from the four destroying angels. The seal has the same meaning in 9:4, where the locusts are harming only those who do not have God's seal on their foreheads. In chapter 14, on the other hand, the name on the forehead indicates belonging to God and to the Lamb and is obviously meant to contrast with the stamp of the beast's name or the number that stands for its name on the right hand of those worshiping it. The people of the beast are clearly distinguished from the people of the Lamb. In the New Jerusalem as well the holy ones will see the face of God and will bear his name on their foreheads (22:4). Hence those who now bear the name of the Lamb on their foreheads, rather than the stamp of the beast, are already identified as the holy ones who are to dwell in the New Jerusalem.

In both chapter 7 and 12:1–15:4, the people of God can be seen on the two levels of earth and heaven. In 7:1–8, the people are on earth: they are those sealed (and counted) with God's seal. Immediately afterward in 7:9–17 there appears in heaven a multitude that no one can count from every nation, tribe, people, and tongue, standing before the Lamb, and so forth. In 14:1–5 the people are likewise on earth, but they hear and learn the new hymn of those who are singing in heaven. Corresponding to this community on earth (14:1–5) there is a victory hymn in heaven in 12:10–11 and 15:2–4, within the structure that we have already examined. As we noted in the introduction, heaven and earth are not only two cosmic dimensions, but they are theological symbols to express the two dimensions of history: the visible or empirical dimension in which the clash between the people of God and the empire is taking place, and the invisible or transcendent dimension, where the victory of the people of God is already assured. It is not as though there are two histories, but rather the single history has two dimensions.

In vv. 2–3 we find the sound accompanying the vision of v. 1. In Revelation the words "hymn" (*odé*), "to sing" (*ádo*), and "harp" (*kithára*) appear only here in 14:2–3, in 15:2–4, and in 5:8–12. Despite their differences, these are three parallel texts and they shed light on one another. The three hymns are sung in heaven and provide us with the meaning of what is happening on earth. In chapters 5 and 15 we are given the content of the hymn, but not in 14:2–3. However, we may well imagine that the content of the new hymn in 14:3 is the same as what we find in the hymns in chapters 5 and 15. Those singing are different: in chapter 5 it is the four living creatures and the twenty-four elders; in chapter 15 it is those who had won the victory over the beast and its image and the number that signified its name. Although 14:2–3 does not say who is singing, it is presumably the martyrs victorious in heaven (who are singing in 12:10–11 and 15:2–4).

A key line, one filled with meaning, is added in 14:3: "No one could learn this hymn except the 144,000 who had been ransomed from the earth." This hymn, which the community on earth learns from heaven, represents the consciousness, identity, and spirituality of this people organized on earth that is resisting the beast. Resisting requires learning this hymn, and only they can learn it. It is like a secret that they discover in heaven and in that hidden dimension of history that is revealed only by faith. Those who resist the beast on earth need to sing the hymn of the martyrs in heaven. There is a contrast between the worshipers of the beast who surrender their subjectivity to it and are transformed into stamped objects and the 144,000 who learn and sing the new hymn that they hear in heaven. They are able to sing because they indeed are subjects and have consciousness, an identity, and a spirituality. The worshipers of the beast, on the other hand, can buy and sell, but they cannot sing.

In the four sentences of vv. 4–5 we are offered an explanation of who these 144,000 in John's vision are. First, "these are they who were not defiled with women: they are virgins." This line sounds horrible to our ears today, and, however it might be explained, it still sounds horrible. Hence it should be eliminated from new translations, and a different reading should be put in its place, one that faithfully expresses the meaning of the original text. In Revelation the verb "defile" (*molyno*) is found only here in 14:4 and in 3:4 with the same meaning. In 3:4 it is Jesus who says:

[However,] you have a few people in Sardis who have not soiled their garments; they will walk with me dressed in white, because they are worthy.

Obviously both texts have a symbolic meaning. The garment expresses the way we live, our practice. According to a constant and broad tradition throughout the Old and New Testaments, what defiles, soils, or contaminates is idolatry. Fornication and prostitution are constant and unmistakable symbols of idolatry. Virginity or purity is the utter absence of idolatry. When Jesus says, "Blessed are the clean of heart, for they will see God" (Matt. 5:8) he is talking about himself. What prevents us from seeing God is idolatry. Hence the saints in the heavenly Jerusalem will see God, for there the idolaters and murders are excluded (21:8). An alternative reading — one that would not be offensive — for this first sentence in 14:4a might be: "these are those who did not contaminate themselves with idolatry, for they are clean of heart."

Second, "these are the ones who follow the Lamb wherever he goes." The verb used here, "to follow" (*akolouthéo*), is the technical term in the tradition of the four Gospels to designate the disciples in the following of Jesus. We have here a sharp opposition between worshiping the beast ("the whole world followed after the beast," 13:3) and following the Lamb. The holy ones follow the Lamb as disciples. The worshipers of the beast, as we have seen, surrender their quality as subjects to him and become objects. The Lamb is here the symbol that stands opposed to, and in contention with, the beast. The community of the 144,000, which is the alternative community to that of the beast (the Roman empire as beast), lives on earth as disciples of Jesus. Christians resist the beast: that is what is meant by the word "resistance" (*hupomené:* in Revelation in 1:9; 2:2, 3, 19; 3:10; 13:10; 14:12). It is resistance to death (see 12:10–11). Paraphrasing Hebrews 12:4 we could say that they resist to the point of shedding blood (see Heb. 12:1–4). However, Christians resist the beast by being disciples of Jesus. It is not said that they have struggled against the beast with weapons in hand. They resisted during this present age by being disciples of Jesus, following the Lamb wherever he goes, singing the new hymn that they learn from the victorious martyrs, who are alive in heaven; but they also resisted with the hope that Jesus will appear to judge the worshipers of the beast (14:6–20) and put an end to it and to the false prophet (19:11–21). They are awaiting the kingdom of the Messiah (20:4–6) and the new heavens and new earth (21–22).

Third, "they have been ransomed as the first fruits of the human race for God and the Lamb." The verb "to buy" (*agorazo*) is used figuratively (to rescue, liberate) in Revelation at 5:9 and 14:3, 4. In 5:9 we are told that the Lamb purchased with his blood persons from every tribe, tongue, people, and nation and has made of them a kingdom, and they will reign on the earth. In 14:4 those ransomed are the first fruits (*aparché*) for God and the Lamb. This is the only appearance of the term "first fruits" in Revelation. In 1 Corinthians 15:20, Paul says that the risen Christ is the first fruit of those who fell asleep, that is, he is the first fruit of those who will rise later. Likewise in 2 Thessalonians 2:13 it is said that God chose the community as first fruit, that is, as the first of a group to follow. In 1 Corinthians 16:15 the household of Stephanas is the first fruit of Achaia, the first converts among others who are to come later. Here in 14:4 the 144,000 are first fruits for God. They are the organized people of God that is resisting the beast, but they are scarcely the beginning (the first fruits) of a multitude who will later follow their example. In heaven they are uncountable (7:9). All of these have been ransomed (liberated) by the blood of the Lamb. Those excluded from the market by the beast and the false prophet are now those rescued and liberated by the death and resurrection of Christ.

Fourth, "on their lips no deceit has been found; they are unblemished." The meaning is the same as that of the first line (and together they enclose the passage): they are those who do not adore the beast, who are not idolaters, who are clean of heart. The lips of Christians are set in contrast with the mouth of the beast, which utters proud boasts and blasphemies. A text contemporaneous with, and parallel to, that of Revelation sums up what we have seen:

[the lawless one] whose coming springs from the power of Satan in every mighty deed and in signs and wonders that lie, and in every wicked deceit for those who are perishing because they have not accepted the love of truth so that they may be saved. Therefore, God is sending them a deceiving power so that they may believe the lie, that all who have not believed the truth but have approved wrongdoing may be condemned. (2 Thess. 2:9–12)

Revelation 14:6–20

This section has a simple structure:

Three angels announce the good news of God's judgment: vv. 6–13

Vision of the son of man seated on a white cloud: v. 14

Three angels execute the judgment of the sickle and the winepress: vv. 15–20

Removing the second part, 14:1–15:4, from the larger section, 12:1–15:4, we find this structure:

Lamb seated on Mount Zion and the 144,000: 14:1–5

Three angels announce the good news of God's judgment: 14:6–13

Son of man seated on a white cloud: 14:14

Three angels execute the judgment of the sickle and the winepress: 14:15–20

Three victors sing the hymn of the Lamb: 15:2–4.

Let us not forget what we said at the beginning of the chapter: in the structure of this passage, 12:1–15:4, which constitutes the center of all of Revelation, we find reflected the structure of Daniel 7 with its fundamental polarity between beasts and the son of man (two myths or symbols to represent mentally the empires and the people of the holy ones of the Most High). In this present section we find this same basic polarity:

beast and false prophet: 13:1–18
son of man and six prophet angels: 14:6–20

In Daniel it is God who executes the judgment. In Revelation and in the synoptic tradition, the son of man carries out the judgment, a symbol with which Jesus himself (personified as the son of man) is identified.

Let us now examine the key elements for interpreting 14:6–20.

Revelation 14:6–13

Proclamations made by three angels divide this passage: first angel (6–7), second angel (8), and third angel (9–11); it then ends with an exhortation (12–13). Although the proclamations are made in heaven or from heaven, the action takes place on earth.

First Angel: vv. 6–7: Strangely he is called "another" angel. The previous one is in chapter 12, where Michael and his angels appear. The six angels in vv. 6–20 are called "another angel." This first angel somewhat resembles the mighty angel in 10:1–7. Both texts begin in the same way: "then I saw another angel" (*kai eidon allon ángellon*). The angel in chapter 10 has a small scroll opened in his hand. Here the angel has good news (*euaggélion*) — the only place where this word appears in Revelation. In Revelation the verb "to evangelize" (*euanggelizo*) is found only in these two passages: 10:7 and 14:6. The "everlasting good news to announce" is a universal good news: "it is for those who dwell on earth and for every nation, tribe, tongue, and people." We have already noted that in Revelation the expression "those who dwell on the earth" is always a technical term for the wicked who worship the beast. Nevertheless, the verb used in that expression is always *katoikountes;* now in 14:6 it is *kathemenos.* Hence the meaning in 14:6 is neutral rather than pejorative and refers to all the inhabitants of the earth, without judging whether they are upright or wicked.

What is unusual is that the content of this "good news" that is "announced" universally is that "the time has come to sit in judgment" (*elthen he hora tes kríseos*). The word "judgment" (*krisis*) is used in Revelation four times: here, in 16:7, in 19:2 (in the expression "true and just judgments"), and in 18:10. We always regard the judgment as something frightful and terrifying, and so it is for the forces of evil. In 16:5–7 the judgment is celebrated in the liturgy, because God has given blood to drink to those who shed blood. Likewise in 19:2 the judgment is celebrated in the liturgy, for the great harlot (Rome) has been condemned and the blood of God's servants has been avenged on her. The judgment is good news for the oppressed, however; for them it means liberation and doing justice. God's judgment is God's liberating intervention in history. The approaching judgment demands three attitudes as seen in the three imperatives in v. 7: "Fear God and give him glory. . . . Worship [*proskunesate*] him who made heaven and earth." This worship of the creator God stands poles apart from those who worship Satan, the beast, and the beast's image (with the same verb in 13:4, 8, 12, 15).

Second Angel: v. 8: A second angel proclaims: "Fallen, fallen is Babylon the great" (likewise in 18:2). The author uses a proleptic or dramatic aorist (*épesen*), that is, he proclaims something future as already happened. Although Imperial Rome (called "Babylon the Great") has not fallen, it is already a city lost and demolished in the minds of Christians. Rome is said to have "made all the nations drink the wine of her licentious passion" (see parallels in 17:2 and 18:3). Throughout the biblical tradition the word "prostitution" or "fornication" (*porneia*) is a symbol for idolatry. Rome is aggressively and furiously idolatrous (licentious *porneia*) and makes all nations drunk with her idolatry. Chapter 18 will develop what is merely stated here.

Third Angel: vv. 9–11: The formula "worship the beast or its image or accept its mark" (in vv. 9b and 11b we have this same expression, thereby framing the passage) is repeated in 16:2 and 19:20. We find the same formula in 15:2 and 20:4, but the meaning is a positive affirmation of those who do *not* worship. This formula summing up 13:11–18 must have been familiar within Christian communities. At the center of 9–11 we find a punishment that will be meted out to one who worships the beast and its image and agrees to be marked with its name. This punishment is described in three frightening, heavily loaded lines:

- will drink the wine of God's fury, poured full strength into the cup of his wrath;
- will be tormented in burning sulfur before the holy angels and before the Lamb . . . forever and ever
- will have no relief day or night.

It is not the horrors of hell that are being described here (nowhere in Revelation is there such a description) but the horrors that one who adores the beast and his image and who accepts its mark has to undergo now in this life. When the beast becomes an idol — Moloch, an absolute and transcendent subject — the worshipers of the beast become things marked; when the beast's image, which is the material representation of the empire's supernatural forces of evil, is worshiped, the worshipers lose their subject quality, their identity, their spirituality. Their identity (mark) is that of the beast. Let us now examine the horrors that the author of Revelation believes must be suffered by those who worship the beast and its image and agree to be stamped with its name.

We have already mentioned the wine of the fury of Rome's idolatry (14:8, 17:2, 18:3). Revelation 12:12 speaks of the devil's fury. Here, however, John is talking about God's fury. He does so with an extremely charged expression: he speaks not merely of fury, but of the wine of fury, wine, moreover, that is poured full strength into a cup; and he adds that it is the wine of God's wrath. He then describes the torment by burning sulfur that one who worships the beast must suffer in the presence of the angels and the Lamb. This is an internal suffering in God's presence. Finally, he says that such a one has no rest day or night.

What does language so heavily laden with hatred mean? John may be describing the deep suffering of the worshipers of the beast, of those who have become stamped objects for adoring an empire transformed into an absolute subject (Moloch). He thus intends to warn his hearers to resist this idolatrous integration into the Roman empire. John may also be reflecting the accumulated hatred of the holy ones who are excluded by the empire, who cannot buy and sell and are persecuted and murdered. Why does he reflect such hatred? One possibility might be catharsis. Like the Greek tragedies, Revelation would then be an exercise of catharsis, that is, reading it within the community would serve as a kind of inner purging, so that by listening the people might be freed of hatred (like a sublimation of the passions in Greek tragedy).[10] John gives voice to that hatred to help his hearers transform their hatred into awareness, such as appears in all the liturgies and hymns in Revelation. I furthermore do not think it is simply hatred; John is also reflecting the desperation of those who are excluded and the enormity of what the poor suffer. Something similar occurs in the Psalms (read, for example, Psalms 22, 35, 55, 59, 79, 109).

Exhortation: vv. 12–13: In vv. 12–13 we find an exhortation. Just as in 13:13, the author urges "resistance" (*hupomoné* should be translated as "resistance" rather than as "patience"). In v. 13 we have a beatitude to overcome his hearers' fear of death (there are seven beatitudes in Revelation: 1:3; 14:13; 16:15; 19:9; 20:6; 22:7, 14). "Yes, said the Spirit": the Spirit steps in as in the seven letters and in 22:17. He must step in to resist the false prophet who acts as the Anti-Spirit.

Revelation 14:14–20

We have three symbols here: the son of man (taken from Dan. 7), the sickle, and the winepress (taken from Joel 4:13–14 in the context of 4:1–17). Like symbols, myths are polysemic (have many meanings); they are always available for and open to new meanings provided that the original context and the overall meaning of the book and the passage in which the symbol appears are respected. The three symbols in this passage are quite abstract; they do not point to anything specific in theological or historical terms.

The son of man figure has no Christological connection, especially if we compare it with the vision of Christ as son of man in 1:10–20 or to the reference in 1:5–7. The visions of Christ in chapter 5 and in 19:11–21 are full of profoundly and intensely Christological symbols. In 14:14, besides the lack of specifically Christological references, there are elements that do not appear in Daniel, such as the white color of the cloud, being seated, the golden crown, and the sickle. Jesus never appears in Revelation with a golden crown, let alone

---

10. Adela Yarbro Collins, *Crisis and Catharsis: The Power of the Apocalypse* (Philadelphia: Westminster Press, 1984).

with a sharp sickle. What we have here is the two-edged sword coming out of his mouth, which always refers to the word (1:16, 2:12, 19:15). It is also striking that the son of man is given an order by an angel. It is similarly striking that in 14:20 it is apparently the angel who treads on the winepress of God's fury, while in 19:5 it is explicitly Jesus (in Isa. 63:1–5 it is God himself).

The symbols of harvest and winepress extend the text from Joel very faithfully without making any specific historical or theological ties. The reference to the place "outside the city" where the winepress is trodden may refer to the text in Joel in which Yahweh's judgment is in the valley of Josaphat, not far outside Jerusalem. The exaggerated character of v. 20, where it is said that blood reaches the height of a horse's bridle for two hundred miles, also has no specific theological or historical tie.

The abstract character (neither historical, Christological, nor theological) of 14:14–20 is intentional on John's part: he insists on the symbolism as such, leaving possible meanings to those reading and listening to Revelation. The fact that the vision of the son of man has no Christological dimension is intended to draw attention to the symbolism of that image in Daniel. In chapter 7 of Daniel the symbol of the human figure (son of man) is poles apart from the symbol of the beasts. The human figure clearly symbolizes the people of the holy ones of the Most High (Dan. 2:18, 22, 27), which after the judgment receives the kingdom and the empire; the beasts, on the other hand, symbolize the four empires (Babylonian, Median, Persian, and Hellenistic: Dan. 7:17 in the light of chapters 2, 8, and 10–12). In Daniel God executes justice by destroying the empires and giving the kingdom of God to the people of the holy ones. In Revelation 14:14 John lowers the Christological profile of the symbol of the son of man in order to give it its original meaning: The son of man seated on the white cloud is the transcendental representation (in awareness and in heaven) of the people of God that resists and opposes the beast, his image, and the number that signifies his name. In the text this people receives the gold crown (power) and the sharp sickle for carrying out God's judgment represented in the symbols of sickle and winepress. In this interpretation we are not ruling out the possibility that the son of man may be Christ. According to the structure already presented, John maintains the relationship between the Lamb and the son of man and the opposition between empire and Christ in the symbolic opposition between beast and son of man. Nevertheless, the author of Revelation conceals this Christological dimension in order to restore the original meaning of the symbol referring to the people of the holy ones. Even in the synoptic tradition, where the title "son of man" is clearly applied to Jesus, the original meaning in reference to the people is not lost. Jesus as son of man is a messianic figure representing the people of God.

Revelation 15:1–4

Here we have two visions: the vision in heaven of a great and awe-inspiring sign (v.1) and that of the victors who sing in heaven the song of Moses and of the Lamb (vv. 2–4). The sign (*semeion*) in v. 1 encloses the passage along with the two signs in heaven in 12:1–3. Thus begins and concludes 12:1–15:4, which is the center of all of Revelation. The sign in heaven is the seven angels who bring the seven plagues, which are the last and with which God's fury is fulfilled. Besides being paired with 12:1 and 3, v. 1 is announcing the next section, which is on the seven bowls (and which we have already examined in an earlier chapter). One of these seven angels shows John the condemnation of Babylon (17:1), and the heavenly Jerusalem (21:9).

Following v. 1 (which serves both to conclude a section and to announce something) come the victors. Each of the letters of the seven churches contains a promise to the victor, which in general points toward the final chapters, 20–22. Revelation 21:7 expressly states, "The victor will inherit these gifts." In these places we have the final (eschatological) reality of the victors. The other two places in which the verb "to be victorious" (*nikao*) appears and in which the believers are the subjects are 12:11 and 15:2–4, which also serve to mark off 12:1–15:4. The victory of the martyrs over Satan is announced in 12:11. They throw him from heaven down to earth, by virtue of the blood of the Lamb and the testimony they gave. Now in 15:2 we have the victory of the martyrs over the beast, his image, and the number that signifies his name. Having first observed the defeat of Satan we now see the defeat of the beast, his image, and the number that signifies his name. These lines framing the whole passage endow it with a tone of victory. What stands at the center of Revelation is the victory of the martyrs over Satan and the beast. The tone of the final song (15:2–4) likewise embodies optimism and a deep faith.

The model for the song of the martyrs is the victory song in Exodus. In this vision, the symbol of the Red Sea appears in heaven, and it is expressly stated that the martyrs are singing the song of Moses (Exod. 15:1–5). This reference to Exodus is preparing the way for the section on the seven plagues, whose theological content and historical meaning is the Exodus. It is the song of Moses but also the song of the Lamb, who at the center of the center of Revelation is seen to be standing on Mount Zion with the 144,000 who follow him wherever he goes (14:1–5). This song in 15:3–4 then points back toward the victory of the martyrs in 12:10–11 at the beginning of the section and toward the community on earth alongside the Lamb, which is learning the song coming from heaven, in the middle of the section (14:1–5). Thus it expresses the culmination of 12:1–15:4.

7

Prophetic Vision of History

Revelation 17:1–19:10

The chapter just concluded took us to the center of Revelation (12:1–14:20). Prior to that we had studied the passages on the trumpets (8:2–11:19) and the bowls (15:5–16:21), which surround this center of Revelation. We are now going to examine the section that follows that of the seven bowls (17:1–19:10), which we have titled "prophetic vision of history." In the overall pattern of Revelation this section is paired with 4:1–8:1, to which we have given the same title. That earlier section began with a liturgy (chapters 4 and 5) and was followed by the prophetic vision of history (in the form of seven seals). Now the pattern is reversed: first we have the prophetic vision of history, and the section closes with a liturgy (19:1–10).

In the seven bowls passage (15:5–16:21) we were told that they were the last bowls because through them God's fury was being accomplished (15:1). Indeed, the seventh bowl tells us of the end of great city: God remembers the great Babylon, giving it the cup filled with the wine of his fury (16:19). What comes now in 17:1–19:10 does not happen after the seventh bowl but announces how this seventh bowl is to come about. Indeed, the seventh bowl and the present section (17:1–19:10) are both about the same thing, the judgment and destruction of Rome, the great Babylon, as it is called.

INTRODUCTION TO THE READING AND STRUCTURE OF REVELATION 17:1–19:10

General Structure of the Text

Overall introduction: 17:1–2: I will show you the judgment of the great harlot . . .

A. The beast and the harlot: 17:3–18
   a. Vision of the beast and the harlot: vv. 3–7
   b. Explanation of the vision: vv. 8–18

B. Judgment upon the great Babylon (the harlot): 18:1–24
   a. Vision of the mighty angel: "Fallen, fallen is Babylon the great"
      reason for its fall: vv. 1–3
   b. A voice: "Depart from her, my people.... Pay her back as she has
      paid others"; mighty is God who judges her: vv. 4–8.

   center: weeping and mourning for the fall of Rome: vv. 9–19
      – mourning of the kings of the earth: vv. 9–10
      – mourning of the merchants of the earth: vv. 11–17a
      – mourning of the ship captains and seafaring merchants:
         vv. 17b–19

   b′. The voice continues: Rejoice over her, heaven, you holy ones,
      apostles, and prophets. For God has judged your case: v. 20
   a′. Mighty angel's action: Babylon will suddenly be thrown down;
      reasons for its condemnation: vv. 21–24

C. Liturgy of final victory: 19:1–8

   a. Liturgy in heaven, vv. 1–5:
      God judged the great harlot
      God avenged on her the blood of his servants
   b. Liturgy on earth, vv. 6–8:
      God established his reign
      The wedding day of the Lamb has come

Conclusion: 19:9–10: These words are true; they come from God

The introduction in 17:1–2 opens not only chapter 17 but this whole section
(to 19:10). The judgment upon the harlot announced here takes place basically in
chapter 18. After the introduction we have a triptych (a painting in three panels):
a vision, a judgment, and a liturgy, followed by a conclusion. The whole passage
is a single uninterrupted, smoothly flowing text.

KEYS FOR INTERPRETING THE TEXTS

General Introduction: Revelation 17:1–2

The angel who speaks is one of the seven angels who carried the seven bowls.
We are thus taken back to 15:1, where the seven angels are a magnificent and
marvelous sign in heaven paralleling the two signs in heaven in 12:1–3 (the
woman clothed with the son and the dragon). These angels draw our attention to
something important that is going to happen on earth. However, 17:1 also stands
in strict parallel with 21:9. In both we find exactly the same line:

Then one of the seven angels who were holding the seven bowls came and said to me, "Come here. I will show you. . . . "

In 17:1 the angel shows John the judgment of the great harlot (Rome); in 21:9 he shows him the bride, the wife of the Lamb (the new Jerusalem). Later (in 17:3 and 21:10) the angel is said to have "carried John away in spirit" (*apénken me en pneumati*). In the first passage he takes him to the desert to see the woman seated on the beast. In the second, he takes him to a high mountain and shows him the holy city Jerusalem coming down out of heaven. This literary parallelism pits the city of Rome against the New Jerusalem coming down from heaven.

Three words are highlighted in the introduction (17:1–2): *pórne* (prostitute or harlot), *pornéuo* (to prostitute oneself), and *porneia* (prostitution or harlotry). The accent is on how universal harlotry is: the harlot is living near many waters (geopolitical space of the empire), the kings of the earth have intercourse with her, and the inhabitants of the earth become drunk with her harlotry. Prostitution here symbolizes idolatry. The word "prostitute" or "harlot" (*pórne*) comes from the verb "to sell" (*pérnemi*). The prostitute is one who sells himself or herself for money, becoming an object in the hands of a subject who has power to buy him or her. In this passage prostitution is female and male: Rome is a harlot, but the kings of the earth are also prostitutes and prostitute themselves with Rome. The kings sell themselves as objects to the city of Rome, which through its money and power has become the goddess Rome: divine and absolute subject. Before describing the judgment upon Rome (chapter 18), the author examines the Roman empire and Rome (17:3–18) to show that it is idolatrous, how it is so, and what that means.

First Panel in the Triptych: Revelation 17:3–18

Vision of the Beast and the Harlot: vv. 3–7

John sees the harlot (Rome) in the "desert." Here the desert is not a symbol of the Exodus, as in 12:6, 14, where the woman (the Christian community) is protected and fed by God. Here it is a symbol of desolation, a place where the demons and savage beasts dwell. The woman is seated on "the beast," the same one that appears in chapter 13 with seven heads and ten horns. The "blasphemous names" are now not on the heads of the beasts (the emperors) but on its body: the very body of the beast is blasphemous and idolatrous.[1] The color of the beast is scarlet (*kokkinos*); the woman is dressed also in scarlet and purple. Gold is emphasized — the root *chrys* (= gold) appears three times: the woman is adorned (*kechrysomene*) with gold (*chrysío*), and is holding a gold (*chrysoun*) cup in her hand. In v. 4b the gold cup is said to be filled "with the abominable and sordid deeds of her harlotry"; and in v. 6a John sees "the woman drunk with the blood of the holy ones and on the blood of the witnesses to Jesus." The

---

1. The beast is neuter in gender but the two participles (*gémonta* = full of names and *échonta* = having seven heads) are masculine. The author is thinking of the beast as a man.

term "abomination" (*bdélygma*) is very well known in the apocalyptic tradition. Daniel (9:27, 11:31, 12:11) speaks of the "horrible abomination" (fearful or desolating abomination), which refers to Baal or Zeus, whose image Antiochus IV Epiphanes placed in the Jerusalem temple. The same expression appears in the synoptic tradition (Matt. 24:15, Mark 13:14), where, however, it refers rather to the idolatrous and criminal presence of the Roman army (the desolating abomination in Jerusalem). Here in Revelation, gold, idolatry, and the blood of the holy ones and martyrs are connected. On her forehead the woman bears a name, which is a mystery: "Babylon the great, the mother of harlots and of the abominations of the earth." Rome is not only a harlot, but the mother of all harlots. Rome is thus seen to be the source and prototype of all the idolatry dominating the empire. The abominations are images of the beast (especially on coins and insignia of the Roman armies).

Having read the text carefully, let us now examine some underlying interpretive keys, beginning with the personification of Rome as a woman and more specifically as a harlot. Rome is called "woman" six times (vv. 3, 4, 6, 7, 9, 18), a "harlot" three times (vv. 1, 15, 16) and the "mother of harlots" once. It is also called Babylon (previously in 14:8 and 16:19). The same theme appears in the Old Testament. Isaiah says of the city of Tyre, "She shall return to her hire and deal with all the world's kingdoms on the face of the earth" (Isa. 23:17). Here prostitution is related to profit and trading in goods. Tyre was the market of the nations, a haughty emporium; its traders were princes and its traffickers nobles (Isa. 23:3, 7, 8, 18). The prophet Nahum (Nah. 3:1–4) presents Nineveh as a bloodthirsty, prostituted city that with its prostitution (clearly meaning idolatry) sells itself to the nations. Ezekiel calls Jerusalem a prostitute: "Therefore harlot, hear the word of the Lord" (Ezek. 23, whole chapter, but especially v. 35). In Revelation, Rome's relationship to the kings of the earth and the inhabitants of the earth is a prostituted (i.e., idolatrous) relationship. The upshot is that Rome becomes a subject, an absolute and divine subject, and all its kings and vassals become objects bought and sold. Imperial Rome is fetishized, as expressed in the veneration of Rome as a goddess. This fetishization turns the whole empire into one huge *porneia,* that is, into massive harlotry, an orgy of idolatry.

What causes the fetishization of Rome as a goddess is its economic and political power: Rome is presented as the woman "seated on" the beast. The color of the woman's clothing is the same as that of the beast (they are spiritually in tune with one another). Nevertheless, what fetishizes the woman is primarily her gold: the woman is adorned with gold (literally: gilded with gold) and she drinks from a gold cup. Finally, the woman draws life from the blood of the saints and the martyrs of Jesus. Blood is what gives life to Rome's economic and political power. Fetishized Rome lives off the blood of its victims, the blood of those who resist the beast, who do not adore its image and do not bear the mark of its name (in other words, are not objects stamped by the system). In short, Rome is like Babylon, Tyre, Jerusalem, Egypt: an idolatrous and criminal city. Such a city can develop only in the desert, where demons and wild beasts alone can survive.

Explanation of the Vision: vv. 8–18

The text and structure indicate that these verses explain the preceding vision (vv. 3–7): "I will explain to you the mystery of the woman and of the beast" (v. 7), but only 17:18 reflects that statement. The rest of the passage delves further into the economic, political, and ideological reality of the Roman empire. More is said of the beast than of the woman.

In vv. 8–11 the author examines the power of the beast, using riddle-like symbolic language. Hence John asks for intelligence and wisdom in order to understand. He asked for the same thing at the end of chapter 13, which in fact parallels this present one. Verse 8 states that "the beast existed once but now exists no longer. It will come up from the abyss and is headed for destruction." These are three successive moments. The first moment — "existed once but now exists no longer" — is mentioned three times (8a, 8b, and 11), an extraordinary amount of repetition in so few verses. The second moment — "it will come up from the abyss" — is repeated with other words at the end of v. 8: "yet it will come again" (*párestai,* literally, "is going to come"). This second moment is the beast's "parousia" (the same root as *párestai*). The third moment, "is headed for destruction," reappears in v. 11.

The same three moments appear in vv. 9b–11, but now employing number symbolism:

1. *First moment* (existed once but now exists no longer): "The [beast's] seven heads represent seven kings: five have already fallen, one still lives, and the last has not yet come, and when he comes he will remain only a short while." These are not seven specific Roman emperors (for example, Caligula, Claudius, Nero, Vespasian, Titus, Domitian, and Nerva, as many writers hold) but the number seven meant to symbolize fullness. The author is living under a powerful emperor. According to the text he is the sixth, that is, he stands between the five who have fallen and the one to come. Here he is presented as number 6 just as he is called 666 in 13:8. The emperor who could round out the seven — meaning perfection — will not last long: perfection is out of reach.

2. *Second moment* (it will come up from the abyss — will come again): "the beast is an eighth king." After the failure of Roman emperor number seven, the beast himself becomes the eighth, trying to surpass number six, but he fails in the attempt, for he "really belongs to the seven." Thus we are drawn inexorably to the next moment.

3. *Third moment*: "is headed for destruction." In other words, the Roman empire tries to be seven but never succeeds. It will always be six, or rather 666. When a seven comes, it does not last; the beast himself (the quintessence of the empire) tries to install an eighth to replace this seventh who has not lasted, but fails because the beast belongs to the seven. Everything over six is either of short duration or is more of the same. Roman political power will therefore always be 666. The beast is a six,

between five failures from the past and a failure to come. The eighth will always be more of the same.

What is said here of the beast, explicitly in v. 8 and in a veiled manner in v. 10, is the antithesis of what is said of God: "who is and who was and who is to come" (1:4). God is the fullness of history, while the beast is the unending emptiness and frustration.

After analyzing the beast's power in vv. 8–11, the author presents a new analysis of history unfolding in three stages: first, alliance of kings with the beast (formation of the oppressive imperial "subject"): vv. 12–13; second, war against the Lamb — the Lamb and the holy ones defeat the beast: v. 14; third, internal war against Rome (crisis of the imperial system): vv. 15–17. Although the third step returns to some aspects of the first, we have here three successive stages that provide us with the logic or rationality of history. Let us examine each of these steps.

First Stage: vv. 12–13:   The beast's ten horns represent ten kings. The number expresses totality: they may be all the kings in the provinces under the empire since they are ultimately part of the beast. Perhaps they also include the imperial officials in the provinces. They likewise include the kings of the whole world who are assembled (or seduced) by the devils who come out of the mouths of the dragon, the beast, and the false prophet (16:14). All these kings who are part of the beast have not yet received a kingdom, but the beast gives them authority (*exousía*) as kings. They are kingdomless kings, but they nonetheless have power as parts of the Roman imperial system. They all share one mindset and purpose: to give their power and authority to the beast. That is why it is said that the kings receive authority for one hour — not because they are to be destroyed, but because they handed their authority over to the beast. The point being made here is the same as that of 13:17: only those who are stamped with the beast's name may buy and sell. Both passages (17:13 and 13:17) are about the beast becoming a "subject" and those who surrender to it being objectified. Its subordinates are objects stamped with the name of the beast; they have no power or authority.

This is a perfect expression of the fetishism of power. Power, which is an object or tool in the hands of responsible human subjects, becomes subject; and the human subjects become objects, with no name, no power, no authority. Fetishizing power likewise means absolutizing it and turning it into an idol, and in the end turning it into an oppressive and criminal power (power becomes beast, Moloch, Baal). Only subjects turned into objects can buy and sell, that is, become part of the market (the empire's economic and political system). Those who resist the beast and continue to be subjects, those who exercise power as responsible subjects, are excluded from the market and condemned to death.

Second Stage: v. 14:   The Roman empire, idolized as beast, and the kings of the earth who have become alienated by surrendering themselves to the beast "will fight with [*polemésousin*] the Lamb." The opposition between the beast of chapter 13 and the Lamb of 14:1–5 is once more taken up. Now it is proclaimed that the beast and the kings will be conquered by the Lamb, who is Lord of lords and King of kings, and also by those who are with him, those who are called, chosen, and faithful. This passage clearly points toward the final war of 19:11–21 (the battle of Armageddon, which is also announced in 16:13–16), where the risen Jesus likewise appears as King of kings and Lord of lords and where he is followed by the armies of heaven, the same as those seen in 17:14: those who are called, chosen, and faithful. This pre-announcement of victory stands in parallel with 12:10–11, where the martyrs defeat the devil in heaven, and likewise with 15:2–4, where those who have conquered the beast, his image, and the number that signified his name are singing in heaven.

Third Stage: vv. 15–17:   The author now returns to the woman in the vision, whom he called a harlot in v. 1. In v. 9 the woman is said to be seated (*káthetai*) on seven hills (representing the seven hills of Rome; now she is said to be seated (*káthetai*) on waters (representing peoples, nations, and tongues). The goddess Rome (whom John regards as a harlot) is seated over the seven hills of Rome, but its universal rule extends from there (particularly across the seas) to the *oikoumene,* or the world populated and organized by the Roman empire. In v. 16 we encounter the description of a future internal crisis in the empire: the ten horns and the beast are going to hate the harlot: they will leave her alone and naked and will eat her flesh and consume her with fire (a passage that draws inspiration from Ezek. 16:39–41 and 23:25–29). The entire Roman empire, with all its local and provincial powers, hates Rome and destroys it. John may not be referring to any specific historical event, but to the internal process of destruction that an empire undergoes when it has turned into beast. The idea in v. 13 is taken up again in v. 17b: all the kings have the same purpose (*gnómen*) of handing their kingdom over to the beast. We have already seen that John is referring to the fetishization of the Roman empire's economic and political power. The idolization of the empire destroys not only the holy ones who stand up to the beast, but it even destroys the beast from within. For John this internal crisis of the Roman empire does not occur by itself, but it is what God wills: he tells us that God put into the minds (*gnómen*) of kings to carry out his purpose (*gnómen*) to hand their kingdoms over to the beast (the same word is used). God continues to inspire kings in this way (leading to the fetishization of the beast and the internal crisis of the empire) "until the words of God are accomplished." The implication is that the internal crisis of the empire is due to the preaching of the Word by those who stand up to the beast.

Second Panel in the Triptych: Revelation 18:1–24

At this point Rome, the great city, Babylon the great, finally meets its judgment. In Revelation terms about judgment (*krino, krisis, krina*) apply primarily to judgment upon Rome (eleven of the sixteen times these terms are used). In the section before us (17:1–19:10) "judgment" (*krima*) appears in 17:1 and 18:20, "judgment" (*krisis*) in 18:10 and 19:2, and "to judge" (*krinein*) in 18:8, 20, and

19:2. The judgment is announced in 17:1, it takes place in chapter 18, and it is celebrated in 19:2. The judgment was announced earlier in 14:7. In 6:10 the martyrs in heaven were pleading with God to do justice (*krino*) and to take vengeance (*ek-dikéo*) for their blood. In 19:2 that appeal is answered:

> for true and just are just judgments [*krisis*]. He has condemned [*krino*] the great harlot. . . . He has avenged [*ek-dikeo*] on her the blood of his servants.

In Revelation the verb "avenge" appears only in 6:10 and 19:2. The liturgy of God's justice that takes place after the third bowl (16:5–7) refers to judgment upon Rome and its inhabitants. The other passages with this terminology about judgment refer to the final judgment (11:18; 19:11; 20:4, 12, 13). The judgment upon Rome takes place now in the present age, before the Parousia of Jesus, the thousand-year reign, and the last judgment (19:11–20:15).

Chapter 18 presents us with a real trial scene: we have the Judge (God), the defendant (Rome), the accusers (the prophets, the holy ones, and all those slain by Rome), the accusation (murder caused by idolatry and the accumulation of wealth), evidence (blood found in the city), the sentence (Rome found guilty), the execution of the sentence (Rome cast down never to be found again), the effects of the judgment on Rome (on kings, merchants, and sailors), the joy that erupts when those for whom justice has been done hear the sentence (v. 20), and the post-trial celebration by those who were oppressed by Rome (19:1–10). This symbolic or mythical representation of the trial of Rome is not a catharsis, a purification of the spirit or sublimation of the passions through a representation, as was the case with the Greek tragedies. Nor is it an outburst of popular rage. What the author seeks in this chapter is to restore the awareness of the Christian community. The central element is the historical thrust of God's justice. The trial involves a discernment into reality and a prophetic vision of history. When we read this chapter today we can understand the consciousness of Christians — how they thought and felt — at the heart of the Roman empire as the first century drew to a close.

Let us now look at each section of this chapter.

Vision of the Mighty Angel: vv. 1–3

John sees an angel coming down from heaven, one who has great authority and whose splendor lights up the whole earth. This angel is similar to the one that appears in 10:1. The angel is a personification of God's action on the earth. The illumination of the whole earth with the angel's glory (God's glory) antici-pates 21:23, where the new Jerusalem is seen to be illuminated with God's glory (see Ezek. 43:1–3: the whole earth shone with the glory of Yahweh returning to Jerusalem). The first thing that happens in the trial is that the earth is lit up in this fashion and darkness is defeated. God's power and glory are revealed here so that the trial may take place. They are signs of hope.

Then the mighty cry of the angel is heard: "Fallen, fallen is Babylon the great!" This fall had already been announced in 14:8 (see Isa. 21:9: "Fallen, fallen is Babylon, and all the images of her gods are smashed to the ground").

We have here a prophetic aorist, presenting what is going to happen in the future as though it has already occurred. In the mind of the community, Rome is a city already fallen, "a haunt for demons, a cage for every unclean spirit, a cage for every unclean bird" (possibly buzzards or vultures). Such is the way Christians felt toward Rome.

Verse 3 explains its fall in three parallel phrases:

– the nations have drunk the wine of her licentious passion;
– the kings of the earth prostituted themselves with her;
– the merchants of the earth grew rich from her drive for luxury.

Almost the very same expressions are found in 17:2 and 18:9. The subjects in these sentences express the concentration of social, political, and economic power: nations, kings and merchants. The three verbs establish a parallel between three actions: getting drunk, being prostituted, and getting rich. It is specifically noted that the merchants become rich with Rome's drive (*dynamis*) for luxury. Drunkenness and prostitution here have a figurative meaning, namely, idolatry. We note the relationship idolatry-wealth-power-luxury. As we have already noted (commenting on 17:1–2), Rome is seen as a prostitute, but the kings are likewise prostitutes. Prostitution here is represented as both female and male. It is important to note this, because if we identify prostitution exclusively with the woman (as happens in patriarchal systems) we may cause violence to be unleashed against prostitutes.

The cause of Rome's fall is idolatry, wealth, power, and luxury. Rome is the center of iniquity, but responsibility nevertheless falls on the periphery: the nations, the kings and the merchants "of the earth." The political and economic powers in the provinces of the empire are also responsible for the fall of Rome. Not only is this city corrupt, but it has corrupted all the powers of the Roman empire. Note the parallel text 18:23b, which again states why Rome falls.

A Prophetic Voice from Heaven: vv. 4–8

John hears a voice speaking from heaven, a prophetic oracle from God, issuing five orders. He is given five imperatives (*exélthate, apódote, diplósate, kerásate, dote*): to depart, pay back, double the measure, measure the cup, and give. It is clear to whom the first of these orders is given and why. "Depart from her, my people." God's people must leave Rome so as not to be in complicity with her sins and to escape from her plagues; Rome's sins rise up to heaven, and God remembers her crimes (*adikémata*). This departure from Rome is not understood in the physical sense, but is to be economic, social, political, and spiritual; the idea is to resist, to refuse to participate, to create alternatives ("I do not ask that you take them out of the world but that you keep them from the evil one," John 17:15). The author draws inspiration from the Old Testament (see Isa. 48:20, Jer. 50–51).

The order to leave Rome is followed by four other imperatives. It is not stated explicitly who must carry out these orders, but since no new interlocutor is introduced it is understood that they are being issued to the "my people" of

v. 4. God's people must do what is being ordered. The first two commands have to do with paying Rome back for what it has done; three times it is stated that she must be paid back double. Into her cup must be poured double what she has poured. In 17:4, Rome the harlot is holding in her hand a gold cup filled with her idolatries, and in 17:6 she is said to be drunk on the blood of the holy ones and the martyrs. In 16:5–6, the text stated: "You are just... in passing this sentence. For they have shed the blood of the holy ones and the prophets, and you [have] given them blood to drink; it is what they deserve." The fourth command is repay Rome in torment and grief in proportion to her boasting and wantonness.

How can the people of God do such things to Rome? Obviously, the people of God must not and cannot use the same violence against Rome that Rome has used against it. The first command was to leave Rome, implying thereby that the combat with her is not on the same ground nor with the same weapons. The people of God actually combat Rome, but its weapons are different and more effective — doubly so, in fact. The best New Testament description of this combat is in Ephesians 6:10–20 (read this passage!). The passage on which we are commenting indicates a particular historical practice of God's people against Rome. Today we would call it nonviolent struggle: cultural, ethical, and spiritual resistance (but not thereby any less effective or real). God's people struggles against Rome as did Jesus: by dying and rising.

Rome's arrogance is described in v. 7. She says in her heart: I am powerful, I am not poor (as represented by widowhood), I will never know grief. The response to such arrogance is pestilence, grief, famine, and fire. The passage ends with a profession of faith: Mighty is the Lord God who judges Rome (*ischurós kyrios ho Theós ho krinas autén*).

Lamentations over the Fall of Rome: vv. 9–19

The text draws inspiration from Ezekiel 26–28 (lamentations over the fall of the city of Tyre). Three groups are wailing: the kings of the earth (political power: v. 9–10), the merchants of the earth (economic power: vv. 11–17a), and seafaring merchants (trading power: vv. 17b–19). The text speaks for itself and needs no further explanation. The threefold refrain, "Alas, alas, great city" is striking, as is the horror felt over the fall of Rome.

It is important to delve further into the central lament: vv. 11–17a (which lies at the center of chapter 18) devoted to the wailing and mourning of the merchants (economic power). Here we find a detailed description of Rome's consumer products:

- metals: gold and silver;
- jewels: precious metals and pearls;
- fine cloth: fine linen, purple silk, scarlet cloth;
- materials: fragrant wood, ivory, expensive wood, bronze, iron, and marble;
- scents: cinnamon, spice, myrrh, and frankincense;

- food: wine, oil, fine flour, and wheat;
- animals: beasts of burden, sheep, horses, and wagons.
- and finally as the ultimate consumer product, slaves and human merchandise. This human merchandise was lower than slaves and probably refers to men and women to be used in the circus and in brothels.

This list of consumer products in the economic realm also reflects a scale of ethical values. At the head of the list is gold, and slaves and human merchandise constitute the ultimate value. The satisfaction of the vices of the rich and the luxury of Rome is what determines the ethics and scale of values of the great city.

Joy of the Holy Ones, Apostles, and Prophets: v. 20

This section (b′) continues 4–8 (b) and is parallel to it. Hence we may assume that the voice speaking here (v. 20) is the same as the one in vv. 4–8. "Rejoice" in v. 20 continues the series of five imperatives in vv. 4–8 (depart from Rome, and resist her). This joy of the holy ones, apostles, and prophets stands in sharp contrast to the lament of the kings, merchants, and sailors in the previous lines. The reason for joy is that in sentencing Rome, God has rendered judgment in the case of the holy ones, apostles, and prophets. Literally, it says: "For God has judged [*ékrinen*] your judgment [*to krima*] against her." This action by God responds to the faith evidenced in v. 8: "For mighty is the Lord God who judges her" (*ho krinas autén*). Mention of the apostles here denotes a ministry or function within the community as in 2:2; it does not refer to the twelve apostles in history, as is the case in 21:14. In the community of Revelation all are called holy ones (as in Daniel 7) and its ministers are prophets and apostles (both men and women).

Action of the Mighty Angel: vv. 21–24

This passage (a′) continues and parallels the initial passage (a) of vv. 1–3. The same mighty angel who illuminates the earth with its is splendor (v. 1) now throws a huge stone into the sea in a symbolic action prophetically presenting the fall of Rome and its disappearance forever. The text is directly inspired by Jeremiah 51:63–64.

In vv. 22–23a we have a song of the people graphically describing the end of life in Rome: gone are all music, artists, craftsmen, lamps shedding light, and wedding celebrations. In response to each proclamation, the people respond "will never more be heard in you." No life — only blood — remains in Rome (v. 24). In v. 23b the reason for the fall of Rome, already given in v. 3 (parallel passage), is reiterated. Verse 24 is the most remarkable in all of chapter 18; it provides us with the ultimate proof that Rome has been found guilty: "In her was found the blood of prophets and holy ones; and all who have been slain on the earth." Revelation is concerned that justice be done not only for the blood of the members of the Christian community, but for all victims of the Roman empire.

Third Panel of the Triptych: 19:1-8

The section (17:ff) that we have titled "prophetic vision of history" ends with a liturgy. This liturgy also closes the present period of history, which in Revelation's account began with 4:1. The liturgy in chapters 4 and 5 parallels this liturgy in 19:1-8. The present age (extending from 4:1 to 19:10) begins and ends with a liturgy. As already noted, the liturgy placed us at the heart of the Revelation community and is a reflection of the liturgies actually experienced by the Christian community at the close of the first century. The hymns in these liturgies are very packed theologically and hermeneutically: they provide us with basic clues for our overall interpretation of the book.

There are two moments in the liturgy: vv. 1-5 and vv. 6-8. Verse 1 and v. 6 each begin with the same phrase: "I heard what sounded like the loud voice of a great multitude, saying: Alleluia!" In v. 1 it is specified that the multitude is in heaven. In v. 6 the voice is described as like the sound of rushing water or peals of thunder. The liturgy in vv. 1-5 is explicitly set in heaven. The one in vv. 6-8 may take place on earth, but the text does not say so explicitly. The liturgy embodies what is commanded in 18:20: Rejoice, heaven (19:1-5), you holy ones, apostles, and prophets (19:6-8).

These verses (1, 3, 4, 6) are the only place in the New Testament where the cry "Alleluia!" appears. This acclamation connects us with the singing of the Hal-lel (Pss. 113-18), which was sung partly before the Passover supper, and partly afterward. What we see in those psalms is closely connected to this liturgy in Revelation.

The liturgy in 19:1-8 stands in parallel, as we have said, with the liturgy in chapters 4-5 (in Revelation the present age opens and closes with a grand liturgy), but this liturgy likewise gathers and sums up numerous liturgies over the course of the present age. The parallels with those liturgies are notable and illuminating. In 6:9-11 the martyrs "cried out with a loud voice, 'How long will it be...before you sit in judgment and avenge our blood?'" These two verbs, "do justice" (*krinein*) and "avenge" (*ek'dikein*) are the central verbs in the liturgy in 19:1-6. Indeed, the verb to avenge (*ek-dikein*) appears in Revelation only in 6:10 and 19:2. In 6:11, the slain martyrs are told to wait a little while. Now the wait is over, and what they asked for takes place.

In 7:9-17 there is also a great multitude in heaven. The term "multitude" (*ochlos*) appears in Revelation only in 7:9 and 19:1, 6 (and also in 17:15, though with another meaning), and always in the expression "great multitude." The author sees great multitudes in heaven celebrating liturgies. In 7:10 they shout in with a loud voice, "Salvation [*soteria*] comes from our God." In Revelation this term appears only in 17:10, 12:10 (a parallel text which we will examine below), and 19:1. It means full and abundant life, and the cry that attributes salvation to God likewise has a political meaning: it is God rather than the empire that assures this *soteria* (the empire was obligated to assure the *soteria* of all citizens). In 7:11 and 19:1-6 the twenty-four elders and the four living creatures join the liturgy, exclaiming Amen.

In 11:15-19 we have another parallel liturgy: when the last trumpet sounds loud voices are heard in heaven: "the kingdom [*basileía*] of the world now belongs to our Lord and to his Anointed, and he will reign [*basileusei*] forever and ever." Here also the twenty-four elders join the celebration, saying, "We give thanks [*eucharistoumen*] to you, Lord God.... For you ... have established your reign [*ebasíleusas*]".[2] In both liturgies we find the expression "the servants ... who fear your name, the small and the great alike." In 11:18 it is said that "the time [has come] to destroy those who destroy the earth." In 19:2 the harlot was condemned because she "corrupted the earth."[3] The seventh trumpet marks the end of the present age, and the reign of God begins. Both the context and the theology are the same as those in 19:1–8: Rome falls and the reign begins.

In 12:10–12 we find another parallel liturgy: "Then I heard a loud voice in heaven say: Now have salvation [*sotería*] and power [*dynamis*] come, and the kingdom [*basileía*] of our God." Here it is the fall of Satan that is being celebrated, whereas in 19:2 it is the fall of Rome, the great harlot. The invitation to the heavens to rejoice appears only here at 12:12 and in 18:20, which announces 19:6. Finally we find the liturgy of God's justice in 16:5–7. Here and in 19:2, God's true and just judgments are acclaimed. In both liturgies the vindication of the blood of the holy ones and prophets (16:6) or of God's servants (19:2) is celebrated.

Four key verbs run through the liturgy in 19:1–8:

v. 2: "God has condemned" (*ékrinen*) the great harlot who corrupted the earth....

v. 2: "God has avenged" (*exedíkesen*) on her the blood of his servants...

v. 6: "the Lord, our God, has established his reign" (*ebasíleusen*)...[4]

v. 7: "For the wedding day of the Lamb has come" (*elthen*), and his bride "has made herself ready" (*hetoimasen*). "She was allowed" (*edothe*) to wear a bright, clean linen garment....

The judgment upon Rome and the vindication of the blood of the martyrs is celebrated in the liturgy in heaven (vv. 1–5), which looks toward the past. In the liturgy on earth (vv. 6–8), which looks toward the future, the coming of the reign and the wedding day of the Lamb is celebrated. The fall of Rome makes possible the beginning of the reign (to be presented in 20:4–6). The parallel between the kingdom of God and the wedding feast is familiar in tradition. In Matthew 22:2 we read: "The kingdom of heaven may be likened to a king who gave a wedding feast for his son" (see Matt. 22:1–14 and Luke 14:15–24). In Isaiah's apocalypse we also have a banquet in which Yahweh "will destroy

---

2. In Revelation, *basileía* (reign) referring to God is found only in 11:15 and 12:10 and *basiléuo* referring to God only in 11:15, 17, and 19:6.

3. The first text uses the verb *dia-phtheiro* (which appears in Revelation only in 8:9 and 11:18), and in the second *phtheiro* is used (the only place in Revelation).

4. This is an incipient aorist: began to reign.

death forever [and] wipe away the tears from all faces" (Isa. 25:6–8). Yahweh's relationship with a new human society expressed in terms of husband and wife is very well known in the Old Testament (see Ezek. 16, Hos. 2, Ps. 45, etc.).

Revelation 19:7–9 speaks of the Lamb's wife (*he guné*), the wedding day of the Lamb, and a wedding feast. This is an anticipation of 21:2: "I also saw the holy city, a new Jerusalem, coming down out of heaven from God, prepared as a bride [*númphen*] adorned [*hetoimasmenen*] for her husband [*to andrí*]," and 21:9: "Come here. I will show you the bride (*numphen*), the wife [*gunaika*] of the Lamb...[the holy city Jerusalem]." Finally, in the epilogue in 22:17 we hear: "The Spirit and the bride say, 'Come!' " Thus we have the man-woman or husband-wife relationship to express the relationship of Jesus as Lamb with the New Jerusalem. The contrast is perfect: the harlot (Babylon-Rome) and the beast standing against the woman (the New Jerusalem) and the Lamb. We are about to see that in the eschatological vision of Revelation, the New Jerusalem is not the church, strictly speaking, but the society that God desires. In the Pauline tradition, and referring to the present age, the bride of Christ is the church (Rom. 7:2–4, 2 Cor. 11:2–3, Eph. 5:25ff.). Revelation 22:17 stands in that same historical context as Paul and also refers to the church.

Final Conclusion: vv. 9–10

Here we come to the end not only of the liturgy but of the whole section that we have entitled "Prophetic vision of history" (17:1–19:10). Revelation 19:9–10 and 17:1–2 are paired, and together they mark the beginning and end of a section. The one speaking in 19:9–10 is the same angel who was speaking in 17:1–2 and is one of the seven angels carrying the seven bowls. Revelation 21:9 and 22:6–9 likewise mark the beginning and end of a section.

The angel's first statement is a beatitude: "Blessed are those who have been called to the wedding feast of the Lamb." In Revelation we have seven beatitudes: 1:3, 14:13, 16:15, 19:9, 20:6, 22:7, and 22:14. This line takes up again in beatitude form the conclusion of the preceding liturgy. Then the angel says, "These words are true; they come from God." We find almost this same expression in 21:5 on God's lips and in 22:6 on Christ's lips. This is a solemn formula for attesting the truthfulness of revelation, and it refers to the whole section (17:1–19:10).

Revelation 19:10 stands in very close parallel to 22:8–9. John tries to adore the angel, but is forbidden to do so:

19:10: Don't. I am a fellow servant of yours and of your brothers who bear witness to Jesus. Worship God.

22:9: Don't. I am a fellow servant of yours and of your brothers the prophets and of those who keep the message of this book. Worship God.

The parallel expression indicates that the prophets are those who bear witness to Jesus. Hence in 19:10 the words "witness to Jesus is the spirit of prophecy" are added. It is likewise obvious that John is a prophet and belongs to a brotherhood of prophets. The angel likens himself to those prophets. The church of Revelation is a church that is basically guided by prophets. The command to adore only God and not the angel demands that we regard church leaders only as servants. We are here warned against absolutizing or divinizing the church. As marvelous as the revelation of the prophets might be, only God is to be adored, not his servants the prophets.

8

Apocalyptic Vision of the Future

Revelation 19:11–22:5

In previous chapters we have analyzed this long "present age" in which the community of Revelation stands, which in the text extends from 4:1 to 19:10. The author has framed this present with a liturgy at the beginning (chapters 4 and 5) and another at the end (19:1–8). In this present the author has already shown us the end: not the end of the world, but *what brings to an end* suffering and persecution in this world. That was what we read at the seventh trumpet (11:15–19) and at the seventh bowl (16:17–21). The seventh trumpet proclaimed to us the coming of the reign and the time for paying recompense to the prophets and the holy ones. The seventh bowl proclaimed the fall of Rome, the great city, the great Babylon. That is what the community is celebrating in the final liturgy in 19:18: God has found the great harlot (Rome) guilty, avenged on her the blood of his servants, and has established his reign, and now the wedding of the Lamb has come. In the prophetic vision of history (6:1–8:1 and 17:1–18:24) this end that brings suffering to an end is told in detail, particularly in 6:12–17 (the wrath of the Lamb that brings about a cosmic cataclysm) and the judgment in chapter 18 (destruction of Rome). None of these is the last judgment; rather they are judgments by which God does justice and ends oppression within history. Similarly in 14:14–20, at the center of Revelation and in the middle of the present age, we find judgment scenes (the harvest, the grape harvest). All these judgments or interventions by God in history to bring an end to suffering are part of the present age, but they are also a foreshadowing of God's last or definitive judgment.

Before the present time (4:1–19:10) stands 1:9–3:22: the vision of the risen Jesus in the midst of the communities (1:9–20) and Jesus' prophetic message to each of the communities (chapters 2–3). This section should not be situated in the past, for it stands at the opening of the present: it is the initial situation, that of the communities on the threshold of the present apocalyptic age that they are going to experience. As the risen Jesus says in the vision: "write what you have seen and what is happening [chapters 2 and 3], and what will happen afterward [4:1–19:10]." In Revelation's overall structure, this initial section *before* the present moment (1:9–3:22) is matched with the section *after* the present moment (19:11–22:5). We have already seen that in the messages to the seven churches, the promise to the victor almost always refers to this final section that we are now going to examine. Moreover, both sections begin with a Christological vision (1:9–20 and 19:11–21): before judging the beasts and the kings of the earth, Jesus judges (discerns, visits) his own communities.

INTRODUCTION TO THE READING AND STRUCTURE OF REVELATION 19:11–22:5

A. The beginning of the future of history: 19:11–20:15

  a. Judgment upon the beast, the false prophet, and the kings of the earth: 19:11–21

    (a) Christ on the white horse: vv. 11–16
        God's great feast: vv. 17–18

    (b) War and annihilation: vv. 19–21

  b. Judgment of Satan and thousand-year reign: 20:1–10

    (a) Satan is tied up for a thousand years: vv. 1–3

        Center: Thousand-year reign: vv. 4–6

    (a') War and annihilation: vv. 7–10

a'. Judgment over the dead, death, and Hades: 20:11–15

    (a') God on the white throne: v. 11
        judgment over the dead: vv. 12–13

    (b') Annihilation of death, of Hades, and of those condemned: vv. 14–15

B. The future of history: 21:1–22:5

  a. New heavens, new earth, new Jerusalem: 21:1–8

description of the city: 21:9–21	– general description: vv. 9–11
	– parts of the city: vv. 12–14
	– forms and measures: vv. 15–17
	– materials: vv. 18–21

a'. Presence of God and of the Lamb: 21:22–22:5

In the text there are two pictures: the first (19:11–20:15) is a somber picture marked by judgment and annihilation, although it has a bright center: the thousand-year reign. The second picture (22:1–22:5) is bright and full of hope, although here as well there are some tragic points that recall the past: 21:8, 27, and 22:3.

In the first picture we have three successive judgments upon (1) the beast, the false prophet, and the kings of the earth; (2) Satan; and (3) the dead, death, and Hades. Christ, riding a white horse, makes the first judgment, and the third is made by God, seated on a white throne. In the first and second judgments those who are going to be judged unleash a war: in 19:19 and 20:9b–10. All the judgments end with an annihilation: at the end of each section the same line is repeated: "they were thrown [*ebléthesan*] into the pool of fire and sulfur." In 19:20b the beast and the false prophet are destroyed; in 20:10 Satan is destroyed; at the end of the third judgment there is a twofold destruction: in 20:14 death and Hades are destroyed, and then in 20:15 those found guilty are destroyed. The first picture is the last of seven visions, containing the expression "Then I saw" (*kai eídon:* 19:11, 17, 19; 20:1, 4, 11, 12) dividing each of the judgments into three parts (the expression is missing from 20:7 and 14, which begins a different part, but not a new vision: 20:7–10 continues the vision in 20:1–3 while 20:14–15 continues the vision from 20:12–13).

We can also divide the second picture (21:1–22:5) into three parts. The first (vv. 1–8) contains two visions, the explanation of the visions, and an oracle from God. The second and larger part (vv. 9–21) presents a description of what the new Jerusalem looks like. The third part (21:22–22:5) shows what cannot be seen there, the universal dimension of the city, the life-giving water, the trees of life, and God's immediate presence in the city. The first and third parts (a and a') are paired. The first match is between 21:1–4 and 22:3–5. The phrase "there shall be no more" (*ouk éstai éti*) is repeated each time:

> ...there shall be no more death or mourning, wailing or pain (21:4)...
> Nothing accursed will be found there anymore.... Night will be no more.
> (22:3, 5)

The reason is that God will dwell in the city (21:3 and 22:3). There is a similar pairing between 21:5–8 and 22:1–2, both of which speak of God's throne and the life-giving water.

KEYS FOR INTERPRETING THE TEXTS

Before looking at each part in detail, it is important to make it clear that the structure of the text that we have examined does not represent a chronological order, a schedule, or a plan. It is a logic rather than a chronology and depicts the logic of God's final intervention in history: it is eschato-logical rather than chrono-logical. It shows us the *ultimate* direction of history, where we are headed, and how the present age comes to an end. As we shall see in greater detail, the author anticipates many of these final events and visions and places them within the present age (4:1–19:10). The future is anticipated. Likewise, the revelation of the future of history is not intended to satisfy unhealthy curiosity, but to make us live the present in a different way. The importance of having a utopia lies not in the utopia in itself, but in how this utopia guides our present history and practice.

Finally, we want to emphasize that in our interpretation of Revelation there is really no second coming of Christ and no end of the world. Rather what we find is a glorious manifestation of Jesus in history. It is not a second "coming" because Jesus has never gone away. There is no end of the world, but rather a new creation. The new heaven and earth and the new Jerusalem is the final stage of history, the triumph or complete fulfillment of history. It is a transcendent state: it lies beyond any human feasibility and beyond death, and yet it is part of our one sole history. There is no end of the world, but rather an end to this world and the creation of a new world. There is no end of history, but rather a new history. Let us now examine all of this in greater detail.

THE BEGINNING OF THE FUTURE OF HISTORY: 19:11–20:15

Christ versus the Beast, the False Prophet, and the Kings of the Earth: 19:11–21

The scene on which we are going to comment is anticipated in 16:13–16 and 17:14. The first passage lies between the sixth and seventh bowl, that is, in the present age (as we noted at that point). In this present age, the "perverse trinity" is at work in an anti-prophetic way:

> ...from the mouth of the dragon, from the mouth of the beast, and from the mouth of the false prophet. These were demonic spirits who performed signs. They went out to the kings of the whole earth [the *oikoumene*].... Then they assembled the kings in the place that is named Armageddon in Hebrew.

This anti-prophetic movement stands as the antithesis of the prophetic movement, which is taking place during this same present age between the sixth and seventh trumpets (10:1–11:13). Hence the present age is witnessing a mortal clash between the prophets and the demons of the structures of evil. This present conflict is resolved in the battle that now takes place in 19:11–21. The site has the mythical name Armageddon. The other passage is 17:14:

> [The kings of the earth] will fight with the Lamb, but the Lamb will conquer them, for he is Lord of lords and King of kings, and those with him are called, chosen, and faithful.

At the center of Revelation (12:1–15:4) we have already observed the Christian community confronting the structures of the empire (the beast and the false prophet). Those who follow the Lamb are here reunited on earth at Mount Zion (14:1–5), and they fight off the beasts while listening to the victory hymns of the martyrs in heaven (12:10–11 and 15:2–4). The final confrontation between Christ and those who belong to him on one side and the beasts and the wicked powers on the other now takes place.

Vision of Christ on the White Horse: vv. 11-16

John sees "the heavens opened." In 4:1 John sees an open door to heaven, and is ordered to go up to heaven. That is merely the beginning of the revelation; now comes the moment for the full revelation. The movement, moreover, is from heaven to earth: the new Jerusalem will come down from heaven to earth and God himself comes to live there. Jesus is riding a white horse. In 14:14 the son of man comes sitting on a white cloud, and in 20:11 God is seated on a white throne. White signifies victory. In 6:2 we saw that the white horse (first of the four horses) represents the Roman empire victorious through violence, economic exploitation, and death. This white horse in 6:2 is the polar opposite of the white horse in 19:11-16; this is parallelism by antithesis. The rider of the white horse "judges and wages war in righteousness." This image of Jesus as a warrior is unusual. We have an antecedent in Isaiah 11:4-5:

> But he [the shoot sprouting from the stump of Jesse]
>> shall judge the poor with justice,
> and decide aright for the land's afflicted.
> He shall strike the ruthless with the rod of his mouth,
>> and with the breath of his lips he shall slay the
>> wicked.
> Justice shall be the band around his waist, and faithful-
>> ness a belt around his hips.

The warrior image of Jesus is somewhat undone since he is presented as unarmed; he does battle with his word alone. In quoting Ps. 2:9 ("he will rule") 19:15 actually uses the word "will shepherd."[1] Thus the image of warrior is softened by that of the shepherd.

The one riding the white horse has three names: in v. 11 he is called "Faithful and True" (*pistós kaí alethinós*); in v. 13 his name is "the Word of God"; and in v. 16 it is "King of kings and Lord of lords." In 1:5 Jesus is called the faithful witness and ruler of the kings of the earth; in 3:15, the faithful and true witness. The title in v. 16 has already appeared in the parallel text 17:14. In v. 15 it is said that with his word — a sharp sword coming from his mouth — Jesus wounds the nations and obliterates the kings of the earth. The centrality of the word in this battle/trial is thus accentuated, as is its political dimension. Jesus is wearing "many diadems" on his head. Satan has seven diadems (12:3) and the beast has ten (13:1). Like his names or titles, Jesus' diadems emphasize his political supremacy. His "eyes" are like "a fiery flame." These eyes and the sword coming from his mouth place this vision of Jesus on the white horse in parallel with the vision of the risen Jesus in the midst of the communities in 1:9-20.

Jesus wears "a cloak dipped in blood" (v. 13); "he himself will tread out in the wine press the wine of the fury and wrath of God" (v. 15). These lines draw their inspiration from Isaiah 63:1-6 (showing how God tramples the enemy peoples in rage and lets their blood run upon the ground; the blood stains his garment;

---

1. The Septuagint uses "to shepherd" while the Hebrew text uses "to break."

the image of the wine presser treading the wine press is also used). This is a violent text, although the author of Revelation radically changes it in applying it to Jesus. He frees us and defeats his enemies by dying as a faithful martyr on the cross. The martyrs conquer Satan, "by the blood of the Lamb and by the word of their testimony" (12:11). His blood has freed us (1:5); he purchased us with his blood (5:9); the martyrs have washed their robes in the blood of the Lamb (7:14). The blood with which Jesus' garment is soaked is his own. It cannot be the blood of the wine press because he has not yet trod it; the same literary device is used when the risen Jesus is presented as the "Lamb that seemed to have been slain" (5:6): it is the risen Christ still bearing the marks of his martyrdom on the cross. The allusion to the winepress simply means that Jesus is now the one who carries out the judgment that God carried out in the Old Testament. Jesus effects this judgment on the cross, and he struggles by means of the power of his word alone. He is not alone in combat, since "the armies of heaven follow him, mounted on white horses and wearing clean white linen." It is the martyrs who follow (*akolouthein*) Jesus. This is clear in the parallel text, 17:14: when Jesus conquers the kings of the earth, "those with him are called, chosen, and faithful." They dress just like the bride of the Lamb (19:8), and the linen represents the righteous deeds (*dikaiómata*) of the holy ones (19:8). In 2:26–27 Jesus promises to give the victor "authority over the nations. He will rule them with an iron rod" (same words in 19:15; cf. 1 Cor. 6:2: "Do you not know that the holy ones will judge the world?")

God's Great Feast: vv. 17–18

"God's great feast" here is the antithesis of the wedding feast of the Lamb (19:9). The word "feast" (*deipnon*) appears only in these two places in Revelation. One either participates in the wedding feast of the Lamb as a guest or is on the menu at God's feast. This symbol of the feast is taken from Ezekiel 39:17–20: God invites the birds and wild animals of the fields to a sacrifice to eat the flesh and blood of heroes, princes, and warriors. Things are turned completely upside down: those who are normally victims to be sacrificed (birds and wild animals) are invited as persons to eat in the sacrifice, while those who normally do the sacrificing (heroes, princes, and warriors) are involved in the sacrifice as victims.[2]

In Revelation the feast is announced with something solemn and universal: "an angel standing on the sun." The menu is the flesh of kings (*basileis*), military officers (*chilíarchoi:* commanders of a thousand, something comparable to generals in an army today), the powerful (*íschuroi*), and cavalry soldiers.[3] Thus political, military, and economic power are all here presented as victims to be

---

2. The literary context in Ezekiel of this feast with the tables turned is like that of Revelation: the dry bones (Ezek. 37), the war against Gog, king of Magog (Ezek. 38–39), and the plan for a future rebuilding of the temple (Ezek. 40–48). The corresponding elements in Revelation are the resurrection of the martyrs (Rev. 11:11 and 20:4–6), the war of Gog and Magog (20:7–10), and the new Jerusalem (Rev. 21–22). There are notable differences as well.

3. Kings, nobles, and military officers appear in the list in Revelation 6:15. Almost the same groups are at Herod's banquet, when John the Baptist is sacrificed (Mark 6:21).

eaten at God's feast (the word "flesh" is repeated five times). The table guests are the birds, conceivably vultures or buzzards (who eat dead flesh). Many think that this feast should be at the end of v. 21, where the birds are said to be eating the bodies after the war, to indicate that the dead are not buried. That is not what God's feast means, however. The antithesis with the wedding feast of the Lamb and the background in Ezekiel give this feast of God a much deeper meaning (hence its centrality in the structure of 19:11–21): those who do not participate as persons in the wedding feast of the Lamb will participate as beasts sacrificed at God's eschatological feast.

War and Destruction: vv. 19–21

The beast, the kings of the earth, and their armies (*stratéumata*) now reappear in a new vision, assembling to make war (*pólemos*) on Christ and his army (*stratéumata*). The two armies stand facing one another, but war does not ensue because the beast and the false prophet are caught and destroyed in the fiery pool burning with sulfur. Why is there no war? Because the war has now been won by Jesus' martyrdom on the cross and the witness of Christians: "They conquered him by the blood of the Lamb and by the word of their testimony" (12:11). Verse 20 offers a marvelous summary of chapter 13:11–18. Many have regarded this absence of war as meaning that Revelation does not envision activity within history. Quite to the contrary, there is no war precisely because such activity is so overwhelming. It is Christ's martyr activity and the practice of Christians that hasten the defeat of Satan and the beasts.

Judgment upon Satan and Thousand-year Reign: 20:1–10

We are now at the center of the section that we have titled "the beginning of the future of history" (19:11–20:15). This center is situated between the vision of Christ riding the white horse (19:11–21) and the vision of God on the white throne (20:11–15). We find two different stories, that of Satan and that of the martyrs. The author inserts the story of the martyrs into that of Satan to connect them. The story of Satan begins in vv. 1–3 and continues in vv. 7–10. This story can stand by itself outside the reign of the martyrs. The connection between the two stories is that the thousand-year reign occurs while Satan is locked up in the abyss for a thousand years.

Story of Satan: vv. 1–3 and 7–10

In Revelation, the story of Satan is told through several stages:

1. Satan in heaven: he fails to kill the Messiah at his birth (12:1–6).

2. Satan is thrown down to earth. Michael, symbolizing the martyrs, defeats Satan, who goes down to earth in great fury, knowing that he has but a short time (12:7–12).

3. Satan on earth: he directly persecutes the Christian community, but fails destroy it (12:13–17); he then gives his power to the beast (13:2); out

of his mouth as from the mouth of the beast and the false prophet come forth the spirits of demons to assemble the kings of the earth for the great battle at Armageddon (16:13–16).

4. Satan is thrown down from the earth into the abyss for a thousand years, is released for a short time, and then is destroyed. This is the story that we have here in 20:1–3 and 7–10: an angel overpowered Satan, enchained him for a thousand years, threw him into the abyss, locking and sealing it, so that he would no longer lead the nations astray and assemble them for war; they rose up against the holy ones, but fire came down from heaven and consumed them, and Satan was thrown down into the pool of fire and sulfur.

This downhill story of Satan evidences Revelation's optimism about history. Chapter 12 and the present passage are paired to form an enclosure. Let us now examine some details from this last stage. The "angel coming down from heaven" in v. 1 reminds us of the angel in 10:1 and 18:1, 21; the angel symbolizes God's transcendent action in human history. The "abyss" where Satan is held previously appeared in 9:1, 2, 11: a star fallen from heaven (possibly Satan himself) has the key to the abyss and opens it, letting out locusts who have as their king the angel of the abyss whose name means Destruction. In 11:7 and 17:8 the beast comes up out of the abyss (in 13:1 he comes out of the sea). Verse 2 reminds us of all Satan's names: the dragon, the ancient serpent, the devil; John does the same in 12:9. Satan's function is to "seduce," deceive, mislead (*planáo*): thus it is in 12:9 and here in vv. 3, 8, and 10. Five verbs are used to describe the imprisonment of Satan: the angel "seized" (*ekrátesen*) Satan, "tied him up" (*édesen*), "threw him down" (*ébalen*), "locked him up" (*ékleisen*), and "sealed him" (*esphrágisen*). This is a high security operation.

After a thousand years Satan is "released." Verse 3 says that he "is to be released" (*dei luthénai*), thus indicating compliance with the will of God who is directing this entire history. Verse 7 takes up where v. 3 left off. Satan is released and "goes out to deceive the nations at the four corners of the earth.... to gather them for battle" (*pólemos*). This is a political action by Satan. Gog and Magog are also involved at this point. These mythical figures are taken from Ezekiel 38–39 (Gog from the land of Magog): Gog attacks Israel when it has returned from exile and is living in security. Gog expresses the persistence of the power of evil, a power that only God can destroy and that is continually lying in wait for God's people.

Satan and his own "come up" (*anébesan*) from the abyss and fire "comes down" (*katébe*) from heaven and consumes them. We see here that coming up is demoniacal and coming down is salvific. Satan is the monster coming up from the abyss; and God's design is the holy city coming down from heaven. Satan and his own "surrounded the camp of the holy ones and the beloved city." This place symbolizes the place on earth where Christians gather (recall 11:1–2 and 14:1–5) and it anticipates chapters 21–22. After Satan and the powers of evil are consumed, Satan is destroyed in the pool of fire and sulfur. This rise of Satan to make war and his subsequent destruction remind us of the existence of the beast in 17:8: "The beast that you saw existed once but now exists no longer. It will come up from the abyss and is headed for destruction." Such is the fate of Satan, the beast, and all the powers of evil, and that is why he is joined to the beast and the false prophet in being destroyed in the pool of fire and sulfur (v. 10). Thus concludes the story of Satan, within which Revelation situates the thousand-year reign.

The Thousand-year Reign: vv. 4-6

Reading and Explication of the Text: We stand before an important passage, one that has had a long history, a text whose liberating power has mobilized many people, especially the poor and oppressed, throughout the history of Christianity. It is likewise a controversial text, heavily apocalyptic in genre and style. We will begin with a careful reading of the text. We present the entire passage (20:4–6) in a literal and grammatically orderly translation for better understanding:

v. 4   I saw some thrones
and those who were seated on them
were granted power to do justice.[4]
I also saw alive[5] those who were beheaded,
for their witness to Jesus and to the Word of God,
and all those who did not worship the beast nor its image
and had not accepted its mark on their forehead or hand;
they came to life[6] and reigned with Christ for a thousand years.

v. 5   The rest of the dead did not come to life
until the thousand years were over.

v. 6   Blessed and holy
is the one who shares in the first resurrection;
over these the second death has no power,
but they will be priests of God and of Christ,
and will reign with him for a thousand years.

Sitting on the thrones are those who were beheaded and who did not adore the beast; now it is said that they are alive. They are granted the power to do "justice." The word justice (*krima*), which we have here translated as "power to do justice," is used three times in Revelation: here in 20:4; in 17:1: "Come here.

---

4. The Greek text reads *krima edothe autois. Krima* literally means judgment, but it denotes the power or authority to do justice. It is the holy ones who sit on the thrones and it is they who do justice.

5. Based on the *Nueva Biblia Española*. Literally the text reads: I saw the souls (*eídon tas psychas*). Souls cannot be seen, and the term *psyché* normally designates life. We find the same expression in a parallel text in Revelation 6:9: I saw alive those slain for the sake of the Word of God.

6. Literally: "they lived." It is not simply coming back to life, but rather implies resurrection. See Revelation 2:8: Jesus was dead and lived (*ézesen*).

I will show you the judgment on the great harlot"; and in 18:20: (speaking to the holy ones) "For God has judged your case against her." At this point it is not God, but the risen ones who have the power to do justice.

Those who do justice in 20:4 are the martyrs, the same ones mentioned in 6:9: "I saw ... the souls of those who had been slaughtered because of the witness they bore to the Word of God." They cry out for God to sit in judgment (verb *krino*) and avenge (verb *ek-dikéo*) their blood. When God destroys Rome he is doing justice for the holy ones, the apostles, and the prophets (18:20), which is likewise the motive of the liturgy in 19:1–8; see especially v. 2: God has judged (*ékrinen*) the harlot (Rome) and has avenged (*exedíkesen*) the blood of his servants. These same martyrs appear in 7:9–17:

A great multitude ... stood before the throne and before the Lamb. ...
"These are the ones who have survived the time of great distress; they have washed their robes and made them white in the blood of the Lamb."

They are also the ones mentioned in 12:11: "They conquered him by the blood of the Lamb; and by the word of their testimony; love for life did not deter them from death." Similarly, it is they who are victorious in 15:2–4: "I saw ... those who had won the victory over the beast and its image and the number that signified its name." All these martyrs died for their faith and now they arise to do justice. In Revelation Jesus himself appears as the first martyr (1:5 and 3:14), he who once died but came back to life (2:8).

In 20:4 we find the reason for the death of the martyrs: they were beheaded

... for their witness to Jesus and for the word of God, and [they] had not worshiped the beast or its image nor had accepted its mark on their foreheads or hands.

The first motive is found in 6:9; the second in 15:2–4. The number of those who do not adore the beast may be greater than that of the beheaded martyrs; many of them may not have been beheaded but they are nonetheless martyrs. All of these are martyrs who have died, whatever may have been the manner of their death. In Revelation there are also martyrs who are still alive on earth. The word "martyr" means "witness," and does not necessarily imply a violent death but rather the willingness to give testimony even to the point of death. There is little difference between a living martyr and one who is dead. The living martyrs in Revelation are first John, who "gives witness [*emartúresen*] to the word of God and to the testimony [*martyría*] of Jesus Christ" (1:2); that is why he is exiled on the island of Patmos (1:9). The devil wages war on earth "against ... those who keep God's commandments and bear witness [*martyría*] to Jesus" (12:17). In 11:3–13 we see the two martyr-prophets representing the whole prophet and martyr church. There is no difference between prophet and martyr, since the prophets are those who "bear witness [*martyría*] to Jesus," which is the spirit of prophecy (19:10). These martyrs who at this moment are still alive will one day die, but they also, because they are martyrs, hope to share in the first resurrection and in the thousand-year reign.

The martyrs "came to life," and, speaking of them, the text adds, "Blessed and holy is the one who shares in the first resurrection." It is explicitly stated that "the rest of the dead did not come to life." The verb "they came to life," which literally means simply "they lived" (*ézesan*), does not have the ordinary meaning of coming back to life, but the emphatic meaning of resurrection. The same verb is used for Jesus' resurrection: "[he] once died but came to life" (*ézesen,* 2:8); similarly in 1:18 "[I am]...the one who lives. Once I was dead, but now I am alive [*zon eimi*]." If we take the meaning of the text seriously, we must understand that the martyrs arise just as Jesus. Hence Jesus is confessed to be "the faithful martyr, the firstborn [*ho protótokos*] of the dead and ruler of the kings of the earth" (1:5). He is called the firstborn, that is, the first to rise from among the dead; others are going to rise after him. This resurrection of the martyrs at the beginning of the thousand-year reign, a thousand years before the final judgment, when all the other dead will arise, is called the first resurrection. It is furthermore stated that the risen martyrs

> ...reigned [*ebasíleusan*] with Christ for a thousand years....they will be priests of God and of Christ, and they will reign with him for [the] thousand years.

There are two ideas here: first the idea of the reign, a joint reign by the Messiah (Christ) and the risen martyrs. This reign is here on earth, in our history, before the final judgment, and it lasts a thousand years. The second idea is that those who have risen reign as priests of God and of Christ. Those who now rise and reign with Christ will have no part in the "second death." In 21:8 we are told that the second death is the burning pool of fire and sulfur, that is, definitive death, returning to nonbeing. The martyrs who died and who now arise for the thousand-year reign have been judged already and are certain that after the thousand years they can enter directly into the new heavens and new earth, into the new Jerusalem.

Overall Interpretation of the Thousand-year Reign: Interpretations of this thousand-year reign currently tend to go in opposite directions: they are either fundamentalist or spiritualizing. The *fundamentalist interpretation* reduces the interpretation of the text to its literal meaning: the thousand-year reign will be a real reign of Christ with his church here on earth, a visible, political reign within history for a thousand years before the last judgment. Christ's second coming will inaugurate this reign. This interpretation is common today within sectarian religious movements and in some neoconservative movements that are both political and religious. The *spiritualizing interpretation,* by contrast, reduces the text to its spiritual meaning: the thousand-year reign is the time of the church between the resurrection of Jesus and the last judgment; the first resurrection is spiritual and takes place at baptism; only the second resurrection is bodily. This interpretation is common in the historical churches, and especially in the Catholic church.

For the first three centuries of Christianity, the prevailing interpretation of the thousand-year reign is on the literal side, along the lines of Jewish apocalyptic. Some interpretations are indeed radical, in a gross millennialism that is generally rejected as heretical. A moderate millennialism nonetheless is part of the church while it retains its original prophetic and apocalyptic inspiration. With the emperor Constantine and the rise of Christendom in the fourth century, the church rejects the original apocalyptic traditions and a purely symbolic interpretation of the thousand-year reign arises. With St. Augustine (d. 430) a spiritualizing interpretation takes hold in the church and it has continued to the present. The original interpretations nonetheless survived in the church, for example, in Joachim of Fiore (d. 1202) whose millennialism was to influence the spiritual Franciscans and later those Franciscans who were to come to the Americas after 1492. The Hussite and Anabaptist movements were also millenarian. The Catholic Church today rejects radical millennialism.

Our interpretation of the thousand-year reign seeks to be faithful to the Jewish and Christian apocalyptic tradition. We are seeking an interpretation that is neither fundamentalist nor spiritualizing, but one in tune with the apocalyptic and prophetic tradition of Christianity during the first three centuries and likewise with the entire apocalyptic tradition in the Bible extending from Daniel to the book of Revelation, respecting the literal, historical, and spiritual meaning of the text.

The immediate background of the text of Revelation is the book of Daniel, where in chapter 7 we find the clash between the empires, represented by the beasts, with the people of the holy ones of the Most High represented by a human figure ("like a son of man"). God's judgment is described: "the Ancient One arrived to do justice in favor of the holy ones of the Most High,[7] and the time came when the holy ones possessed the kingdom" (Dan. 7:22). God's justice consists in the destruction of the empires, represented by the beasts, and in the handing over of the reign to the people of the holy ones, represented by the human figure (see Dan. 7:14, 26–27. God's judgment is not the end of the world, but the end of the empires and the beginning of God's reign within this world and our history. God ends the oppression of the empires and of Antiochus IV Epiphanes and gives the reign of God to the holy ones. We have the same pattern in chapter 2 of Daniel: a stone that destroys the statue (symbol of the empires) becomes a great mountain, which is the reign of God (see 2:34–35, 44). In chapters 8 and 9 of Daniel the end is followed by the restoration of the sanctuary. In Daniel 12:1–3 the theology is developed further: after the death of Antiochus IV Epiphanes, Michael assures the salvation of the people. The text then reads:

---

7. The Greek text of the Septuagint (version of Theodosion) says: *krima édoken hagíois.* Revelation 20:4 reads *krima edothe autois.* In Daniel the verb is active: God does justice on behalf of the saints. In Revelation the verb is passive: the martyrs receive the power to do justice.

Many of those who sleep
  in the dust of the earth shall awake;
Some shall live forever,
others shall be an everlasting horror and disgrace.

The holy ones are truly resurrected (see also Isa. 26:19). The wicked do not arise, but awaken as corpses to suffer horror and eternal disgrace. The most outstanding of the holy ones are those who lead the many to justice, those who not only arise, but who also shine like the stars. The reign of God and the resurrection of the holy ones takes place on earth, and it is as historical as the restoration of the sanctuary in chapters 8 and 9. An apocalyptic pattern of history begins with Daniel: period of persecution (rule of the beasts), judgment of God bringing oppression to an end, resurrection of the holy ones and beginning of God's reign. All subsequent apocalyptic literature repeats this pattern.[8] This pattern of a messianic reign on the earth is also found in the prophets: see Isaiah 11:1–9 and 65:17–25, Ezekiel 33–39, etc.

In many places the New Testament points toward this reign of God on earth before the last judgment. In Matthew 19:28 we read:

Amen, I say to you that you who have followed me, in the new age [*paliggenesía* = "regeneration"] when the son of man is seated on his throne of glory, will yourselves sit on twelve thrones, judging the twelve tribes of Israel.

"Regeneration" means moving from death to life, collectively: the world that comes back to live after the flood or the rebirth of the people of Israel after the exile.[9] The parallel text in Luke (22:28–30) reads:

It is you who have stood by me in my trials; and I confer a kingdom on you, just as my Father has conferred one on me, that you may eat and drink at my table in my kingdom; and you will sit on thrones judging the twelve tribes of Israel.[10]

To judge (*krino*) means to do justice: to liberate the oppressed and convict the oppressors. In the reign of God (Luke) or on the day of resurrection (Matthew), Jesus' disciples render justice over the people of Israel. The same idea appears in Acts 3:21:

---

8. Pablo Richard, "El Pueblo de Dios contra el Imperio: Daniel 7 en su contexto literario e histórico," *Revista de Interpretación Bíblica Latinoamericana* (San José, Costa Rica-Santiago de Chile) 7 (1991): 25–46.

9. See F. Büchsel *paliggenesía* in *Theologisches Wörterbuch Neues Testamentes* 1, 685.

10. Matthew and Luke follow Q, which may have said: "You who have followed me ... in the kingdom will sit upon twelve thrones, to judge the twelve tribes of Israel." See Ivan Havener, *Q: The Sayings of Jesus,* Good News Studies 19 (Collegeville, Minn.: Liturgical Press, 1986).

...Jesus, whom heaven must receive until the times of universal restoration [*apokatástasis*] of which God spoke through the mouth of his holy prophets from of old.

This restoration originally referred to the restoration of God's people after the exile. Later it was projected into a time to come, when the Messiah would bring about universal restoration. Jesus' parousia was to be for the sake of that restoration, which coincides with Matthew's regeneration (*paliggenesis*) and with the setting up of the reign of God that Luke speaks about. Likewise in Mark (13:24–27) the son of man comes not for the last judgment or the end of the world but for the assembly of all his elect. Revelation 20:4–6 fits into this apocalyptic tradition coming down from Daniel and reflected in the synoptic tradition. At the time of regeneration (Matthew), at the time of the kingdom (Luke), or at the time of the universal restoration (Acts), which begins with Jesus' resurrection, the disciples are involved in the reign of Jesus and judgment over the people of Israel. The same thing can be seen in 1 Corinthians 15:21–26:

In Christ all [shall] be brought to life, but each one in proper order: Christ the first fruit; then, at his coming, those who belong to Christ; then comes the end, when he hands over the kingdom to his God and Father, when he has destroyed every sovereignty and every authority and power.... The last enemy to be destroyed is death.

In Revelation this tradition is embodied in a clearer and more historical form. The reign described in Revelation 20:4–6 is being announced from the very beginning of the book. Revelation 1:6 salutes Jesus Christ "who has made us into a kingdom, priests for his God and Father." Here the whole community is acknowledged to be a reign (*basileía*) and to be a power, and all are priests for God. This is not a "reign of priests," but a community established with power, in which all are priests (idea taken from Exod. 19:6 and Isa. 61:6). Also in 5:9–10:

with your blood you purchased for God
those from every tribe and tongue, people and nation.
You made them a kingdom and priests for our God,
and they reign [var. will reign] on earth.

In these two texts the present community is made into a reign: it has power to reign and in it all are priests. This present reality of the community made possible even now in time, thanks to the death and resurrection of Christ, proclaims the reign of Christ with the martyrs described in 20:4–6. In 3:21 we find a promise that clearly proclaims the reality of the end: "I will give the victor the right to sit with me on my throne, as I myself first won the victory and sit with my Father on his throne." We later have an explicit reference to the reign of the Messiah and of God in the seventh trumpet. We already noted, when commenting on that passage, that the seventh trumpet announced not the end of the world, but the end of oppression in this world and the beginning of God's reign:

> The kingdom of the world now belongs to our Lord and to his Anointed,
> and he will reign forever and ever.... We give thanks to you.... For
> you have assumed your great power and have established your reign
> [*ebasíleusas*]. (11:15–17)

This text also proclaims the thousand-year reign.

We thus have a single tradition extending from Daniel to Revelation and cul-
minating in Revelation 19:11–20:15. All the passages are about a reign of the
Messiah together with the holy ones on earth. This reign comes after the beasts
are destroyed (Dan. 7 and Rev. 19:11–21), after the seventh trumpet sounds and
brings the present age to an end. Throughout the apocalyptic tradition, this reign
is a time of hope. What kind of reign is this? We rejected the literal interpretation of a radical millennialism as found in fundamentalist sects, but we likewise
rejected the purely symbolic interpretation that spiritualizes the thousand-year
reign. This latter interpretation is characteristic of an established church that
his lost its original apocalyptic and prophetic inspiration. We proposed a prophetic and apocalyptic interpretation of the thousand-year reign consistent with
the original tradition of Judaism and Christianity — but what kind of a reign
is that?

Briefly, we may say that the thousand-year reign is the utopia of all those
who struggle against the idolatry and oppression of empires in order to establish
God's reign on earth. It is the hope of a community that believes in a God who
does justice now in history, a God who destroys empires and gives power to
the people of the holy ones and the martyrs. In general, it is the utopia of the
poor and oppressed that *ultimately* it is possible to bring about order in this
world, to restore the order of God the creator and of the liberating Messiah
Jesus. The utopia of the thousand-year reign has nothing to do with destructive
and horrifying visions of the end of the world. This vision is not about the end
of the world, but about a reign of God that ends the idolatry and criminality of
empires in this world. This is not a passive utopia, since essential to it is that
the martyrs, the holy ones, and all those who did not adore the beast and did
not accept its mark be incorporated into the reign of the Messiah. It is not a
violent and vengeful utopia, for the martyrs arise to reign as a people of priests
of God and of Christ: they are not warriors, nor are they a power elite, since
this is a priesthood encompassing the entire people of the saints. This utopia
is also complex: before the thousand-year reign, Rome/Babylon will have been
judged, thus bringing the present age to an end (chapter 18). Likewise, before
the reign we have the glorious manifestation (parousia) of Jesus, who destroys
the beast, the false prophet, and the kings of the earth who are loyal to the beast
(19:11–21).

The thousand-year reign comes into being at a time when Satan is defeated:
before the reign Satan is chained and thrown into the abyss (20:1–3); after the
reign, Satan is released, goes out to battle the holy ones, and is destroyed (20:7–
10). Then, after the thousand-year reign comes the last judgment: destruction
of the cosmos, judgment upon the dead, and destruction of death and Hades
(20:11–15). Finally, we have the new creation: the new heaven and earth and the

new Jerusalem. The utopia of the thousand-year reign is a transcendent utopia: it is beyond all human possibility and feasibility and assumes that the parousia of Jesus and bodily resurrection of the martyrs have taken place. The fact that this utopia is transcendent does not make it un-historical: the thousand-year reign is beyond the destruction of Babylon and the beasts and the defeat of Satan, but it is not beyond history; it takes place in history and is part of our history.

The utopia of the thousand-year reign is expressed in symbols, but a purely symbolic interpretation that would deny this utopia its historical actuality is not thereby justified. The symbols point to a reality in history: in Daniel 7, for example, the beasts symbolize empires and the human figure symbolizes the people of the holy ones. The term "thousand-year reign" in Revelation 20:4–6 is likewise symbolic: it designates a particular completed period of history (according to the rabbis, human history would have seven millennia, like the seven days of creation: the thousand-year reign would be the last millennium of human history). Not everything is symbolic, however: the resurrection of the martyrs is as real as that of Christ; the judgment that the martyrs are to make is as real as God's judgment throughout salvation history; and Christ's reign with the martyrs is just as real.

Thus, although the utopia of the thousand-year reign is transcendent and is beyond all human feasibility, a spiritualizing and ahistorical interpretation of that utopia is not thereby justified. As we said, the utopia is beyond oppression and death, but not beyond history, for it takes place in history: it is the final stage of history before the last judgment. We may also say that the utopia is historical in the sense that it gives direction to our present history; it is beyond all human possibility, but nevertheless guides our human activity and thinking in a particular direction; the utopia is transcendent, but it actually makes us live history differently. The utopia is beyond death and depends on God's action, but it can also be advanced and lived now in the symbols of faith. The first resurrection of the martyrs is not symbolic but is as real as that of Jesus, and yet it can be lived symbolically in baptism. Baptism is not the first resurrection (as St. Augustine said, thus denying the real and utopian character of this resurrection), but it does announce that resurrection symbolically and enables us even now to live in faith and sacrament that first resurrection that marks the beginning of the millennium.

The real and historical character of the utopia does not entail a literal and material interpretation of the thousand-year reign, as maintained by fundamentalists and in gross or radical millennialism. The thousand-year reign is not a stage situated chrono-logically in history, with exact beginning and ending dates. We already said that the section of Revelation extending from 19:11 to 22:5 is not a chronology but a logic: it is the rationality or logic of what is to happen at the end of history. This vision is not chrono-logical but eschato-logical. We have here the meaning or ordering of what will happen when history reaches its fullness. Revelation 19:11–22:5 symbolically organizes the future, and it represents the utopia in a historical manner; it is a symbolic plan for transcendent hope; it is a utopian reconstruction of consciousness, a reconstruction of consciousness that takes its bearings from utopia. The meaning of Revelation is perverted and destroyed when we put dates on Jesus' parousia, on the thousand-year reign, or on the (misnamed) end of the world. Such an effort to set dates and establish precise stages is an idolatrous effort that reifies the future and destroys the utopian and transcendent meaning of Revelation. Jesus asks us for vigilance, not fortune telling; he asks us to discern the signs of the times, but God alone knows the time of fullness:

> But of that day and hour no one knows, neither the angels of heaven, nor the Son, but the Father alone. (Matt. 24:36)

Revelation makes known to us the meaning of history in order to maintain hope and utopia alive, not to sow fear and terror:

> But when these signs begin to happen, stand erect and raise your heads because your redemption is at hand. (Luke 21:28)

Final Judgment upon the Dead, Death, and Hades: 20:11–15

There are three parts to this judgment: the vision of the white throne (v. 11), the judgment upon the dead (vv. 12–13), and a threefold destruction of death, of Hades, and of those convicted (vv. 14–15). God appears seated (*kathémenon*) on a large white throne, in a parallel with 19:11, where Jesus is seen riding (*kathémeonos*) a white horse. White is a symbol of victory. In 19:11–16 Jesus is followed by the martyrs (see 17:14), mounted on white horses. Jesus battles the beast, the false prophet, and the kings of the earth. In 20:11 God appears alone, and in fact "the earth and sky flee from his presence." God is alone in a cosmic emptiness. Where Jesus battles living powers, God now judges the dead, death, and Hades. Between the judgment by Jesus (19:11–21) and the judgment by God (20:11–15), other thrones make their appearance, and on them the martyrs are seated in order to do justice during the thousand-year reign (20:4–6).

Verse 12 speaks of "the dead." There is no explicit mention of resurrection, but it is mentioned in 20:5: "The rest of the dead did not come back to life until the thousand years were over." The dead are "standing" (*hestótas*), thus suggesting their resurrection. The dead are judged "by what was written in the scrolls." These scrolls represent God's memory — God forgets nothing. Everything done by humankind is written down. Things do not happen because they are written (there is no predestination here), but they are written because they happen. This memory of God inspires hope in the righteous and terror in the wicked. Twice it is said that they "were judged according to their deeds." At judgment it is not people's good ideas or intentions that count but what they do; it is orthopraxis that saves us, not orthodoxy. In addition to the scrolls (plural), there is also "the book of life." Revelation 13:8 speaks of those who adore the beast, "whose names were not written from the foundation of the world in the book of life, which belongs to the Lamb who was slain" (similarly in 17:8). In 3:5, Jesus promises the victor that he will never erase his name from the book of life. The only ones who enter the new Jerusalem are those "whose names are written in the Lamb's book of life" (21:27). The use of this term is traditional (see Exod. 32:32, Ps. 139:16, Luke 10:20, Phil. 4:3, Heb. 12:23). The book of life is not a registry of works but is more personal in nature, and in Revelation it appears as a book that belongs to the Lamb. It is not a book containing the names of those predetermined, those whom God is to have decided shall be saved from the beginning of the world. Those who appear in the book of life are those who have made an option for life and for the God of life. This book is mentioned here in 20:12 to give hope and to take away the fear of those who have chosen life.

Verse 13 has, as it were, a second judgment, a repetition of the one made in v. 12. I do not think that these are two judgments nor is it a case of superimposed literary sources. The repetition enables the author to bring in the sea, death, and Hades (*ho hades*). The sea had not yet fled, as had the earth and sky in v. 11, for it had not yet given up its dead. It disappears in 21:1. Death and Hades are annihilated. Finally, anyone who chose death, that is, "anyone whose name was not written in the book of life," is annihilated. The annihilation of death is especially important in this final vision of history. It comes back in 21:4: "there shall be no more death or mourning, wailing or pain, for the old order has passed away." The same thing was already announced in Revelation 7:17 and in the beautiful passages in Isaiah 25:8 and 35:10. This is also explicit in 1 Corinthians 15:26: "The last enemy to be destroyed is death." The definitive death of death is a bright sign of hope in this somber "last judgment" scene.

THE FUTURE OF HISTORY: 21:1–22:5

Let us begin with a careful reading of the text. To that end, we recall and broaden the structure already noted at the beginning:

a. New heavens, new earth, new Jerusalem: 21:1–8

description of the city: 21:9–21
- general description: vv. 9–11
- parts of the city: vv. 12–14
- forms and measures: vv. 15–17
- materials: vv. 18–21

a'. Presence of God and of the Lamb: 21:22–22:5

Here John is presenting us the future of history in its final stage in a striking reconstruction of heaven, of utopia, and of hope. In this final section of Revelation, the author finishes rebuilding the awareness of the community, which is now listening to the book being read. At this point we offer some keys for interpretation, section by section.

A New World

The terms "heaven" and "earth" do not have a mythical meaning here, but are used to designate the cosmos or nature as a whole. John sees a "new" cosmos. This cosmos is new because "the former heaven and the former earth have passed away" (there is an allusion to 20:1b). It is also stated that "the old order has passed away" (v. 4). The first and second cosmos stand in opposition. A new Jerusalem is also mentioned. What does it mean that the cosmos and Jerusalem are new? Five very similar sentences provide us with the answer:

> The sea was no more (21:1).
> There shall be no more death (21:4).
> There shall be no more mourning, wailing, or pain (21:4).
> Nothing accused will be found there anymore (22:3).
> Night will be no more (22:5 and 21:25).

These sentences all mean practically the same thing. Sea and night here have a cosmic and mythical meaning. The sea is identified with the abyss. In 11:7 and 17:8, the beast rises out of the abyss. In 13:1 the beast emerges from the sea. In 9:1, 2, 11 and in 20:1, 3 the abyss is a satanic place, the place were Satan is locked up. The sea symbolizes chaos. In the new cosmos, the sea, the abyss, and chaos are all destroyed. The new creation defeats chaos. Night, which is synonymous with darkness, has a similar mythical meaning. God definitively defeats the darkness and illuminates with his presence those dwelling in the new Jerusalem (22:5; see John 9:4–5, which speaks of night in a mythical sense when no one can work and in which Jesus defines himself as the light of the world; see also John 1:4–5: "this light was the light of the human race; the light shines in the darkness, and the darkness has not overcome it").

The definitive defeat of death (announced in 20:14; cf. Isa. 25:8; 1 Cor. 15:26) is also revealed. The cosmos is new because life in this cosmos has defeated death; life is said to be victorious beyond death. It is similarly stated that every "mourning, wailing, and pain," has been banished. This refers to the collective cry of the people, like the cry of the people in Egypt (Exod. 3:7). In the new cosmos and in the New Jerusalem there is no exploitation or oppression. Moreover, "He will wipe every tear from their eyes" (v. 4). God does this only for those who have tears in their eyes, that is, for those who had compassion and wept over the oppression and the cry of the people. There is nothing "accursed" (*katáthema* in Greek; *jejem* in Hebrew) there any more. This is a reference to Zechariah 14:10: "There will be no further curse: Jerusalem shall abide in security." The curse weighing over the earth since the beginning (Gen. 3:17) is overcome.

In short, earth and heaven are new and Jerusalem is new, because life triumphs over death, order over chaos, and light over darkness within them; compassion is victorious over all wailing, crying, and pain; and there is no longer any curse. What is transcended here is not matter or bodiliness, but death, chaos, darkness, suffering, the curse; heaven, earth, and city remain; history continues, but now with death and the curse removed.

The Holy City, the New Jerusalem

The Holy City

The new Jerusalem is first of all a *city*. Revelation no longer speaks of the Jerusalem of history, which had been destroyed in 70 C.E. and which John regarded as comparable to Sodom and Egypt as symbols of Rome, since Jesus had been crucified in Jerusalem (11:8). In Revelation Jerusalem is a myth, a symbol for the people of God or the community. In 11:1–2 (as we saw when discussing that passage) the prophet John protects the community, symbolically called a holy city. In 14:1 Mount Zion also symbolizes the assembly site of the community of those who follow the Lamb. The symbol of Jerusalem as a city expresses community, people, humankind organized; today we might speak of social relationships or a vision or model of society. Chapter 21 opens with two visions: John first sees a new heaven and a new earth, a new cosmos or nature; he then sees a new city, the holy city Jerusalem, a new society or humankind organized. We thus have a coupling of cosmos and city that combines the two dimensions of human history: nature and humankind. History is not limited to being a society of men and women, but also includes the cosmos or nature. The new cosmos and the new humankind are bodily. Transcendence, as we have said, means overcoming death, chaos, and darkness, not overcoming bodiliness and history. In the new world created by God there is bodiliness and social relations, but they are now without death, chaos, darkness, and oppression.

In the overall structure of the book Jerusalem is clearly a symbol or myth opposed to Babylon. The Babylon of history, the capital of the empire of Nebuchadnezzar that battled Jerusalem and destroyed it in 586 B.C.E. becomes a symbol or myth of the idolatrous and criminal city, the huge powerful city. Chapters 21–22 of Revelation are the antithesis of chapters 17–18. Babylon is a prostitute (symbol of the idolatry of money) and is riding on the beast (Roman empire); Jerusalem is holy (anti-idolatrous) and is the bride and wife of Christ. With its idolatry Babylon corrupts the kings of the earth. The kings of the earth come to Jerusalem dragging behind them the splendor and treasures of the nations. Babylon becomes drunk on the blood of the holy ones and the martyrs. Murderers and idolaters are excluded from Jerusalem. John uses the Babylon myth to designate the city of Rome in history; analogously, he uses the Jerusalem myth to designate in history the new humankind in the new world created by God.

I Saw... the New Jerusalem, Coming Down out of Heaven from God (v. 2)

In Revelation the terms "heaven" and "earth" have two meanings, a cosmic meaning: heaven and earth signify the whole of the cosmos or nature; and a mythical and symbolic meaning, which is theological: heaven and earth signify the two dimensions of history (earth: the empirical, visible dimension of history; heaven: the transcendent invisible dimension of history). In v. 1 heaven and earth are used with a cosmic meaning, to designate the whole of nature or creation (the cosmos). New heaven and new earth point to a new creation, a new cosmos. In v. 2, "I saw. . . . the new Jerusalem coming down out of heaven, from God," the term "heaven" has a mythical and symbolic meaning. We should not remain on the level of the space-time representation of the myth, but move on toward understanding its theological meaning. As we said, heaven and earth point to the two dimensions of history: heaven is the deep transcendent dimension of history; earth is its empirical and visible dimension, that of appearance. There is only one history, but it has two dimensions: one empirical and the other transcendent. The new Jerusalem comes down from heaven to earth: theologically this means that it goes from its transcendent condition to an earthly condition: it enters into the empirical, visible dimension of history. If we take vv. 1 and 2 together we have the convergence of a twofold transformation. On the one hand (v. 1), we have the transformation of heaven and earth (the cosmos) into a new heaven and new earth, meaning a cosmos without death, chaos, darkness, oppression (see the previous section). On the other hand, the new Jerusalem comes down from heaven to earth, meaning the transformation of the heavenly Jerusalem into an earthly Jerusalem. However, the earth and heaven that now receive the new Jerusalem is a transcendent cosmos, that is, one without death, chaos, and darkness. The new Jerusalem enters into the earthly and empirical dimension of a history that is now transcendent. As we have said, Jerusalem is a myth signifying the new community or social organization, located now not in heaven but on earth. The city is new because there is no longer any death, chaos, darkness, and oppression in it. In short, the transcendent can become visible in history because the cosmos has triumphed over death, chaos, and darkness. We experience the earthly city, the new social organization of humankind, in a world without death or oppression. Everything proper to heaven becomes visible on earth. The distinction between heaven and earth disappears; now everything is earth, although it is a transcendent earth without death.

It is quite significant that in spatial and temporal terms the myth moves downward from heaven to earth. We come to the final and transcendent stage of history when heaven symbolically comes down to earth. What is salvific and liberating comes downward and ends on earth. We find just the opposite in the contrary myth of Babel. In Genesis 11:1–9 humankind wants to build a city with a tower that reaches up to heaven. That city wants to scale heaven from earth. Now in Revelation the city comes down from heaven to earth. The Bible begins with an idolatrous and oppressive city that wants to reach heaven; it ends with a transcendent city coming down from heaven to earth. A different tradition appears in Paul, since he speaks of a rapture into the heavens: "then we . . . will be caught up . . . in the clouds to meet the Lord in the air" (1 Thess. 4:17).

Jerusalem: God's Dwelling Place on Earth — No Temple

The new Jerusalem is the new "dwelling place of God on the earth" (21:3). God no longer dwells in heaven or in a temple, but in the new transcendent society, created by God in the new world. Literally the text reads: "Behold, God's tent" (*skené*) on the earth and "he will place his tent" (*skenósei*) on it. This is not the "temple that is the heavenly tent of testimony" (*ho naós tés skenés tou marturíou*) that appears in heaven in 15:5. In 21:22, John explicitly says that he saw no temple (*naón*) in the new Jerusalem. Hence "tent" does not have the literal meaning of tent of testimony as sanctuary or temple but the figurative sense of "dwelling place": the new Jerusalem is God's dwelling place on earth. See Leviticus 26:11: "I will set my Dwelling among you, and will not disdain you. Ever present in your midst, I will be your God, and you will be my people." Closer yet is the line in John 1:14: "the Word became flesh and made his dwelling [*eskénosen*] among us."

The same idea of God's dwelling on earth can be seen in 21:11 in the theme of God's glory: the holy city Jerusalem comes down from heaven from God "with the splendor of God." In 21:23 we are told that the new Jerusalem needs no sun or moon for light "for the glory of God gave it light, and its lamp was the Lamb." Revelation 22:5 goes further in saying that the inhabitants of the new Jerusalem do not need light from lamp or sun, "for the Lord God shall give them light." The whole city shines with the glory of God. God's glory is his essence, what God is. God fills the new Jerusalem, the new humanity that lives in a transcendent new world created by God. Paul expresses the same thing in his short apocalypse (1 Cor. 15:20–28): all history reaches its culmination when "God will be all in all things" (*ho theos pánta en pásin*). This is not, however, a kind of pantheism, in which God might dissolve into, or spread throughout, the new city, since 22:4 reads "they will look upon his face." Paul's statement is thus fulfilled: "At present we see indistinctly, as in a mirror, but then face to face" (1 Cor. 13:12). Also, "We do know that when it is revealed we shall be like him, for we shall see him as he is" (1 John 3:2). "Blessed are the clean of heart [free of idolatry], for they will see God" (Matt. 5:8).

John says: "I saw no temple in the city, for its temple is the Lord God almighty and the Lamb." This is a sharp break with Jewish tradition, since a Jerusalem without a temple is unthinkable for the Jews. God replaces the temple with his visible and direct presence throughout the city. He replaces not only the temple of the Jerusalem of history, but replaces any possible or imaginable temple. The new Jerusalem is a symbol of God's new universal community, the new people, the new society, the new humankind, the new historical project created by God in the new heaven and earth. God's glory utterly fills this project; God has his dwelling place on earth in this new society; God is all in all in this new people of God. Here there is no need for temple, nor church, nor for any kind of mediation between the people and God. God fills all, and all see God's face directly. The old historical temple in Jerusalem drew boundaries to mark off a series of differences and separations: between Jerusalem as holy city and the rest of Palestine, between the temple itself and the city, between the Holy of Holies and the temple courts — which had separate courtyards: one for priests, another for Israel, another for women, and yet another for pagans. Since there is no temple in the new Jerusalem, all these distinctions and differences vanish. Distinctions between holy and profane, priest and lay person, Christian and non-Christian likewise vanish. Now the whole city is holy, all are priests, and all see God and bear God's name on their forehead.

Nothing could be further from the truth than to identify the new Jerusalem with the church now — so it is claimed — glorified in the new world. Many writers cite Ephesians 2:19–21 in concluding that the new Jerusalem is the church. Ephesians is speaking of the church, of course, but in this present age in history: it is a holy temple, built upon the foundation of the apostles and prophets, with Christ as the capstone. In Revelation 21–22 we have the future of history, the transcendent city, and it is explicitly stated that there is no temple. In the new Jerusalem Christ is not the capstone, as he is in the church, but rather the lamp spreading light over the whole city. The only possible comparison with Ephesians 2:20 is Revelation 21:14, which says that the wall of the city (not the city itself) is built upon twelve stones, which bear the names of the twelve apostles of the Lamb. The apostles are not the wall's foundation, which is rather the memory and tradition of the apostles. Likewise engraved over the twelve gates of the city are the names of the twelve tribes of Israel. What it means is that the new Jerusalem, as new people of God, is the fullness of the historical people of God prior to the new creation.

Water and Trees of Life

In 21:6 God says, "To the thirsty I will give a gift from the spring of life-giving water." The same thing is said in the community liturgy in 22:17 (like 7:17). Water here symbolizes the life that God offers to all who seek it. The interesting thing is that it is offered as a gift, that is, money has nothing to do with it. It is God who assures life, not the market. A beautiful text of Isaiah is reflected here:

> All you who are thirsty
>   come to the water!
> You who have no money,
>   come receive grain and eat;
> Come, without paying and without cost,
>   drink wine and milk! (Isa. 55:1)

This is the utopia of those prevented from eating and drinking and from leading a secure life, those without money. Now in Revelation this is the ultimate life, guaranteed by God beyond death and oppression. In Ezekiel 47:1–12 the river of water flows out of the temple, but since there is no temple in the new Jerusalem, 22:1 says that "the river of life-giving water... [was] flowing down from the throne of God and of the Lamb." In Jeremiah 2:13 God is a spring of life-giving water. In John 7:37–39 Jesus shouts:

> "Let anyone who thirsts come to me and drink. Whoever believes in me, as Scripture says, 'Rivers of living water will flow from within him.' " He said this in reference to the Spirit.

Verse 22:2 says that "on either side of the river grew the tree of life." This tree gives abundant fruit: twelve times, once a month, and it is further said that "the leaves of the trees serve as medicine for the nations." In the new Jerusalem there now appears the tree of life that God offered in his life-giving design for humankind in Genesis 2:9. When humanity chooses the project of death, it loses access to the tree of life (Gen. 3:24). At this point the tree of life is now seen to be producing fruit twelve times a year. God's project of life for humankind is achieved in the church. The leaves from these trees serve as medicine to heal the nations that were sick as a result of Babylon's idolatry.

Description of the New Jerusalem: 21:9–21

We have already noted that the city symbolizes humankind, God's universal people, a new design or transcendent social system with no death, no chaos, no darkness, no exploitation, no pain. In the passages preceding (21:1–8) and following (21:22–22:5), John has unveiled for us the essential aspects of the new Jerusalem. Here he seeks to rebuild the city along new lines using things that are real, although highly charged symbolically. The writer utilizes this model of rebuilding a city as a tool for rebuilding hope, utopia, God's transcendent and eschatological design for all humankind. The rebuilding of the city is fundamentally a rebuilding of the collective consciousness of the people of God that is reading and hearing Revelation. Let us now look at the central symbolic elements in this reconstruction.

Verses 9–11 offer a general description of the city. The introduction in vv. 9–10 has a structure parallel to 17:1–3. This parallelism is deliberate with the aim of demonstrating the antithesis between Babylon and Jerusalem. Chapter 17 was about the judgment over Babylon, the famous harlot. Here we have the new Jerusalem, the bride of the Lamb coming down out of heaven, full of the glory of God. Babylon represents the city full of idolatry and crime; Jerusalem symbolizes the city filled with God's glory, where the river and trees of life are located. We have already stressed that the two cities are at odds.

The various parts of the city are described in vv. 12–14. The central element is the wall, which has twelve gates with twelve angels hovering over them and is inscribed with the names of the twelve tribes of Israel. The wall also sits on twelve stones, which bear the names of the twelve apostles of the Lamb. Here we have a symbolic reconstruction of the people of God. The number twelve, which expresses totality or social perfection, is repeated six times. The names of the twelve tribes symbolize the people of God in its origins, while the names of the twelve apostles symbolize the people of God, rebuilt by the death and resurrection of Jesus (see 7:1–8 and 14:1–5). Upon this tradition the new Jerusalem, God's new transcendent design, is now erected.

In vv. 15–17 we find the shapes and measurements of the city. It is 12,000 stades — i.e., about 1,500 miles — in length, breadth, and height, and hence it is a gigantic cube (or perhaps also a pyramid). The measures are excessive to indicate symbolically the perfection of the new city. The wall is about 144 cubits high, that is, about 70 meters. It is an insignificant and symbolic wall: it recalls tradition (the names of the twelve tribes and the twelve apostles).

The fourth and last part (vv. 18–21) gives us a description of the materials of which the city is made. The most striking thing is the use of gold; in v. 18 pure gold is used as a construction material in the city, and in v. 21 the city square is pure gold and passersby walk on it. Gold thus loses its exchange-value and its fetishism and becomes use-value. The two verses mentioning gold serve to enclose this passage, whose central portion speaks of a multiplicity of precious stones, signifying the light and beauty of God's glory filling all. The background text is Isaiah 54:11–17, where we find a symbolic vision of the new Jerusalem: the precious stones of the city signify that all her children will be disciples of Yahweh and that this city will be established in justice and will live securely without oppression and terror.

The Inhabitants of the New Jerusalem

The new Jerusalem is God's dwelling in the midst of the men and women living there (21:3).[11] God renews the covenant with them collectively in 21:3: "He will dwell with them and they will be his people and God himself will always be with them." In 21:7, God renews the covenant in a personal manner: "I shall be his God, and he shall be my son; I shall be her God, and she shall be my daughter."[12] As in the Old Testament, the covenant signifies mutual recognition: the people recognize God as God and God recognizes the people as people. The people recognize what God has done for them, and God entrusts the people with responsibility for their own future. In the new Jerusalem, humankind as totality — and each person individually — attain full personhood vis-à-vis God.

In 21:24–26 (in the light of Isa. 60) we are told that "the nations" (*ta ethne*) will walk in the light of the new Jerusalem and that "to it the kings of the earth will bring their treasure." These are the kings and nations that were not contaminated with Babylon's idolatry. They are assumed to have put up resistance against Rome. All the nonidolatrous cultures of the earth from all the ages will come to enrich the new Jerusalem, symbol of transcendent humankind.

Three verbs characterize the activity of inhabitants of the new Jerusalem in 22:3–5: they will worship him (*latreúsousin*), they will look upon (*ópsontai*) his face, and they will reign (*basileúsousin*) forever. In the new Jerusalem all are priests, all see God, and all reign. There are no hierarchies, no differentiations, no power elites, and no oppressed. That is why God's glory can fill the whole city, and God can be all in all.

Those Excluded from the New Jerusalem

In 21:8, 27, and 22:15 are listed all those who are excluded from the new Jerusalem and destroyed forever. We will take the list in 21:8 as a basic reference

---

11. We have consciously used inclusive language. We must free the text from the patriarchy imbued in it — and especially free translations.

12. See Rosa Kitzberger, "Wasser und Baume des Lebens: eine feministich-intertextuelle Interpretation von Apk.21/22," mimeographed text sent by the author. In Isaiah 43:5–7 Yahweh speaks of his sons and daughters whom he brings back from exile (similarly 49:22). In Zechariah we have a beautiful vision of the Jerusalem to come, where old men and old women and boys and girls play in the streets and main square.

point, adding details from the other two. Seven groups or categories of persons are listed in 21:8:

1. Cowards (*deilós*). In Matthew 8:26, when calming the storm, Jesus reproaches the disciples: "Why are you terrified [*deiloí*], O you of little faith?" (similarly Mark 4:40). This is fear for lack of faith, not a psychological type of fear. In the context of Revelation it refers to one who fails to resist the beasts for lack of faith and courage, one who does not have the strength and faith to give public witness, even with martyrdom. They are defeated by the system.

2. The unfaithful (*á-pistos*). Jesus' expression. "O faithless and perverse generation!" is preserved throughout the synoptic tradition (Matt. 17:17). Jesus calls Thomas unbelieving (John 20:27). These are not atheists, but those who have no faith, who do not believe in anything.

3. The depraved (*ebdelygménos*) — those given to depravity or abomination (*bdélygma*). The "desolating abomination" was the idol that the Romans placed in the temple (Matt. 24:15; Mark 13:14). The depraved are those who worship the oppressive idol.

4. Murderers (*phoneús*). This term occupies the center of the list. The three previous and three subsequent terms refer to idolaters. Murder is always an immediate consequence of idolatry, generally in a social sense, i.e., meaning oppression. Idolatry is the root of all social sin.

5. Prostitutes (*pórnos*). In prophetic and apocalyptic literature, prostitution symbolizes idolatry: one who sells oneself for money to another and thus becomes an object in the hand of the other who pays and becomes one's master.

6. Sorcerers (*pharmakós*) — synonymous with idolatry. It connects fetishism and idolatrous practices, such as magic.

7. Idol-worshipers (*eidololátres*). In the Bible an idolater is one who perverts the meaning of God or who substitutes other gods (money, power, market, etc.) for God. Ephesians 5:5 speaks of a "greedy person (*pleonéktes*), that is, an idolater" (similarly in 1 Cor. 5:11). Colossians 3:5 speaks of "the greed [*pleonexía*] that is idolatry." In the New Testament, idolatry is almost always connected to money

The categories listed above as 4, 5, 6, and 7 are also found in 22:15): sorcerers, the unchaste, murders, and idol-worshipers. The vehemence of the expression "Outside are the dogs," applies to all of them.

The seven categories are ultimately summed up in one: "the deceivers of every sort" (*pseudés*), as also in the parallel text 22:27: "all who live and practice deceit." In the apocalyptic tradition, deceit is basically idolatry: it is deceit vis-à-vis God, it is religious perversion. The fate of the seven groups listed in 21:8 "is in the burning pool of fire and sulfur, which is the second death." As we said before, this pool or second death signifies eternal annihilation. When history reaches its climax in the new heaven, new earth, and new Jerusalem, there is no other space outside this new world. What does not enter into this new world is definitively annihilated, reduced to nothing. That, according to Revelation, is hell — it is not an eternal *place*. There can be no negative *eschaton;* only the good can be eternal. Hell, according to Revelation, is total annihilation.[13]

The Biblical Tradition on the New World and the New Jerusalem

The theme of hope and utopia is basic throughout the Bible. The spirit of the entire biblical tradition is this pursuit of a new and transcendent world. The images and symbols for this pursuit are always cosmic and social: new heaven and earth and new city (new Jerusalem). Perhaps the Old Testament passage closest to Revelation 21–22 is Isaiah 65:17–25. Its opening line is, "Lo, I am about to create new heavens and a new earth." This cosmic sign is explained in social terms: rejoicing and happiness in Jerusalem and in its people, an end to weeping and crying, the promise of a long life ("No longer shall there be in it an infant who lives but a few days.... He dies a mere youth who reaches but a hundred years"); exploitation overcome ("they shall live in the houses they build, and eat the fruit of the vineyards they plant; They shall not build houses for others to live in, or plant for others to eat; ... [they] shall long enjoy the produce of their hands. They shall not toil in vain"); nearness to God ("Before they call, I will answer"); cosmic and social peace ("The wolf and the lamb shall graze alike"). Along the same line, 2 Peter 3:13 states: "We await new heavens and a new earth in which righteousness dwells."

There is nonetheless a great difference between the passage in Isaiah and the one in Revelation; the utopia in Isaiah is a world without oppression, but death is still at hand; in Revelation the utopia is a world with neither oppression nor death (no chaos and no darkness). Both present a transcendent world. The word "trans-cendent" literally means "what is beyond." It assumes that there is a limit beyond which lies the transcendent reality. In Isaiah that limit is oppression. The transcendent world (new heaven and earth) is a world without oppression. God's breaking the chains of oppression proves divine transcendence. In Revelation the limit is death. The transcendent world is now a world without death. God's destruction of death demonstrates divine transcendence. Understanding the transcendence in Revelation means starting with the transcendence in Isaiah. We understand the transcendence of a world with no death only from a liberating perspective.

The utopia of a new Jerusalem has a long tradition. The first stage was the hope of rebuilding Jerusalem after it was destroyed in 586 B.C.E. The passages in Jeremiah 30:1–31:22 and chapters 16, 36–37, and 40–48 of Ezekiel date

---

13. Wilfrid J. Harrington, O.P., *Revelation*, Sacra Pagina 16 (Collegeville, Minn.: Liturgical Press, 1993), 232–35.

from this period. The whole optimism of Deutero-Isaiah is focused on a new Jerusalem (Isa. 40–55). The aim is no longer to rebuild the old city but to build a new city. With Third Isaiah, Jerusalem is a myth, an apocalyptic symbol of a new society (see especially Isa. 60–62 and the text just considered, 65:17–25). The same is true of Zechariah 14. John will break this tradition when he presents the new Jerusalem with no temple.[14]

---

14. See Ariel Alvarez Valdés, "La Nueva Jerusalén del Apocalpsis: Sus raíces en el A.T.: El período de la 'Jerusalén reconstruida,'" *Revista Bíblica* (Argentina) 47 (1992): 141–53.

Conclusion

Now that we have finished the reading of Revelation, I want to conclude by focusing on two questions: what is the central message of Revelation and what is the principal meaning of Revelation for our time?

THE CENTRAL MESSAGE OF REVELATION

The central message of Revelation, what constitutes its main axis, is *the eschatological reality, here and now, of the resurrection of Jesus.* It is eschatology already realized in the resurrection of Jesus. Jesus is alive, alive in his own body, which means that he is alive in the Christian community and in history, both in the human dimension and the cosmic dimension of history. Jesus is alive in his body in the midst of our history, but he is also glorified, he has regained his divine condition, he has power. This strength and power of the resurrection also becomes historical in the pouring forth of the Spirit and in the realization of the project of Jesus: the reign of God on earth. The resurrection of Jesus also makes the resurrection of the martyrs possible, those who in Jesus and with Jesus now participate in the transformation of our history. Let us briefly consider these points in the texts of Revelation.

As we have already seen, Revelation 14:1–5 makes up the center of the central part of Revelation (12:1–15:4). The risen Christ appears at this center (as a Lamb who is standing, alive), and with him the community of believers (the 144,000 marked with the seal), those not tainted with the idolatry of the empire (according to our translation) who follow the Lamb wherever he goes. This entire crowd is now gathered together on earth, on Mount Zion, as a symbol of the church. The risen Christ leads the community in the present time in his confrontation with the monster, the beast, and the false prophet. We are at the center of Revelation and at the center of present history (this present time is developed from Revelation 4:1 to 19:10). Chapter 12 recounts the defeat of Satan and the arrival of liberation, power, and the reign of God. All this is made possible by the death and resurrection of Jesus (represented by the painful birth of the male child, 12:1–6). The martyrs also are part of this victory in the present time: "they conquered him by the blood of the Lamb and by the word of their testimony" (12:11). This same presence of Christ and his martyrs, as conquerors of the beast, appears in the hymn of 15:1–5.

The presence of the risen Christ in the midst of the communities is the central theme of the first part of Revelation (1:9–3:22). Jesus says, "Do not be afraid. I am...the one who lives. Once I was dead, but now I am alive " (1:17–18). The risen Christ sends seven messages to the seven churches. It is an apocalyptic visit of the risen Christ to each of the churches, now, at the moment that the present time begins. Christ becomes present in the midst of each community, and it is he who truly leads the churches: "Behold, I stand at the door and knock. If anyone hears my voice and opens the door, [then] I will enter his house and dine with him, and he with me" (3:20).

In the liturgy of chapters 4 and 5 inaugurating the present time (which goes from 4:1 to 19:10) the risen Christ is the central figure. He appears in the fullness of wisdom and power to interpret all of history (in the symbol of taking the book and breaking its seven seals). In the section on the seven seals (6:1–8:1) it is the risen Christ who breaks each seal and reveals to us the reality of both heaven and earth. In the liturgy that closes the present time (19:1–10), the fourth motive of celebration is the coming of the Lamb's wedding day (v. 7). "Blessed are those who have been called to the wedding feast of the Lamb" (v. 9).

The fundamental eschatological reality of Revelation is not therefore the end of the world but rather the resurrection of Christ in the present history of our world. Revelation is not the fearful book of the last judgment but rather the book of hope and joy because Christ has risen and this good news changes the meaning of present history. The eschatology of Revelation therefore is realized in the present time. This is the time begun by the resurrection and thus is a time of grace, a *kairos,* in which it is possible to build the reign of God in history. If Christ has risen, the time of the resurrection and the reign has already begun.

The last part of Revelation (19:11–22:5) indeed speaks of the future. This future is the end of the present time; it is not, however, the end of history but rather of the suffering and oppression within history. The eschatological is not the end, but rather *what puts an end* to the beasts and Satan and all their followers who have controlled the world. Moreover, the end is not simply judgment and destruction but also and fundamentally a new creation: a new heaven and earth, a new Jerusalem (21:1–22:5). Apocalyptic eschatology is not only the revelation of future realities, but also the revelation of the direction of all of present history through those future realities. Concern for the future is a concern for the direction of all of history toward that future. Eschatology is what gives meaning and direction to the present realities. The question about utopia is not whether it can or cannot occur in history but rather about its ability in the present to provide direction to the meaning of history, the meaning of our thought and action. Let us briefly consider the apocalyptic texts that deal with this future eschatology that provides direction to the present.

The prevailing religious ideology reduces all future eschatology to the unique and terrifying reality of the last judgment. Revelation, on the other hand, presents the future of history in a complex series of different and successive stages in which the meaning of history is progressively revealed. Future apocalyptic eschatology is a program for the future, a plan of hope and utopia to provide meaning and fullness to the present time. In chapter 8 above we distinguished two basic stages in the apocalyptic description of the future: the beginning of the future of history (19:11–20:15) and the future of history (21:1–22:5). The future begins with three different judgments: (1) the judgment of the beast, the false prophet, and the kings of the earth; (2) the judgment of Satan; and (3) the final judgment of the dead, of death, and of the place of the dead. In the midst of these judgments we have the thousand-year reign (20:4–6), which we have interpreted as the utopia of the poor in which they can finally build the reign of God on earth, before the last judgment. After this beginning of the future, we have the definitive future (21:1–22:5). There is no judgment here, but rather a new creation: new heaven and earth and a new Jerusalem that comes down from heaven to earth. It is not the end of history, but rather a new creation within history. It is a transcendent world, not because it is beyond history but because it is beyond death within history. This new creation is the final achievement of our history.

What is the reason for this complex series of stages in the future of the world? There are two basic reasons: on the one hand, to give greater meaning to present history and, on the other, to distinguish the elements of the future that can be anticipated and lived in the present. When the future is presented as a unique and absolute given then the future crushes and destroys the present. The apocalyptic presentation produces the opposite effect: the vision of the future inspires and gives direction to the present time.

THE MEANING OF REVELATION FOR OUR TIME

We want to conclude with a reflection on the meaning and importance of Revelation for our time. We will provide only a few brief and provisional guidelines.

In the first place the book of Revelation is important for moderating the radical and fundamentalistic apocalypticism that has invaded our society, especially now that the end of the twentieth century and the end of the second millennium is approaching. Revelation is customarily manipulated by fundamentalistic sects, both Protestant and Catholic. A historical and liberating interpretation of Revelation can help us overcome these deviations and generate a positive and constructive reflection on Revelation in our churches. This is what happened in the second century when the book of Revelation tempered the Montanist current in the church, which was a radical apocalyptic tendency.

The book of Revelation can also help us to rebuild a new vision of history, without fear, without anguish, without radicalism, and without fundamentalistic dogmatism. Revelation teaches us to live the *present* time as a *kairos,* as an opportune and decisive moment, in the light of eschatology realized in the resurrection of Christ. Revelation teaches us also to live the *past* as a history of salvation and to ask how that history is taking place today. But most important is to interpret Revelation so that we can correctly confront the *future* and so overcome all the manipulation that creates anguish, fear, and terror. Revelation teaches us to imagine the present and final eschatology with a sense of joy and hope. It also helps us to rebuild the transcendent utopia of the reign of God on earth and of the new creation. It teaches us to rethink the judgment of God now in the present time and the final judgments in the future with a sense of exodus and hope.

Revelation is indispensable for building a theological, prophetic, and apocalyptic analysis of our present situation. Revelation teaches us that there is only one history and that this history has both transcendent and empirical dimensions (what Revelation calls heaven and earth). Revelation teaches us how to un-conceal the invisible forces, satanic or divine, that are working in history today. It gives us the criteria to discern where the monster, the beast, and the false prophet are in our present situation, and where God is as well. Chapters 12–14 are an especially privileged instrument of this apocalyptic analysis of the economic, political, social, and ideological situation. Revelation's analysis of the false prophet (13:11–18) is a masterpiece of religious-ideological analysis of the reality of domination, helping us to understand the modern theory of fetishism.

Revelation has taught us to appreciate the language of symbols, myths, and visions and thus to overcome an overly rationalistic and conceptual language. We have discovered the positive power of myth for rebuilding the consciousness of a people and a sense of hope and utopia. We have also discovered the importance of symbols and visions for transmitting strength, spirituality, and profound convictions.

Revelation has also enabled us to achieve a different reconstruction of the origins of Christianity, less Hellenized and more popular. Our collective imagination regarding our origins has excluded primitive Christian apocalypticism, which has led to serious aberrations in ecclesiology over the centuries. To recover Revelation is to recover a fundamental and founding dimension of the origins of Christianity. We can say the same about the primitive Christian wisdom movement, which is very close to prophetic Christian apocalypticism and likewise has been forgotten in the official history of the church.

Finally Revelation is having a decisive influence especially in the so-called Third World (the poor countries and the poor within those countries) in the reconstruction of liberating theologies. There is a very significant movement away from the prophetic dimension and toward the apocalyptic dimension (as we have systematically understood it in this book). Revelation is playing an important role in the rebuilding of civil society in general and of hope and spirituality in particular. The book of Revelation is helping to create a new historical and liberating language. And for all these reasons Revelation is coming to be the preferred book of the Base Christian Communities and of all the ecclesial movements that hope to transform the present situation and reform the church, movements that are born among the poor, the oppressed, and the excluded (both women and men).

Bibliography

On Revelation and Apocalyptic

ACFEB (Association Catholique Français por l'étude de la Bible). *Apocalpyses et Théologie de l'Espérance: Congrès de Toulouse (1975)*. Lectio Divina 95. Paris: du Cerf, 1977.

Alegre, Xavier. "El Apocalipsis, memoria subversiva y fuente de esperanza para los pueblos crucificados." *Revista Latinoamericana de Teología* (San Salvador) 26 (1992): 201–29; 27 (1992): 293–323.

Alvarez Valdés, Ariel. "La Nueva Jerusalén del Apocalpis: Sus raíces en el A.T.: El período de la 'Jerusalén reconstruida.'" *Revista Bíblica* (Argentina) 47 (1992): 141–53.

Arens, Eduardo. *Apocalipsis: ¿Revelación del fin del mundo? Estudio exegético-crítico del texto en sus contextos*. Lima: Centro de Proyección Cristiana, 1988.

Barr, David L. "The Apocalypse as a Symbolic Transformation of the World: A Literary Analysis." *Interpretation* 39 (1984): 39–50.

Beassley-Murray, G. R. *The Book of Revelation*. New Century Bible Commentary. Grand Rapids: William B. Eerdmans, 1974.

Beker, J. Christiaan. *Paul's Apocalyptic Gospel: The Coming Triumph of God*. Philadelphia: Fortress Press, 1982.

Boesak, Allan A. *Comfort and Protest: The Apocalypse from South African Perspective*. Philadelphia: Westminster Press, 1987.

Boring, M. Eugene. *Revelation*. Interpretation: A Bible Commentary. Louisville: Westminster John Knox, 1989.

Brown, Raymond E. *Las iglesias que los Apóstoles nos dejaron*. Bilbao: Desclée de Brouwer, 1986; English original: *The Churches the Apostles Left Behind*. New York: Paulist, 1984.

Caird, G. B. *A Commentary on the Revelation of St. John the Divine*. Harper's New Testament Commentary. San Francisco: Harper & Row, 1966.

Collins, John J. *The Apocalyptic Imagination: An Introduction to the Jewish Matrix of Christianity*. New York: Crossroad, 1987.

Collins, Adela Yarbro. "The Political Perspective of the Revelation to John." *Journal of Biblical Literature* 96, no. 2 (1977): 241–56.

———. *The Apocalypse*. New Testament Message: A Biblical-Theological Commentary. Wilmington, Del.: Michael Glazier, 1979.

———. *Crisis and Catharsis: The Power of the Apocalypse*. Philadelphia: Westminster Press, 1984.

———. "Roma como símbolo del mal en el cristianismo primitivo." *Concilium* 220 (November 1988): 417–27.

Comblin, José. *Cristo en el Apocalipsis*. Barcelona: Herder, 1969; French original: Tournai: Desclée, 1965.

Croatto, J. Severino. "Apocalíptica y esperanza de los oprimidos: Contexto socio-político y cultural del género apocalíptico." *Revista de Interpretación Bíblica Latinoamericana* (San José, Costa Rica-Santiago de Chile) 7 (1990): 9–24.

———. "Desmesura y fin del opresor en la perspectiva apocalíptica: Estudio de Daniel 7–12." *Revista Bíblica* (Argentina) 39 (1990): 129–44.

———. "El discurso de los tiranos en textos proféticos y apocalípticos." *Revista de Interpretación Bíblica Latinoamericana* (San José, Costa Rica-Santiago de Chile) 8 (1991): 39–53.

De Castro, P., Flávio Cavalca. *Apocalipse hoje.* Aparecida, Brazil: Santuário, 1982.

Dunn, James D. G. *Unity and Diversity in the New Testament: An Inquiry into the Character of Earliest Christianity.* 2d ed. London: SCM Press; Philadelphia: Trinity Press International, 1990.

Dupont, Jacques. *Les trois apocalpyses synoptiques.* Paris: du Cerf, 1985.

Ewing, Ward. *The Power of the Lamb: Revelation's Theology of Liberation for You.* Cambridge, Mass.: Cowley Publications, 1990.

Foulkes, Ricardo. *El Apocalipsis de San Juan: Una lectura desde América Latina.* Buenos Aires: Nueva Creación; Grand Rapids: William B. Eerdmans, 1989.

Gager, John G. *Kingdom and Community: The Social World of Early Christianity.* Englewood Cliffs, N.J.: Prentice-Hall, 1975.

Gorgulho, F. G. S., and Ana Flora Anderson. *No tengan miedo: Apocalipsis y comunidades cristianas.* Buenos Aires: Paulinas, 1978.

Hanson, Paul D. *The Dawn of Apocalyptic: The Historical and Sociological Roots of Jewish Apocalyptic Eschatology.* Rev. ed. Philadelphia: Fortress Press, 1983.

Harrington, Wilfrid J., O.P. *Revelation.* Sacra Pagina 16. Collegeville, Minn.: Liturgical Press, 1993.

Hellholm, David, ed. *Apocalypticism in the Mediterranean World and the Near East: Colloquium Uppsala, August 1979.* Tübingen: J. C. B. Mohr, 1983.

Horsley, Richard A. *Jesus and the Spiral of Violence: Popular Jewish Resistance in Roman Palestine.* San Francisco: Harper & Row, 1987.

Horsley, Richard A., and John S. Hanson. *Bandits, Prophets, and Messiahs: Popular Movements in the Time of Jesus.* Minneapolis: Winston Press, 1985.

Isenberg, Sheldon R. "Millenarism in Greco-Roman Palestine." *Religion* 4 (1974): 26–46.

Käsemann, Ernst. *Ensayos exegéticos.* Salamanca: Sígueme, 1978. German original: Göttingen: Vandenhoeck and Ruprecht, 1960, 1964.

Köster, Helmut. *Introducción al Nuevo Testamento: Historia, cultura y religión en la época helenística e historia y literatura del cristianismo primitivo.* Salamanca: Sígueme, 1988. German original: Berlin and New York: Walter de Gruyter, 1980. English translation: *Introduction to the New Testament.* Philadelphia: Fortress Press, 1988.

Lacocque, André. "Naissance de l'apocalyptique." *Lumière et Vie* 160 (1982): 4–12.

Lambrecht, J., ed. *L'Apocalpyse johannique et l'apocalyptique dans le N.T.* Bibliotheca Ephemeridum Theologicarum Lovaniensium 53. Louvain: University Press, 1980.

Léon-Dufour, Xavier. "Autour de L'Apocalypse de Jean." *Revue des Sciences Religieuses* 71 (1983): 309–36.

Marshall, I. Howard. "Is Apocalyptic the Mother of Christian Theology?" G. F. Hawthorne, and O. Bets, eds., *Tradition and Interpretation in the New Testament.* Grand Rapids: William B. Eerdmans, 1987. 33–42.

Mesters, Carlos. *Flor sin defensa: Una explicación de la biblia a partir del pueblo.* Bogota: CLAR, 1984. English version: *Defenseless Flower.* Maryknoll, N.Y.: Orbis Books, 1989.

———. *El Apocalipsis: La esperanza de un pueblo que lucha: Una clave de lectura.* Santiago: Rehue, 1986.

Muelenberg, Leonardo. "A Igreja diante do desafío do Império Romano: Um esboço social." *Revista Eclesiástica Brasileira* (Petrópolis, Brazil) 50, no. 199 (September 1990): 629–42.

Nickelsburg, George W. E. *Jewish Literature between the Bible and the Mishnah: A Historical and Literary Introduction.* Philadelphia: Fortress Press, 1981.

Paul, André. "L'Apocalyptique, source majeure du Christianisme." *Lumière et Vie* 160 (1982): 13–24.

Perrin, N., and D. C. Duling. *The New Testament: An Introduction.* 2d. ed. New York: Harcourt, 1982.

Pikaza, Xavier. "Apocalipsis de Juan: Origen y fin de la violencia." *Carthaginensia* 8, nos. 13–14 (January–December 1992): 609–39.

Pixley, Jorge. "Las persecuciones: El conflicto de algunos cristianos con el Imperio." *Revista de Interpretación Bíblica Latinoamericana* (San José, Costa Rica-Santiago de Chile) 7 (1990): 89–102.

Prigent, Pierre. "Au temps de l'Apocalypse." *Revue d'Histoire et de Philosophie Religieuses* 54 (1974): 455–83; 55 (1975): 215–35 and 241–63.

Richard, Pablo. *La fuerza espiritual de la Iglesia de los Pobres.* San José, Costa Rica: DEI, 1988.

———. "Lectura popular de la Biblia en América Latina: Hermenéutica de la liberación." *Revista de Interpretación Bíblica Latinoamericana* (San José, Costa Rica-Santiago de Chile) 1 (1988): 30–48.

———. "Teología en la teología de la liberación." *Mysterium liberationis: Conceptos fundamentales de la teología de la liberación.* San Salvador: UCA, 1990. 1:201–222. English translation: "Theology in the Theology of Liberation," *Mysterium Liberationis: Fundamental Concepts of Liberation Theology.* Maryknoll, N.Y.: Orbis Books, 1993. Pp. 150–67.

———. "El Pueblo de Dios contra el Imperio: Daniel 7 en su contexto literario e histórico." *Revista de Interpretación Bíblica Latinoamericana* (San José, Costa Rica-Santiago de Chile) 7 (1991): 25–46.

———. "Hermenéutica bíblica india: Revelación de Dios en las religiones indígenas y en la Biblia (después de 500 años de dominación)." *Revista de Interpretación Bíblica Latinoamericana* (San José, Costa Rica-Santiago de Chile) 11 (1992): 9–24.

———. "Crítica de la hermenéutica occidental: Hermenéutica del Espíritu." *Pasos* (San José, Costa Rica) 49 (September–October 1993).

Rowland, Christopher. *The Open Heaven: A Study of Apocalyptic in Judaism and Early Christianity.* London: SPCK, 1982.

———. "Mantener viva la peligrosa visión de un mundo en paz y justicia." *Concilium* 220 (November 1988): 429–42.

———. *Radical Christianity: A Reading of Recovery.* Maryknoll N.Y.: Orbis Books, 1988.

———. *Liberating Exegesis: The Challenge of Liberation Theology to Biblical Studies.* Louisville: Westminster John Knox, 1989.

Ruiz Bueno, Daniel. *Actas de los mártires.* Bilingual text. 9th ed. Madrid: BAC, 1987.

Snoek, Juan, and Rommie Nauta. *Daniel y el Apocalipsis: Una lectura introductoria.* San José, Costa Rica: DEI, 1993.

Schüssler Fiorenza, Elisabeth. *The Book of Revelation: Justice and Judgment.* Philadelphia: Fortress Press, 1985.

———. *Revelation: Vision of a Just World.* Proclamation Commentaries. Minneapolis: Fortress Press, 1991.

Thompson, Leonard. "A Sociological Analysis of Tribulation in the Apocalypse of John." *Semeia* 36 (1986): 147–74.

———. *The Book of Revelation: Apocalypse and Empire.* New York and London: Oxford University Press, 1990.

Vanni, Ugo. *Apocalipsis: Una asamblea litúrgica interpreta la historia.* Estella: Editorial Verbo Divino, 1982. Italian original: Ed. Queriniana.

———. *L'Apocalisse: Ermeneutica, Exegesi, Teologia.* Bologna: Dehoniane, 1988.

Wainwright, Arthur W. *Mysterious Apocalypse: Interpreting the Book of Revelation.* Nashville: Abingdon Press, 1993.

Wanamaker, C. A. "Apocalypticism at Thessalonica." *Neotestamentica* 21 (1987): 1–10.

Theoretical and Historical Background for Revelation

Alcina Franch, José, ed. *El Mito ante la antropología y la historia.* Madrid: Siglo XXI, 1984.

Assmann, Hugo, and Franz Hinkelammert. *A idolatria do mercado: Ensaio sobre economia e teologia.* São Paulo: Vozes, 1989.

Barabas, Alicia M. *Utopías indias: Movimientos socio-religiosos en México.* Mexico City, Barcelona, and Buenos Aires: Grijalbo, 1987.

Comblin, José. *Tiempo de acción: Ensayo sobre el Espíritu y la Historia.* Lima: CEP, 1986. Portuguese original: Petrópolis, Brazil: Vozes, 1982.

———. *A força da palavra.* Petrópolis, Brazil: Vozes, 1986.

De Santa Ana, Julio. *La práctica económica como religión: Crítica teológica a la economía política.* San José, Costa Rica: DEI, 1991.

Dussel, Enrique. *Etica comunitaria.* Madrid: Paulinas, 1986. English translation: *Ethics and Community.* Maryknoll, N.Y.: Orbis Books, 1988.

———. *Las metáforas teológicas de Marx.* Estella, Spain: Verbo Divino, 1993.

Gutiérrez, Gustavo. *Teología de la liberación: Perspectivas.* Salamanca: Sígueme, 1973. English translation: *A Theology of Liberation: History, Politics, and Salvation.* Rev. ed. Maryknoll, N.Y.: Orbis Books, 1988.

Hinkelammert, Franz J. *Las armas ideológicas de la muerte.* 2d ed. San José, Costa Rica: DEI, 1981. English translation: *The Ideological Weapons of Death: A Theological Critique of Capitalism.* Maryknoll, N.Y.: Orbis Books, 1986.

———. *Crítica a la razón utópica.* 2d. ed. San José, Costa Rica: DEI, 1984.

———. *Sacrificios humanos y sociedad occidental: Lucifer y la Bestia.* San José, Costa Rica: DEI, 1991.

Hoornaert, Eduardo. *La memoria del pueblo cristiano: Una historia de la Iglesia en los tres primeros siglos.* Madrid: Paulinas, 1986. English translation: *The Memory of the Christian People.* Maryknoll, N.Y.: Orbis Books, 1989.

Irarrázabal, Diego. *Rito y pensar cristiano.* Lima: CEP, 1993.

Llanque Chana, Domingo. *La cultura aymara: Destructuración o afirmación de la identidad.* Lima: Idea-Tarea, 1990.

Miranda, José P. *Marx y la Biblia: Crítica a la filosofía de la ópresion.* Salamanca: Sígueme, 1975. English translation: *Marx and the Bible: A Critique of the Philosophy of Oppression.* Maryknoll, N.Y.: Orbis Books, 1974.

Pixley, Jorge. *Historia sagrada, historia popular: Historia de Israel desde los pobres (1220 a.c.–135 d.c.).* San José, Costa Rica: DEI, 1991.

Richard, Pablo. *Morte das cristandades e nascimento da igreja.* 2d ed. São Paulo: Paulinas, 1984. English translation: *Death of Christendoms, Birth of the Church.* Maryknoll, N.Y.: Orbis Books, 1987.

Siller Acuña, Clodomiro L. *Flor y canto del Tepeyac: Anotaciones y comentarios al Nican Mopohua.* Mexico, D.F.: Servir-Estudios Indígenas-Cenami, 1981.

Sung, Jung Mo. *La idolatría del capital y la muerte de los pobres.* San José, Costa Rica: DEI, 1991.

———. *Neoliberalismo y pobreza: Una economía sin corazón.* San José, Costa Rica: DEI, 1993.

Tamez, Elsa. *Contra toda condena: La justificación por la fe desde los excluidos.* San José, Costa Rica: DEI-SBL, 1991.

Trigo, Pedro, and Gustavo Gutiérrez. *Arguedas: Mito, historia y religión: Entre las calandrias.* Lima: CEP, 1982.

Scripture Index